PRAISE FOR *Taste,*

"*Taste, Memory* may well be the most beautiful book ever written about *food biodiversity* and how it has 'landed' on earth, in our mouths and in our hearts. Once you have read and digested David's book, you will never again regard this two-word phrase as an abstraction, but as a vital element of our common food heritage, one that continues to nourish and enrich our lives."

—from the foreword by **GARY PAUL NABHAN**

"As we increasingly seek to reconnect to our agrarian roots and restore our relationship with the land, we need guides who have been down the path before us and already negotiated some of the tangles along the way. There is no better guide than David Buchanan. *Taste, Memory* is the captivating work of a writer who is alert to the world around him and ready to learn from it. Buchanan's elegant celebration of the 'ongoing conversation,' as he calls it, between generations of heirloom food plants and the families that have lovingly kept them alive, will inspire a new generation to nurture the happy marriages of plants and place that make communities lively, resilient, and deeply meaningful."

—**ROWAN JACOBSEN**, author of *Fruitless Fall* and *American Terroir*

"*Taste, Memory* is not the typical storybook novel about finding redemption on an isolated old farm, but a 21st-century success story built around collaboration, innovation, and vibrant new models for sustainable farming. David's book helps us explore agricultural models past and present, in order to help us find our own unique niche, rhythm, and flow in the emerging local food economy. His ability to help us appreciate the nuances of heirloom crops and regional flavors reminds us that we can help to preserve agricultural and food traditions for the future . . . one seed, one bite, and one backyard at a time!"

—**JOHN FORTI**, garden historian, "The Heirloom Gardener"

"With a scientist's intellect and the heart of a 21st-century Noah, David Buchanan goes beyond biodiversity to explore the true place of *Taste, Memory,* a sensory experience that ties all of mankind together at life's dinner table. Using taste as his compass, Buchanan uncovers authentic endangered flavors, making us all long for another serving."

—**POPPY TOOKER**, New Orleans food activist and host of *Louisiana Eats*

"Buchanan shows us that reconnecting with the sources of our food reconnects us with what it means to feel alive. His unbridled enthusiasm for all things agricultural—from a forgotten peach variety to the proper soil balance for a rooftop farm—is infectious."

—**CURT ELLIS**, FoodCorps

"Taste is one of the great joys in life, a sense and sensibility that all of us share. But it is a common pleasure we are in real danger of losing, as our modern world seems bent on a collision course with ever greater homogeneity and the lack of distinctive local flavors and cultures. In this thought-provoking book, David Buchanan captures taste experience from whence it once flowed, from an overpowering, life-enhancing diversity."

—TOM BURFORD, orchardist, historian, and author of *The Apples of America*

"Every peach, every turnip, every ear of corn becomes a local food in the fullest sense when gardeners and fruit growers opt for regional advantage. There are stories to be told here, be it the lore of the Fletcher Sweet apple or the enduring affair of 'that blonde' cucumber from the Boothbys. How well David Buchanan weaves the human element into this celebration of plant selection and provincial cuisine. Good eating goes hand in hand with our dance with place. Let *Taste, Memory* bring appreciation for varietal delight to your dinner table."

—MICHAEL PHILLIPS, author of *The Holistic Orchard* and *The Apple Grower*

"In *Taste, Memory,* David Buchanan shares his quest to promote fruit and vegetable biodiversity in New England. 'Plant it to save it' is his mantra. In his thoughtful meditation and memoir, Buchanan reveals a powerful commitment to collecting and conserving the apples, blueberries, rutabagas, potatoes, and other foods long part of this rocky and harsh landscape. As important, though, is his clear-sighted understanding of the necessary innovations that will be required to preserve the fantastic Baldwin apples, Bordo Beets, and Amazon Chocolate tomatoes not just for this generation, but for the next seven generations. An important book."

—AMY TRUBEK, author of *The Taste of Place: A Cultural Journey into Terroir*

"David Buchanan takes on his subject, some of it prickly, with grace and eloquence. *Taste, Memory* is hard to put down. It is beautiful read that illuminates the challenges to and importance of biodiversity, a subject that David frames with our taste buds and personal food histories. A wonderful book, and an important one!"

—DEBORAH MADISON, author of *Vegetable Literacy* and *Local Flavors*

"A Greek proverb states, 'A society grows great when old men plant trees whose shade they know they shall never sit in.' David Buchanan's book about food, agriculture, community, and connections to soil and climate embodies the spirit and vision of the Greeks. Beyond weaving an engaging narrative about farming, the past twenty years of his life reflect the extraordinary changes occurring in American agriculture and a rediscovery of taste and quality in food. We are indeed fortunate that, as a young man, he has many years to plant apples, peaches, and other notable foods!"

—JEFFREY P. ROBERTS, author of *The Atlas of American Artisan Cheese*

Taste, MEMORY

Taste, MEMORY

FORGOTTEN FOODS, LOST FLAVORS, AND WHY THEY MATTER

DAVID BUCHANAN

FOREWORD BY GARY PAUL NABHAN

Chelsea Green Publishing
White River Junction, Vermont

Project Manager: Bill Bokermann
Editor: Benjamin Watson
Copy Editor: Laura Jorstad
Proofreader: Helen Walden
Indexer: Margaret Holloway
Designer: Melissa Jacobson

Printed in the United States of America
First printing October, 2012
10 9 8 7 6 5 4 3 2 1   12 13 14 15 16

Our Commitment to Green Publishing
Chelsea Green sees publishing as a tool for cultural change and ecological steward-ship. We strive to align our book manufacturing practices with our editorial mission and to reduce the impact of our business enterprise in the environment. We print our books and catalogs on chlorine-free recycled paper, using vegetable-based inks whenever possible. This book may cost slightly more because it was printed on paper that contains recycled fiber, and we hope you'll agree that it's worth it. Chelsea Green is a member of the Green Press Initiative (www.greenpressinitiative.org), a nonprofit coalition of publishers, manufacturers, and authors working to protect the world's endangered forests and conserve natural resources. *Taste, Memory* was printed on FSC®-certified paper supplied by Thomson-Shore that contains at least 30% postconsumer recycled fiber.

Library of Congress Cataloging-in-Publication Data
Buchanan, David, horticulturist.
 Taste, memory : forgotten foods, lost flavors, and why they matter / David Buchanan ; foreword by Gary Paul Nabhan.
  p. cm.
 Includes index.
 ISBN 978-1-60358-440-1 (pbk.) — ISBN 978-1-60358-441-8 (ebook)
 1. Gardening—Anecdotes. 2. Biodiversity conservation—Anecdotes. I. Title.

 SB455.B926 2012
 635—dc23
                              2012025581

Chelsea Green Publishing
85 North Main Street, Suite 120
White River Junction, VT 05001
(802) 295-6300
www.chelseagreen.com

Contents

Foreword

When I close my eyes and reimagine my periodic pilgrimages to David Buchanan's plantings, I see him walking with me through a lush, and luscious-tasting, garden in a sunny opening of the Northern Forest, as moist breezes and latent humidity from the sea suffuse all the colors around us with a rich brilliance. David is leading me between the rows to show me a Waldoboro Greenneck rutabaga, whose ancestors, they say, washed up on the Maine coast after a shipwreck way back in 1886; today, he tells me, this colorful turnip-like oddity is making a comeback on the local-food scene. Next, he shows me the diminutive ground-hugging foliage of a Marshall strawberry, still struggling to get off the endangered list, but once prized as the best-tasting cultivated berry in all of America. Finally, he leads me over to his fledging nursery—now spread among three properties and thriving—which harbors some of Maine's rarest but most delicious apples. Their names are as memorable as the sauces, pies, and hard ciders that are made from them.

For David, working to save, celebrate, and savor the remaining living riches of the agrarian world is something that's visceral as well as intellectual, ethical, and, perhaps, spiritual. His sweat mingles with their floral fragrances and herbal high notes. We have inherited rather ugly terms from the sciences to describe these unusual-tasting, sometimes oddly shaped and garishly colored heritage crops: *agrobiodiversity; endemic floral cultigens; economic botanical heirlooms; plant germplasm; phytogenetic resources;* and *landraces.* Such labels only serve to obfuscate what the agrarian poet Wallace McCrae calls "things of intrinsic worth"—shrouding them with a kind of tyranny that comes from an overreliance on esoteric jargon. Walking through David's garden, though, helps put faces back on these plants, tastes back in our mouths, and synesthetic memories back into our dreams.

Suddenly, through David's well-paced storytelling, these plants have once again become living neighbors of ours, part and parcel of our communities, our feasts, and folklore. And yet, David is cautious not to keep them suspended in some romanticized past, as if tending heirloom vegetables and heritage fruits were merely an effort to freeze the genetic and cultural landscape by a mutant cohort of agricultural Luddites. He, like many of us, wants to see these genetic, cultural, and culinary legacies continue to evolve, adapt to new conditions, and gain resistance to previously unforeseen diseases. David wants them to diversify and proliferate and reach beyond his own garden beds, to stun and inspire others wherever their journey takes them.

Over the years David Buchanan has scoured archives and abandoned orchards in search of the rarest of the rare. He is both a seasoned sleuth of botanical lore and a nationally recognized conservationist of historically cultivated plants, but his book is about the future, not about the past. It sows seeds of hope, not despair. It is about how David's own life has been changed by his daily practice of meditating over plants, of tending the garden, cherishing the seedlings, and harvesting the fruits to share with people who have never known them before. He is not alone in these pursuits, but shares the skills, sentiments, and sensibilities of some of America's most remarkable (agri)cultural treasure keepers: Will Bonsall, John Bunker, Tom Burford, Betty Fussell, Rob Johnston, C. R. Lawn, Russell Libby, Glenn Roberts, Robin Schempp, Poppy Tooker, and Ben Watson. He also is intimate with the local gardeners, home cooks, honey spinners, fruit canners, cheesemakers, and brewers on his own home turf. These folks may not be as widely touted as the Iron Chefs and Extreme Eaters on TV and YouTube, but they are surely the ones who enliven and enrich our communities through their fostering of regional and ethnic foodways.

Taste, Memory may well be the most beautiful book ever written about *food biodiversity* and how it has "landed" on earth, in our mouths and in our hearts. Once you have read and digested David's book, you will never again regard this two-word phrase as an abstraction, but as a vital element of our common food heritage, one that continues to nourish and enrich our lives. In turn, we must nourish it, or it will surely fade away. As Poppy Tooker famously says, "You've got to eat it to save it." *Taste, Memory* offers the rationale and the inspiration you need to embark upon your own voyage of food discovery.

Gary Paul Nabhan
June 2012

One

SEEDS OF AN IDEA

*A*ugust 1992. Emerenciana Sandoval greets me with a radiant smile in her kitchen and asks if she can make me breakfast. "*¿Comer?*" she asks as she mimes eating eggs and tortillas with her fingers. "Are you hungry?" her daughter-in-law, Catalina, adds. Of course they know this is a formality. I'm always hungry, and each of us understands that it wouldn't be polite for me to say no. I've tried to refuse many times, knowing they have no money and many mouths to feed, but somehow a plate piled high always winds up in front of my place at the counter. They worry about me, living in the foothills of Washington State's North Cascade Mountains forty miles away, without a resident mother or wife to feed me and watch out for my well-being. Emerenciana warns me to beware of devils—something to think about while walking alone through the woods on dark nights.

Behind their home is a large garden ringed with nodding sunflowers where they grow plants like lettuce and tomatoes, herbs, summer squash, corn, beans, and potatoes. I stop by whenever possible to help and to learn from their experience. Everything about food production is new to me. Looking back while writing this nearly twenty years later, I recall their two sheep and the fire pit

Emerenciana's son Miguel used to cook the ram when it began to harass the children; their machete-built chicken coop, made from salvaged dimensional lumber but resembling something straight from the highlands of Oaxaca; and the perch we caught together in the alkaline lakes a few miles from their home in Okanogan, Washington. I think of the corn and bean seeds they and their friends carried with them from Mexico, and the care they took to maintain food traditions while working long hours in nearby orchards and packing houses. These are some of my earliest gardening memories.

The night before, the Sandovals set out a cot on the screened porch for me while everyone else slept wherever they found space in the two-bedroom house. Preschooler Leticia usually curls up on the couch next to her grandmother, whereas Adan and his brother Marcus share a bedroom with their parents. In the morning the blinds are pulled and it's hot inside, noisy and crowded as the women prepare breakfast and the three children play with their father. Marcus, the oldest at six and deaf from birth, angles for my attention by hanging on to my shirt and signing frantically. We eat breakfast together without hurry. Later Miguel throws a bag in his Isuzu truck and drives away to the orchards, dropping Catalina off at a packing shed on the way. Adan and Marcus catch a bus to school, while Emerenciana stays home to make tortillas and watch over Leticia.

I grab a straw hat and head for my truck, parked in the shade of a large willow tree. It's a 1970 Chevy half-ton pickup nearly the size of my house, a guilty pleasure for a young guy trying to live lightly off the grid. Although I'd purchased it for $600 to use as a farm truck, gradually it came to replace my less-reliable car. A friend of mine recently tore its door off while backing up at high speed over uneven ground, catching it on a stump as he leaned out to see where he was going with his good eye, but he fixed it by bolting in another door from the salvage yard that sort of fit and nearly matched. With a new engine dropped in by a local mechanic for $1,400, this truck—nearly as old as I am—roars along good as new.

My boots mirror the truck in spirit. They're covered in leather patches stitched artlessly by a local "cobbler"—mismatched suede, cowhide, whatever scraps he had lying around. If at first it seemed that he'd ruined my favorite thrift-store boots, soon it became clear that instead he'd transformed them into folk art. Wearing beat-up cowboy boots used to feel like an affectation to me, a displaced easterner, but the year before they'd prevented a nasty fall down Miguel's well. After I'd climbed into the concrete casing to check on a malfunctioning irrigation pump, a wooden ladder rung snapped under my weight, throwing me backward. One of my heels miraculously caught on the steel bar that bisected the well to secure the pump, about three feet below the broken rung. I landed on it light as a feather, hooked on the bar with one foot, my hands pressed against the smooth concrete walls in the half-light. Try that in a pair of running shoes.

As I pull out of the Sandovals' driveway, my destination for the day is the town of Pullman in eastern Washington, about a four-hour drive away. Pullman is home to the USDA Western Regional Plant Introduction Station, a genebank repository for crops like beans, peas, and safflower, collected from around the world. Maybe this doesn't sound particularly exciting, but my goal in traveling there is to broaden my gardening knowledge, to see firsthand all kinds of foods I've read about in USDA records—plant diversity that's hard to imagine in the abstract. I also hope to pick up some interesting, commercially unavailable seeds to grow at home and with the Sandovals.

With spray planes buzzing overhead I cross the Omak River and follow the road as it quickly gains elevation, leaving behind irrigated orchards, alfalfa fields, and pastures to enter the dry scrublands of the Colville Reservation. The sun shines in a cloudless sky, just as it does around here most days from April to October. Central Washington lies in the rain shadow of the North Cascades (their height wrings moisture from the air as it rises, leaving this side of the range dry and clear). The land turns to arid bitterbrush and sage in the highlands to the east as the road skirts the Columbia River and the Grand Coulee Dam. The truck windows are down to catch a breeze as the day heats up. Gradually the landscape transforms into a beautiful sea of wheat in the Palouse region at the eastern edge of the state. Giant six-wheeled tractors roll over cultivated hills past abandoned barns and derelict gabled houses, signs of small farms long ago lost to competition and consolidation.

The plant introduction station occupies a nondescript warehouse somewhere on the campus of Washington State University. It's surrounded by student parking lots, one of which I sleep in that night, in the open bed of my truck. Recalling my visit today, I have a vague memory of the handmade display rack one of the scientists used to show local schoolkids the endless variety of shapes, colors, and sizes of beans in the collection, and of his helpfulness as he answered questions and fetched requested varieties for me—vivid green chickpeas from India, fuzzy little brown chickpeas from Iran, an old unnamed bean from Tennessee, eye-catching red and white Bolivian beans, and a dozen other must-have varieties. Greedy for beans, lentils, and chickpeas, I was smitten by odd and forgotten legumes.

For several years these plants grew in my gardens. I maintained them even after returning to the East Coast to live in Boston's North End and work for a museum as a writer and fund-raiser. They survived two seasons at my parents' home north of the city while I gardened on weekends, hauling paper bags filled with compost and produce back and forth by train. They stayed with me after I married and moved to the nearby city of Salem, though by then the collection had diminished. Gradually, one by one, varieties began to disappear: Some failed to adapt to New England; others couldn't germinate after long stretches stored in a cabinet. It's hard to say exactly when the last of them went—probably after my divorce and move to Maine, where I stopped gardening altogether for a few years.

Life's like that. Mine was for a time, anyway. In our haste and mobility we lose threads that tie us to the past, watch a season or two slip by without a much needed new coat of paint on the house, neglect those things that demand constant attention and care. This is one reason we have genebanks—to back up our inattention and shifting priorities. Today I could grow these beans again by digging up their accession numbers and ordering replacements from the government. But my collecting interests have evolved; my goals have changed. If I were to grow chickpeas now it would be mostly out of nostalgia, because staying motivated to grow dry pulses (edible seed crops) for the table isn't easy. Why should we go to all the trouble to preserve some obscure Iranian chickpea already in someone else's collection? It's a lot of work! How many of us are willing to grow and thresh beans for soup, as long as we can buy pinto beans for pennies at the supermarket?

Over the years, even as my concern about maintaining genetic diversity and preserving disappearing agricultural traditions has increased, I've struggled with some fundamental questions. What should agricultural diversity look like, and how is it relevant to the modern world of supermarkets, giant tractors, and irrigated mega-farms? What role can the individual play, and what place should niche crops and heritage foods (also known as heirlooms—typically described as foods dating back at least fifty years and untouched by modern breeding) have in our markets and on our plates? How do we summon the energy and will to keep this bounty alive? Many years have slipped by since my visit to Pullman, and I'm looking for some answers.

Leave behind the granite and brick facades of the waterfront retail shops and restaurants in Portland, Maine, wind your way past the galleries and performance spaces that appear to sprout up overnight along Congress Street, and enter the leafy Victorian residential neighborhood of the West End. There on a side street you'll find a small nineteenth-century house, set at the back of its urban lot under a giant catalpa tree. Come at the right time and you'll find me and my fiancée, Karla, picking greens from our small garden, throwing sticks for our black lab, Tica, or sitting and drinking coffee on one of my carved wooden benches. It's probably not your idea of a farmhouse.

The fact is, I've always lived fitfully divided between the pleasures of the city and the country. Deep inside I'm still the Princeton student who moved to a barn in western Massachusetts soon after graduation in the late 1980s, infatuated with the natural world and not ready for office life, yet not quite at home with rural living. Still torn like the young guy who lived in a tiny cabin in the North Cascade Mountains for six years, trying to hide from hippie friends my too-straight habits, like listening to Jessye Norman on a CD player rigged up to a solar panel, or my need for daily showers. ("How do you always look so clean?" my first farm employer asked at the end of a long day hoeing knee-high weeds in ninety-degree heat.)

If you tell me most farmers shouldn't live like this, that to plant an orchard or tend a market garden it makes sense to surround yourself with a little land, I won't argue with you. For me the words *urban farming* seem contradictory, strangers at the table, a mystifying idea even for someone caught up in it. My move to Portland ten years ago was motivated by a desire to live in an up-and-coming small city and eat at its restaurants, not grow food to be served in them. Days spent in Washington State tending large gardens seemed like a distant memory, and it never occurred to me that in this place the preoccupations of my time in the West might come roaring back to life.

What started innocently enough a few years ago as a small garden on borrowed land, however, has blossomed over the past two years into a quasi-farm and conservation project—an awkward, sprawling enterprise that covers roughly two acres of other people's backyards near the city. This wasn't something planned or exactly intended, and even now it's hard to explain how it happened. Why I'm running around today, for example, hauling heavy coolers full of Summer Crookneck squash, tomatoes, sweet peppers, and new potatoes into commercial kitchens, cornering busy chefs. "Already in the weeds," the first one tells me (kitchen shorthand for "Can't talk, see you later"). At the restaurant next door the kitchen is running in overdrive, but they buy everything except the peppers while I weigh things out and dodge the prep cooks, who call out, "Step back!" "Watch out!" and "Duck!" as they fly past me.

Out by the service entrance near the trash bins sits my station wagon, filled with a grower's paraphernalia, the clutter of a market gardener: buckets overflowing with bits of string, torn gloves, salvaged vinyl siding for tree labels, coolers, hand tools, and lists of recently planted row crops. Wads of cash from the farmers' market lie hidden under a towel and in the glove compartment—not a good idea in our neighborhood, where once I found someone rummaging through my car at 5:30 AM and chased him across the schoolyard next door, wondering what to do if I caught him. From April to November canvas tarps cover the pale beige seats of my Subaru Outback, a car purchased without farming in mind.

In practice my new enterprise is more like a collaborative community project than a working "farm," because it's pieced together out of a broad patchwork of shared land use and reciprocal arrangements. When I need a clean, licensed space to set up a cider press, I wrangle a deal with a friend who's renting a commercial kitchen. If picking a few dozen bushels of apples justifies owning such a nice little press, I team up with one of Karla's friends, the owner of a recently abandoned orchard a few towns away. All of these arrangements are informal, based on goodwill and handshakes, even for borrowed fields planted with dozens of rare fruit trees, so they depend on hedged bets and diversification. Such casual partnerships can feel tenuous and difficult, but in the end there's a kind of beauty in the way they weave food production into the community.

There are advantages and disadvantages to borrowing land and equipment like this. On the positive side, while building connections and creating partnerships (and letting me live in the city), it keeps costs very low. There's no need to rent a commercial kitchen, own a van to transport food and nursery plants to the market, or buy a tractor, rototiller, and mower. I make use of these things by tapping into the right networks and looking for win–win situations. If this sometimes feels precarious, cobbled awkwardly together rather than organized around a clear plan, it has the benefit of keeping me focused on what matters most while the business grows. For the time being, borrowing equipment and land helps me avoid unnecessary expenses, and saves time that can be put to better use.

It was never my goal to become a farmer, and that's not exactly what I'm up to here. This project is more like an attempt to come to grips with an old obsession, to find a way to connect biodiversity to something larger than my own gardens. It's as much about collecting rare varieties of fruit trees, berries, and vegetables as it is a working farm. Call it an effort to bring regionality, cultural difference, and flavor back to the plate, and discover what place these foods deserve in the modern world. I'm trying to make good on plans embarked upon long ago in Washington State and nearly forgotten, to discover meaning in unusual and forgotten foods by building something of value around them.

Determining what grows successfully in any given place, and what will be a commercial success, is the primary challenge for any grower. Throw in a desire to collect and experiment with unusual foods, and this can lead at times in conflicting directions. How much should we bend to the market and winnow out underperforming plants, at the expense of greater diversity in the field? To what extent should we emphasize efficiency and uniformity over anything odd, quirky, regional, niche? Commercial growers willing to work with rare plants and animals need to discover some kind of middle ground, and make enough profit to justify the time. What will this compromise look like?

Seven miles, a fifteen-minute drive, separate my leased fields from our house. Although it's a good bike ride, half an hour on roads with wide shoulders and moderate hills, most of the time I jump in the car. There's all the gear to consider, plus our dog Tica. And then riding a bike home after a long day in the fields isn't very appealing. Today I load a few stray boxes from a vegetable delivery, pack my lunch, persuade Tica to leave her bed on the porch, and drive over the Casco Bay Bridge, the roughly half-mile span that separates Portland from its neighbors to the east and south. Its highest point offers sweeping views of Portland's working waterfront and skyline, Casco Bay, the Fore River, and whatever weather hangs over nearby Cape Elizabeth.

The weather isn't looking very promising on this late-summer day. Clouds are gathering on the horizon, the flag raised over the bridge is whipping in the wind, and as I reach the turnoff from Route 77 toward my fields, it's starting to rain. A storm isn't unwelcome after last month's heat and drought, but the unexpected change kills plans to start bud-grafting fruit trees this morning. Although a quick search online doesn't turn up much information to discourage me, opening the bark on young trees in the rain, potentially exposing them to fungal infections, doesn't seem like a bright idea.

The road off Route 77 passes the first of my fields. This is a new site for me, roughly a third of an acre of newly tilled and cover-cropped ground behind a grand old barn and beautiful nineteenth-century farmhouse. Its owners are letting me grow here without charge, hoping to see the space better used, and understanding that organic fruit trees suit the character of their land better than a large expanse of lawn. Last month I hired a nearby farmer to till the sod, then raked in a buckwheat cover crop to build organic matter and provide forage for Karla's two beehives. In two years I'll start planting trees. My other fields are located a few doors from each other another mile or so down the road, but they occupy very different worlds. The first, more than an acre of vegetables and fruit trees, sits behind another imposing old farmhouse and large barn, surrounded by seven acres of lawns and gardens immaculately tended by the owner and hired gardeners. The second, twenty-five acres of fields and woods, privately owned but conserved as open space by the local land trust, is more like a giant community garden, its space shared by a children's camp, a nonprofit educational group, my third-of-an-acre nursery and gardens, the farmhouse tenant, several beekeepers, and an Ethiopian immigrant who gardens there with his family. It gets very busy, and although this is one of the prettiest little farms in the Portland area, it suffers from a lack of general upkeep.

I pull into the driveway at this last site, park by my gardens, and walk over to the nursery beds and greenhouse. Roughly four hundred recently grafted fruit trees grow in carefully tended rows, where they'll remain for a couple of years before I can transplant them to permanent sites in nearby fields. Here I'm also growing potted fruit trees and berry bushes for market sales, and certified-organic vegetables and berries. Tomatoes, peppers, basil, and eggplant fill the nearby greenhouse, a seventy-five-by-fourteen-foot hoophouse constructed from a bent steel frame covered by a single layer of plastic.

I check my potted plants to make sure they received enough water from the rain, and a few minutes later two friends arrive: Colin Reid, a young guy interested in orchards and hard cider, and Jake Hoffman, a musician who's been coming out to the fields in his spare time to help out. They'd been looking forward to grafting trees this morning, but understand the last-minute change in plans. We talk about other tasks to tackle instead. Colin and I start with a quick inventory of young apple trees, reviewing plans for the new orchard up the road. My goal is to develop a mix of rare and endangered American apple varieties, with a focus on the production of sweet and hard cider.

"What were you thinking of grafting this morning?" Colin asks. It's a more-than-reasonable question, but the answer is a work in progress.

"Not sure, guess I'll know when we do it," I tell him, which is, unfortunately, the honest and unsatisfactory truth. They both laugh at this.

Here's my quandary: With last spring's sixty additions to the apple collection, there are roughly 120 varieties in these fields from which to choose for additional grafting. Until we can learn about their growing habits and sample their fruits, though, figuring out which to select is a shot in the dark. Who can say how well fruit as obscure as Fall Wine (aka Musk Spice, House, and Uncle Sam's Best)—an antique American apple once nearly lost to cultivation and still quite rare—will grow in this location? What kind of cider will it produce? Will it yield consistently? Should we plant two trees, or twenty? Fall Wine has history and a good story going for it—no small advantage for any producer marketing directly to customers. But how much of my borrowed, limited growing space does it deserve?

While Colin and I look over apple lists, Jake transplants strawberry runners into new beds. The same question comes up. Although strawberries don't require years of waiting to reveal their secrets, and each of these varieties has grown here for at least three seasons, deciding which to plant can be elusive. "I don't know, let's plant all of them, why not . . . ," I tell him. Two of the berries are commercially unavailable and extremely rare. One of these stands out for its exceptional flavor and historical interest, but it's nearly extinct in part because its yield is somewhat lower than the others, and the fruit is very juicy, hard to pick and handle. Does its fine flavor and rarity justify giving it equal space, or would it be more prudent to go the easier route with more forgiving strains? What exactly am I trying to accomplish?

On some level these concerns seem pretty mundane, encountered by everyone from the commercial wheat farmer looking to increase yields to the home gardener searching for flavorful varieties in the nursery catalog. From another perspective, though, they get at some fundamental truths about agriculture and biodiversity, and lie at the heart of my growing project. What place does a cantankerous old apple or too-delicate strawberry have in our kitchen gardens, farm fields, and markets? Now that the computer brings so much information to our fingertips, and access to foods of all sorts, what should we choose to grow?

The good news for gardeners is that many of the best foods will always be the province of home growers, rewarding those who go to the trouble of maintaining them by yielding the finest quality and flavor. There's justice in that. Many rarities simply can't adjust to the realities of the market, even at the most local of levels—a thin-skinned heirloom tomato, an ugly old baking apple, or an exceptionally juicy peach. Every garden that includes these foods has a significant role to play, and in the case of heirloom crops that's in keeping with their original spirit. After all, it was small-scale independent farmers and gardeners who developed them, often for their own sustenance and pleasure.

I don't consider myself an advocate for any one particular way of producing food, so this book isn't a manifesto about how to transform the world. It's more like an exploration of what we've lost while moving away from daily hands-on contact with the land, or, to put it more positively, what we have to gain by reconnecting at some level with it. My farm project isn't about just saving seeds or old fruit varieties, but searching for a creative connection with land and plants that, until the last few generations, was at the heart of most people's lives. In practice this means collecting not only older varieties, but also new foods—most often those developed by public breeding programs, with direct farmer participation—as long as they emphasize flavor, high yields, and natural disease and pest resistance. My goal is to create the best plant collection for this particular time and place, not develop an isolated museum of curiosities.

It's my hope that reading about these experiences will encourage others to view healthy food production, on any scale, as a careful balance of thoughtful selection of plants and animals with the demands of a particular landscape and climate. To me, biological diversity is the driving energy behind the locavore movement, the regionalism that distinguishes the cuisine of a particular place from anywhere else. For those of us who are willing to adapt and are open to experimentation, the next heirloom peach, or a cross between some fine old pear and a wild seedling, may yield something sublime. This true sense of place in food becomes increasingly clear to me every time I taste the complex flavors of old raspberries and blackberries, the sweetness after frost of heirloom beets and rutabagas, and the snap between my teeth of an excellent green bean.

In my eyes forgotten apple trees bred on isolated Maine farmsteads, or hard ciders blended from their fruits, are among humanity's richest creative achievements. Growing and producing such foods, and making them available to others, helps maintain long-standing traditions. Would Portland chefs have sought out the heirloom beans I grew in Washington to gain an edge in their competitive business? Will Fall Wine apples live up to their promise in my orchard? Colin, Jake, and I can't answer such questions until we commit to grafting the trees, planting the strawberries, and seeing what happens. There's no perfect answer. We just do it.

Ultimately, what's more fundamental to who we are and what we believe than what we choose to eat? This book is about my efforts to live amid diversity, find a place for rare and unusual varieties in our fields and markets, and discover meaning and stories in our forgotten foods. It begins with a step back to explain how I came to this place, and then asks this question: Where do we go from here, and how can we keep this richness alive?

Two

DISCOVERING FORGOTTEN FOODS
WITH THE ARK OF TASTE

*A*s I walk up and down a narrow waterfront street beside the
Piscataqua River in downtown Portsmouth, New Hampshire, it seems like it should be easy to spot the Black Trumpet
Bistro bar and restaurant. Given its reputation (chef-owner Evan
Mallett has recently been named a semifinalist by the James Beard
Foundation for its annual Best Chef in the Northeast Award), the
bistro's modest entrance in the service and delivery side of the
block comes as a surprise. If you miss its sign, hanging over what
looks more like a hole in the brick wall than a front door, you could
wander around here all day without a clue as to what lies inside.

Originally this building housed a nineteenth-century chandlery
that sold wares to ships in the city's busy harbor, which explains
the unassuming back-street orientation toward the nearby docks.
In the 1970s it was home to James Haller's celebrated restaurant,
Blue Strawbery, known for its emphasis on regional and seasonal
ingredients that helped define the New American cuisine. These
days a steady stream of traffic enters and leaves the nearby downtown shopping district by two busy arterial roads that connect to
the I-95 corridor, both of which turn their backs to the working

waterfront. Tourists and nearby UNH students come to shop at independent boutiques or the Banana Republic, visit brewpubs or wine bars, check out museums or handicrafts, and eat seafood or burgers. It's all too easy to miss some of the best that the city has to offer. There's the pine nut risotto and duck cassoulet at Black Trumpet Bistro, or, more modestly, the Hansel-&-Gretel gingerbread waffle with pomegranate molasses and "real" whipped cream at a nearby restaurant called the Friendly Toast.

Chef Evan greets me cheerfully at the door and steers me toward a table set with pastries and coffee. I pour myself a cup and stand a little awkwardly, wondering exactly what I've gotten myself into. The restaurant is closed at nine o'clock on a Saturday morning in September 2009, and I'm here as a newly confirmed member of Slow Food USA's Ark of Taste Committee. For several years I've been involved with Slow Food, an international organization devoted to everything that fast food isn't, like preserving food traditions, supporting small-scale producers, and celebrating the pleasures of the table. Joining this committee ratchets things up a notch, though, because we're here today to evaluate neglected and forgotten regional foods. This requires knowledge of culinary history and agriculture, not to mention a discriminating palate. Since I've never been able to say much beyond "this tastes good" to describe any food, that last point makes me especially nervous.

The narrow interior of the Black Trumpet Bistro's first-floor dining room is all smoke-blackened brick and timber, white tablecloths, and wall-mounted racks of wine. Two other committee members sit at the solitary long table set for twelve, engrossed in conversation, but otherwise the room is empty. What could they be talking about? Pomegranate molasses, or whether whipped cream processed mechanically can be considered "real"? I feel kind of fraudulent, a little nervous about the day ahead. How hard will it be to bluff my way through hours of taste comparisons without falling flat on my face?

Evan puts me at ease, smiling warmly as he asks about the Boothby's Blonde cucumbers in my bag, my contribution to the day's evaluations. They're a little tired looking and on the small side (three to four inches each), the last fruits remaining on the vines in a friend's farm fields. Some unseasonably cool early-fall weather made it hard to find a few decent samples, and these have lived for a week at the back of our refrigerator. Evan seems unconcerned as he picks up the bag and whisks it away to the kitchen, adding the cucumbers to the full roster of foods we'll taste and evaluate over the course of the day. I wonder how he plans to prepare them, and what else this meeting has in store.

There isn't long to wait. As Evan disappears through the swinging doors to the kitchen, the rest of the Ark of Taste committee arrives with breakfast sandwiches from the farmers' market—ten people plus two guests. Some look tired, having flown in from places as far away as California and New Mexico. One by one they introduce themselves and take their seats at the long table. Arie McFarlen, a rancher from South Dakota, serves on the board of directors of the American Livestock Breeds Conservancy and the National Family Farm Coalition. She's sitting beside Elissa Rubin-Mahon, a forager from California who specializes in wildcrafted and rare heirloom fruits. At the other end of the table is Kraig Kraft, an agricultural ecologist who studies Mesoamerican crop domestication and maintains a blog titled *Chasing Chiles*, about his search for native peppers in Mexico. That everyone is passionate about foods of one sort or another seems to be their only common link.

Our goal for the day is to review two dozen foods from around the country, ranging from Kraig's selection of native New Mexican chiles to Maine's Long Pie pumpkin. Each variety or product has a nomination form that describes its history, current production, reasons for inclusion, and level of endangerment. Those that pass today's final scrutiny—above all, for their distinctly delicious flavors—will board the Slow Food USA Ark list. These in turn will become part of a program managed by Slow Food International's Foundation for Biodiversity, based in Italy. The Ark of Taste's mission is to identify and preserve "forgotten flavors" from around the world; "endangered products that have real economic viability and commercial potential." According to the international website, its listings are "a metaphorical recipient of excellent gastronomic products that are threatened by industrial standardization, hygiene laws, the regulations of large-scale distribution and environmental damage." The Ark is a mouthful.

A few preliminaries—coffee refills, introductions—and we launch quickly into nomination reviews. Evan reappears from the kitchen carrying the first variety of the day, a sort of palate cleanser and light introduction to the tastings ahead. He's holding a five-gallon bucket shipped from Iowa with a Chelsea watermelon packed inside. This arrived overnight from the Seed Savers Exchange, an organization that preserves heritage varieties of fruits, vegetables, and flowers by connecting backyard plant collectors with others willing to exchange plants and seeds. SSE put together the melon's nomination sheet, which tells us the variety came originally from the former Czechoslovakia and was once grown on the sandy hills north of Chelsea, Iowa. According to the story—and all these foods come with stories—farmers at the turn of the twentieth century loaded their melons onto horse-drawn "triple box" spring-loaded carts, drove them to town, and sold them on the streets.

It's difficult to imagine how they managed to transport these watermelons without Styrofoam peanuts and bubble wrap. Our two samples arrived here in identical condition, each cracked in half despite the thick newsprint padding in their plastic containers. They're as delicate as eggs. Evan holds the pieces together for inspection with a rueful smile, then disappears back into the kitchen to slice them. Soon he returns to pass a plate around, and we start eating and throwing out comments. It's my kind of meeting. We move quickly, cover lots of ground, and share interesting information. I feel comfortable here. Although much of the melon's juice has run off into the newsprint, the fruit is still very sweet: delicious, if almost too sugary for my northern taste, accustomed to not-quite-ripe melons grown in Maine's chilly soil. But the greatest surprise isn't the red flesh itself. We eat through it, down to the rind, and keep going as someone discovers that the delicate skin, roughly the thickness and consistency of a cucumber's, is more than edible. Some discuss pickling. I glance around the table to find there's nothing left on anyone's plate, nothing but seeds.

In short order Evan brings plate after plate to our table: smoked Lake Michigan whitefish, roasted Macomber rutabagas, Burford pears. He's spent several years helping to rescue this rutabaga, a highly endangered, commercially unavailable variety named for two sixth-generation farmers from Westport, Massachusetts. It's surprisingly delicious, earthy and sweet, with a crunch reminiscent of a radish. In Westport's seaside soils Macomber is said to develop a distinctive flavor from the salt air. The variety is much prized regionally, and local farmers guard it jealously, arguing over which lines are the most true to type. I'm startled to realize that it's in my own collection under the name Westport (a recent acquisition through the Seed Savers Exchange). It's growing in my gardens for the first time this season, so this is my first taste.

We follow these foods with three types of mayhaw jelly, a traditional staple in the Southeast made from a wild fruit in the hawthorn family. Production of the jelly is in decline despite its rich aroma and flavor. Then several of Kraig's favorite New Mexican native chiles, little balls of fire sampled raw in small pieces from a shared plate. We taste Bodega Red potatoes, unique in that they arrived in this country directly from South America, unlike most other potatoes that came from the Southern Hemisphere by way of Europe. Then we're on to Newtown Pippin apples, an eighteenth-century variety native to what is today part of Queens, New York, and once known as "the Prince of Apples." These were said to be a favorite of George Washington, Benjamin Franklin, and Thomas Jefferson (although, as fruit historian and nurseryman Tom Burford wryly points out, we can't really know the mind of Jefferson, a man known for his diverse tastes). Queen Victoria thought so highly of the Newtown Pippin that she had the British Parliament exempt its import duty to make it more widely available.

Fast, free-flowing conversation follows each new nomination. As a longtime collector and heritage food grower, I'm deeply impressed by the level of knowledge here. Could Long Pie pumpkin be identical to another variety called Algonquin? How close is the Macomber to Pennsylvania's Sweet German rutabaga, described by Fearing Burr in 1863? Chefs in the room discuss flavor and culinary potential, while growers speculate about horticultural shortcomings that might prevent broader acceptance. Some foods pass with resounding approval, and others are tabled pending additional research.

Only one food definitively fails to pass, based on its taste. Maybe if we'd sampled Boothby's Blonde cucumbers back in August, straight from the field? It's true these last remaining fruits don't have a lot of flavor—they're a little watery and bland—but what does everyone want from a cucumber, anyway? They're pretty, with a greenish flesh and vivid yellow skin, and isn't that enough? The committee members come to a general agreement, though: Boothby's Blonde doesn't have what it takes for the Ark of Taste. Thumbs down. Reluctantly, I have to agree. I try not to take it personally.

Tastings continue through the afternoon. A beautiful loaf of bread sits on the side table at our room in the Black Trumpet Bistro: wood-fired, thick-crusted, dark and irresistible. I start leafing through my notes to figure out when we'll slice into it. Must be the Turkey Hard Red winter wheat from Kansas, because the other possibility, White Sonoran wheat from Arizona, is lighter and traditionally used for flat bread. Whatever this is, a little bread would be perfect as a foil for all the fruits and vegetables Evan presented to us through the morning—particularly the roasted Burford pears and raw bits of Red Wethersfield onion we've sampled directly from a shared plate.

Sitting next to me at the table is Glenn Roberts, the founder of Anson Mills, a South Carolina company working with organic heritage grains to produce foods ranging from Antebellum Coarse Grits to Ni-Hachi Sobakoh, the buckwheat flour foundation for Japanese soba noodles. He's disarmingly friendly and warm, infectiously enthusiastic about heritage grains and good food of all kinds. Glenn left behind a thirty-year career in historic restoration and restaurant and hotel concept design to found his company, starting with a few grinding wheels in a rented warehouse behind a car wash in Columbia, South Carolina. He's the kind of guy who's equally at home wearing work boots in the field and sitting at a boardroom table.

Glenn launches into rapid overviews of Turkey and Sonoran wheat, revealing that he had a hand in both nominations. Flavor profiles, sources, baking qualities, nutritional content—you name it, he's a walking encyclopedia. He guides us through intricate details about growing habits and tastes, speculates about the origins of these grains, and lays out historical details from memory. Glenn can puzzle out different names for a particular line of wheat, identify its truest representatives, and distinguish fine points of flavor. He goes off on tangents that leave the rest of us subdued and quiet while we try to take everything in. Because he's a natural storyteller, he keeps everything interesting as he recounts the details of each variety.

In the case of Turkey wheat Glenn explains that's he's been working with Thom Leonard of the Heritage Grain and Seed Company in Lawrence, Kansas, to clean up and certify seed for increased production. This grain once dominated plantings throughout much of the Great Plains, but today only one adventurous farmer is growing it on any scale beyond tiny, hand-harvested plots. Glenn describes Bryce Stephens's hundred acres of Turkey wheat in Jennings, Kansas, as likely the largest planting in decades, and it's clear we're lucky to have enough to taste today. The loaf of bread on our table is a living cultural relic, a food that brightened winter days in sod huts from Oklahoma to Nebraska. It's *Little House on the Prairie* wheat.

Glenn tells us that Turkey is a class of wheat rather than a particular variety. In other words, there are variations among strains, but all those that share the name arrived on the Kansas plains with Mennonite settlers fleeing nineteenth-century persecution in the Crimea. Because of their relatively high yields, hardiness, and excellent flavor, these seeds were among their most prized possessions. Farmers across the Midwest would grow Turkey wheat for the next seventy-five years, and its success helped establish the Great Plains as the breadbasket of the world, until the advent of modern dwarfing varieties in the middle of the twentieth century.

Turkey wheat grows nearly six feet tall in the right conditions. Seedheads sway in the wind on tall, willowy stems—the amber waves of Great Plains mythology. In wet conditions on highly fertile ground the plants' height can lead to "lodging," or a tendency to fall over, which can complicate harvesting and reduce productivity. In dry conditions with limited fertility, however, Thom Leonard finds that yields of Turkey wheat approach those of modern semidwarf varieties. Its tall growth helps suppress weeds and produces more organic matter to return to the soil over time, while deeper roots increase nutrient uptake. According to Thom and Glenn, Turkey wheat promises to become a valuable crop once again as we seek to reduce irrigation and move away from petroleum-dependent fertilizers. And then, if it can produce a beautiful loaf like this from my own kitchen . . .

It's hard to go wrong with any kind of bread coming from a wood-fired oven, in my opinion. This loaf more than lives up to its promise, though: chewy and moist, with a crisp crust, and richly flavored. Its taste is especially eye-opening next to the flat bread made from Sonoran wheat, which is light, nutty, and nearly free of gluten. Glenn describes the latter as "lingering sweetness on the back palate . . . and a haunting minerality." We instantly understand that these grains can't be used interchangeably, because the Kansas bread is dark, earthy, and strongly flavored. Both are delicious, but contrasting, occupying entirely different culinary and ecological niches.

My relationship with heritage foods has until now been what you might describe as "curatorial." Sure, I want to eat them, but first and foremost my goal has been to help preserve them from extinction. Glenn's motivations are similar, but his ambitions are much greater. His efforts to bring grains like these back into commercial production are part of something new in conservation, a glimmer on the horizon. By engaging producers and chefs with heritage varieties in the field and at the market, he wants to return these foods to cultural relevance. Turkey wheat isn't simply an old variety making a comeback. It represents a new business model, a way to develop a brand around genetic conservation. This, to me, is revolutionary.

A final nomination to the Ark of Taste also arouses my curiosity. On a side shelf in our tasting room sits a half-filled, dark green wine bottle with its label removed. If it's not left over from a staff party, this must be the fermented cider of the Harrison apple. Renowned nurseryman Tom Burford nominated this apple for the Ark, as well as the Burford pear we tasted earlier, named for his great-grandfather. The notes he's prepared describe Harrison as the source of one of the finest of American hard ciders, which "commanded the highest price in the New York market" as a single-variety cider in the nineteenth century. At one time Americans recognized distinctions between single-variety and blended ciders, much as we do in today's wines. Dark and rich, Harrison's juice was also often blended with that from another antique apple, the Graniwinkle, to produce a much sought-after drink.

Tom Burford and his father spent many years searching for a Harrison tree. Although the variety once grew widely in the mid-Atlantic and eastern seaboard, by the middle of the twentieth century it had all but disappeared, gone the way of so many older food varieties, and was nearly extinct. In the case of cider apples this was not only by chance and neglect, but also by design. Beginning in the middle of the nineteenth century, prohibitionists targeted apple orchards and made them the symbolic focus of many of their campaigns. Unlike beer, the grain-based beverage of choice for new immigrants in industrial cities, fermented cider was a rural, land-based drink, and cider trees like Harrison were easy marks for hatchet-wielding teetotalers.

By the 1980s the only known source for Harrison apples was a Vermont collector who had rescued scions (dormant cuttings) from a single New Jersey tree in 1976, which was cut down soon thereafter. Tom Burford continued the search for Harrison trees, and in 1989 visited an acquaintance in Paramus, New Jersey. After dinner the land's owner suggested he take a walk behind the house to examine a neglected old orchard, thinking there might be some unusual fruits growing there. According to an article about his work in the *Charlottesville News*, Burford said, "I just about fainted. It was the gut feeling: This is a Harrison. So I was mute for a while and I went back and told [the owner] I think you have a very rare apple out there that's one I've been looking for and one my father looked for for many years." On the condition that he wouldn't reveal his source, he collected scions and grafted them onto new rootstocks. Several years later this original tree died as well, and the Harrison apple lived on only in the trees propagated by these two collectors.

If Glenn Roberts's reintroductions of heritage grains are one kind of success story in the heritage food movement, Harrison apples could represent its latent potential. This cider seems to have everything going for it. The taste is of the highest quality, its history is rich, and the tree has good horticultural properties. Harrison is resistant to some prevalent apple diseases, and it bears annually and well. One early-nineteenth-century New Jersey tree was said to have produced more than one hundred bushels (an ordinary yield would be in the range of twenty). Despite all this, Harrison has yet to catch hold again. A few specialty nurseries now carry the tree, and a handful of cider makers, particularly in Virginia, are experimenting with plantings. Nevertheless, it's been more than twenty years since the rediscovery of this fine old apple, and it hasn't quite gained traction and found its niche.

Enter Ben Watson. Or, more precisely, give him a moment to push back his chair, grab a few glasses, and head for the side table. The chairman of our Ark of Taste committee is, conveniently, also one of the country's preeminent cider experts. Ben's been working closely with Tom Burford to encourage wider use of the Harrison, and he's shepherding this nomination closely. He brought with him a half bottle of unlabeled fermented Harrison cider from Albemarle Ciderworks in Virginia (my partner Karla asked me later, "Was it full the night before?"), and he measures this carefully into glasses for sampling. Each of us receives a few ounces of this very rare drink, a taste from another century, and we wait to begin the tasting until Ben can walk us through the nomination.

Ben's a genial guy, well suited to his role as spokesman for what was once the country's most ubiquitous drink, the mainstay of farm orchards from colonial New England to the midwestern frontier. Our review of the nomination is as convivial as a round at a neighborhood bar, and he makes clear to us that this is part of the appeal of real cider. It's a drink every bit as accessible as good craft beer, but with the natural food pairing you'd expect only from wine (thanks to cider's acids and tannins, which break down fat and help clear the palate). "Cheers," he says, after explaining the backstory and details of Harrison's history. With that we begin our tasting.

The cider has the color of an ale, dark and complex, with the full, exceptional mouthfeel most people probably associate with wines like Grenache or Syrah. It's a drink best appreciated with good company and a laden table. Until this meeting, two years ago as I write this, like so many other Americans I'd associated hard cider with wine coolers: overly sweet, light, clear, one-note drinks that taste above all like apple juice and alcohol. Harrison may have been the first real cider I'd encountered, and it was nothing like the commercial hard "ciders" most of us know in this country, produced as often as not from concentrates. Tasting this drink was an eye-opening experience that captured my imagination. It may not be an exaggeration to say that it's changed the direction of my life and work.

Not even a month later, in October 2009, I find myself in a sports bar in downtown Syracuse, New York, wondering what the hell I was thinking while holding a glass of commercial "draft cider" in my hand. The moment it hits the mahogany counter, I think *What a mistake.* The glass is frosty and crystal clear, the color of a Bud Lite, and the drink is obviously heavily carbonated. One sip and I start looking around for someone to take it off my hands. Karla glances at me, instantly reads my mind, and points to our Indian grad student friend. She leans over to whisper in my ear, "Nidhi loves sweet drinks. Give it to her." Sure enough, this turns out to be Nidhi's thing. "It's delicious," she says. Plenty of people seem to agree with her and enjoy drinking sweet commercial ciders, and it's true they go down easily enough. Not for me, though. I order a Guinness to get the taste out of my mouth.

The next day I hop in the car and head west. Karla will be tied up all day in meetings with her thesis advisers at the SUNY College of Environmental Science and Forestry, so I'm on my own, free to go exploring. My destination is the New York State Agricultural Experiment Station a few miles from Geneva, a romantic-sounding town at the northern tip of Seneca Lake.

Low-hanging clouds on the horizon accentuate changes in the landscape we've noticed since crossing the New York state line, where we left behind the small farm fields and wooded slopes of New England. Here vistas broaden, agricultural land becomes increasingly fertile and expansive, and everything starts to flatten out. On the outskirts of Geneva, about an hour west of Syracuse, only streams, windbreaks, and woodlots interrupt the farm fields. Everything is agricultural. Farms are still quite small by the standards of the Midwest, where a farmer might work many thousands of acres, but to New England eyes open fields are everywhere. No one has to scramble to find half an acre of tillable ground to plant a garden, or a scant quarter acre for orchard trials. Even near Syracuse, where urban sprawl takes its toll, agricultural land is everywhere.

Less than five minutes from downtown Geneva I reach the experiment station and park beside a complex of offices and research buildings. Even a cursory glance at the surrounding campus suggests an awkward blend of old and new, an uneasy divide between technologies. What appear to be abandoned and decrepit glasshouses share space with new climate-controlled structures, while one-story cinder-block offices surround a fine old barn. Hardly anyone is around, and there are plenty of parking spaces available. This could be due to the season—early October—or maybe it's simply the quiet of a rural area seen from the perspective of a visiting urban dweller.

In fact the site is actively used for research, and Cornell University shares space here with USDA offices and the National Genetic Resources Program. I walk among the greenhouses and peer through the steam-covered glass, trying to get a better look at what's going on inside. Trays of seedlings confirm that these are in full use, continuing a tradition that stretches back to the 1880s. The station has a rich and varied history from an agricultural perspective. It was here in the late nineteenth and early twentieth centuries that researchers collected, evaluated, and improved foods ranging from grapes to beef cattle, and published the wonderful illustrated series that includes *The Apples of New York, The Peaches of New York, The Cherries of New York,* and others in the same vein.

The Geneva USDA program is part of a nationwide genebank network that preserves everything from thousands of accessions of *Abelmoschus,* or okra (native to Africa, Asia, and Australia), to four of *Zingiber,* root ginger (native to Southwest Asia). Somewhere in between are the green Indian chickpeas and the red and white Bolivian beans that the Pullman USDA collections curator gave me for my own gardens nearly fifteen years ago. Their network comprises twenty plant stations spread throughout the country, each specializing and focusing on crops adapted to a particular region. The Arctic and Subarctic Plant Gene Bank in Palmer, Alaska, doesn't try to preserve crops better suited to the Desert Legume Program in Tucson, Arizona, or the National Germplasm Repositories in Puerto Rico and Hawaii.

Anyone concerned about wise use of government resources should visit the USDA's plant genetic resources websites and read about these collections. A cursory glance at the bare-bones Geneva web page puts to rest any fears that they've wasted tax dollars on anything approaching a sophisticated PR effort. The main heading reads "Plant Genetic Resources Unit (PGRU): Welcome to the

Plant Genetic Resources Unit!!" The latter is in bold red lettering. Below is a modestly stated goal: "The two missions of the PGRU are the preservation of germplasm of selected crop plants and the breeding and improvement of apples. Specific activities include acquisition, documentation, maintenance, characterization, breeding, enhancement and distribution of the assigned crops. PGRU maintains approximately 20,000 different accessions, representing over 300 species."

If this sounds pretty casual, working with such a large collection is a tremendous challenge. I wonder what resources they have at their disposal here in New York. Walking into their headquarters in a nondescript one-story concrete block building on the Geneva research station grounds, it's immediately clear that it doesn't get much more basic than this. The researchers do their seed processing in a steel utility barn beside the farm fields. How many staff does the station have? Not a lot, as it turns out—if anything, this is a severely underfunded operation.

Bill Garman, a research technician responsible for growing and evaluating vegetable collections, greets me in his office. "Give me a minute," he tells me, "and we'll drive over to the nearby fields." It's late in the season to gain a good impression of his work, but many crops are still in the ground thanks to the warm fall. He grabs his coat and baseball cap, we head outside, and I jump in my car to follow him in his truck. After a couple of miles on county roads we turn off onto a gravel drive, unmarked beside ordinary split-level ranch homes. It looks more like the utility entrance to a warehouse or an electrical substation than a genetic research facility, and maybe that's exactly the point. If you can't find your way here, in all likelihood you belong somewhere else.

We pull up beside the barn and I join Bill in his truck, engine running with the heat on. It's cold and wet, downright gloomy. Slowly we head down a rutted access road along the field's edge while Bill talks about his work and the vegetable collection under his supervision. "I started in these fields fifteen years ago," he tells me. He tended plants and ran equipment, eventually working his way up to the farm manager position. Previously he'd sold farm machinery and agricultural chemicals, and he retains the open, easygoing manner of a salesman. It's partly the time of year, but this morning he's in no great hurry, happy to look over the fruits of the season's labor.

"Wish we didn't have to let the tomatoes run over the ground like this," he says, apologizing for the tangle of vines sprawled across the black plastic weed barrier. He doesn't have the time, staff, or budget to tie the hundreds of varieties growing here to vertical supports. Since he grows these plants primarily to regenerate seed and evaluate their characteristics, it's enough to let them run, even if it makes the plot look pretty unruly. Bill also regrets managing weeds primarily with herbicides, but it's equally necessary to save labor costs. I tell him I'm impressed by what he accomplishes with such a limited budget and skeleton crew. If he has to spray to preserve rare squashes, tomatoes, and cabbages, so be it. That decision was effectively made elsewhere.

We can only see so much from the cab of the truck: the forlorn look of a late-season vegetable field, row after row of netted cages that isolate plants and prevent insects from crossing pollen between varieties, and rutted, muddy access roads. It isn't raining at the moment, but a heavy mist hangs low over the whole scene. Soon Bill needs to get back to the office. I'm more than ready to jump out to have a closer look at everything. My camera tucked under my coat for protection from the weather, and a bag with notebook and pen in hand, I'm on my own. There's no one else out here, though Bill tells me he plans to return soon to clean seeds in the barn. It's 10 AM and I've got roughly an hour and a half before the gates will be locked for the rest of the weekend.

The ground is saturated, and it doesn't take more than a few minutes for my leather boots to become completely waterlogged in the heavy dew. Should have thought to throw rubber boots in with my gear, but honestly it doesn't really matter. The scene in front of me is captivating—row after row of plants I've never seen before, like wild tomatoes with fantastic shapes from South America. They aren't edible, or barely so, but the shapes, textures, and colors alone are enough to set them apart from any tomatoes in the supermarket. These are something from a children's book, fantasy vegetables—grape-like clusters of purple-tinged fruit, spiny globes with the appearance of seed husks, fuzzy little fruits with encircling stems that resemble the body and legs of caterpillars.

Many of the plant varieties in these fields may never again grace anyone's table, if they ever did. They're here for their resilience and resistance: to disease, pests, drought, or heavy rain. Some may hold the keys to future breeding success. As Bill Garman grows and preserves them, others record information about their attributes, like susceptibility to diseases such as anthracnose and bacterial canker, level of cracking in the mature fruits (which would quickly relegate commercial tomatoes to the seconds bin), and size, shape, and yield. There are dozens of descriptors, and, yes, they include taste, though it's a bit of an afterthought and a little vague. Instead of quantifiable codes and numeric values, the category simply requests "comments on unusual or noteworthy flavor." What's the breeder of the future to do when searching for a more alluring aroma, or a hint of chocolate on, say, a scale of 1 to 9? At least the USDA records levels of sugars, ascorbic acid (vitamin C), and total acidity, which begins to get at the essence of a good tomato.

Next to the wild Peruvian tomatoes are celeries of different hues and textures, ranging from the large supermarket varieties familiar to most of us to culinary types best used in small quantities for seasoning. I didn't know it was possible to produce so many large celeries in this climate. In my own gardens I've grown only wilder "smallage" varieties, with tough, strong-flavored stalks and leaves typically used in soups or stews. Those growing here were collected all over the world, and their names reflect their diversity. Glademaster 136 sounds to me like an automatic weapon. Golden Spartan brings to mind a football team. And what are we to make of the Seler odm. Globus Nr2/LRN 734? I'd like to cook with the Golden Detroit and the curiously named Listen from Macedonia. Could the latter be the name of a village where it was collected?

Forty large, rectangular steel-framed cages, each roughly ten by thirty feet long and five feet tall, cover nearby rows. Each is fitted with heavy nylon insect screening to allow the staff to maintain control over pollination. Private seed preservation gardens often use something similar on a smaller scale. They tack spun polyester row cover to wooden cages to create an effective insect barrier. These USDA cages are much larger and more durable, with heavy-duty zippers securing UV-treated fabric. Inside are nucs (short for "nucleus hives"), cardboard bee boxes holding small colonies, including a queen. The bees ensure pollination within the cage. In such a planting arrangement scientists know that an insect-pollinated crop, say a broccoli, will be pollinated only with other plantings of the same type within the cage. They can add several other insect-pollinated species in the same space (like a water-melon, a turnip, and an onion), knowing these can't cross with one another—but only one of each type. If not for these precautions wild pollinators would quickly cross varieties of the same species, resulting in the loss of distinct identities.

Only a part of these fields is caged, because each kind of vegetable has different pollination requirements to remain true to type. Those that aren't insect-pollinated either rely on the wind to disperse their pollen (plants like corn and spinach, which need to be isolated from other varieties by at least a mile, and aren't grown at this research station), or are largely self-pollinating (beans, tomatoes, peppers). Biennials like celery, carrots, and rutabaga require two seasons to set seed, so these can be grown unprotected in their first season, then transplanted to cages or isolated from other varieties the fol-lowing year. The larger the collection, the more complicated the rotations and isolation required to keep each seed variety true to type. You can't just plant everything out and call it preserved.

At this time of year the *Cucurbita maxima*, the winter squashes, catch the eye even under their insect netting. Colorful Macedonian squashes look like Turban varieties, hues of orange and green with the distinct Turk's-cap shape, while other squashes resemble noth-ing so much as giant pale pumpkins. Their labels (barely legible through the screens) identify them as cultivars collected around the world, from countries like Italy, Burundi, and China as well as the United States. Later I look the collection up online and find over eight hundred accessions, including some of my favorites, like Marina di Chioggia from Italy. Its name is misspelled here, and there's no infor-mation about its wonderful rich flavor and flaky texture, the vivid color of its skin and flesh, or its culinary history. But there it is none-theless. Marina di Chioggia is an outstanding squash, known for making some of the finest gnocchi and for roasting. Also in the col-lection are familiar Hubbards and Buttercups, American heirlooms like the Candy Roaster (listed here as "Candy Roadster"), imports with names like Probistipska and Lisicka, and numerous unnamed varieties—like the PI135365—that provide nothing but accession numbers (*PI* being an abbreviation for "Plant Introduction").

As fascinated as I am with these foods, my attention is continually drawn to the far side of the field. Somehow it hadn't occurred to me that the USDA's preservation orchards (apple, grape, and cherry collections) might be here at the same site as the vegetables. Yet just a few hundred yards away, stretching across the horizon, is a fifty-acre expanse of trees and vines, one of the largest fruit collections in the world. It doesn't take long for me to decide bolting asparagus can wait. It's October, peak apple season, and this is an opportunity to see fruits I may never lay eyes on again. I feel like a kid at an unwatched candy store, and like a kid I tell myself I'm only going over to take a look.

An encircling eight-foot-high wire fence rises along the edge of the large field. It protects the site from browsing deer, but there's nothing other than a meadow dividing the vegetables from the apples, cherries, and grapes. I snap photos while crossing the open space, then ascend a low hill into the nearest block of trees. The apples in this area are taller than the rest, many over twenty feet, with an appearance distinctly different from the others. It feels like I'm hiking into a forest in Western Asia. These trees were collected directly from the wild in Kazakhstan, which is the genetic homeland, birthplace, and center of diversity of the cultivated apple (*Malus* x *domestica*, or *M. pumila*) that we all know today. Most of the apples here have already dropped to the ground, but some trees remain covered with wild fruits of all sizes and shapes. A surprising percentage appear ready for the table, as appealing as any abandoned fruit growing on forgotten farms around Maine. From my vantage point these Kazakh trees stand watch over their tamed descendants farther down the hill. Below me row after row of dwarfing trees eight to twelve feet tall spread out in neat rows. It's a beautiful scene, rolling fields filled with midsized trees loaded with unpicked fruit.

The USDA maintains two trees of each variety—a true apple ark. Most are planted on twelve- or nine-foot centers between trees, an average spacing in a modern orchard—neither the high-density trellising of dwarfed trees nor the open spacing of full-sized standards. If that sounds like a close planting, consider how much ground it covers, with several thousand trees spaced three to four paces apart. I do a little quick math (which in my case generally means inaccurate math) and come to the conclusion that to view each of the more than three thousand apple varieties planted here (over six thousand trees) would require several miles of walking. It won't be possible to cover everything today. There's nothing to do but pick a place at random and get started, so I choose a row and follow it, zigzagging back and forth between varieties and reading labels on the fly. I search for recognizable names and stop only to examine and photograph fruit that catches my eye or sounds familiar.

The fields are eerily empty. Commercial orchards swarm with pickers in early October, yet here there's no one around, even though most trees are hanging full of ripe fruit. Before dropping me off in his vegetable plots, Bill Garman explained that the fruit collections are as lightly staffed as his own farm fields, with a handful of scientists and technicians responsible for the ongoing maintenance of thousands of varieties of apples, sour cherries, and grapes. This explains in part why there's no one else out here, despite the peak season for fruit evaluation. That, and it's Columbus Day, a holiday for federal and state workers. Plus it's started to rain.

Since this is a sort of living museum, in keeping with that spirit I've resolved to look but not touch or taste. My willpower holds up for a couple of minutes, until I come across an Ashmead's Kernel, a variety I've been meaning to taste for a long time. Such a beautiful apple, and it has a long and rich history dating back at least three hundred years in England. Its two trees are heavily laden, with dozens of apples scattered over the ground in varying states of decomposition. They're impossible to resist. How likely is it that anyone has plans for all the nice Ashmeads lying amid the recently sprayed, blackened weeds around the trunk? I pick up a fresh drop, have a taste, and lay it back inconspicuously, bite-side down. This is my favorite kind of apple: golden, russeted, with a perfect balance of sweetness and acidity. Fantastic.

My pace accelerates as row after row flies by. All sense of time disappears. It's simply impossible to take everything in; there's too much to see. I'm walking very fast, almost running, veering off to read the small print on plastic ID labels. My feet are soaked but my raincoat shields my camera from the light rain. I'm keeping it close at hand for photographing identification tags and fruit. Upon reaching an interesting tree I stop to shoot the fruit, then the label (to identify it later), and move on quickly. I take bites from the choicest of the drops and stay true to my decision not to remove fruit from the trees. Maybe the apples will be on the ground tomorrow, but it seems right to avoid disturbing any still hanging on the branches.

And then suddenly it's 12:30 and I'm reminded that Bill said the staff would leave by 11 AM, locking the gates behind them. My car parked by the barn is on the wrong side of the fence. If Bill has been looking for me, he'd need a bloodhound to track me down among the trees. Quickly I turn on my heel and start heading for the entrance, but then stop short again after a hundred yards. Halfway down another set of orchard rows there's another car parked on the grass. Someone is walking beside it, examining trees. So there's someone else out here after all. Whoever it is, they're heavily bundled in rain gear, slowly wandering from tree to tree, apparently also entranced by the orchard.

Jessica Rath looks up into one of the trees, consults her notes, and takes a photograph. Then she picks one of the fruits and tastes it. And drops it on the ground. "Hey," I call out, "do you know when the gates close for the day?" Three o'clock, she tells me, don't worry, there's plenty of time remaining ahead of us. Maybe Bill had to head out early, or he just wanted to be sure I wouldn't do exactly what I've done, lose all sense of time and get lost out here.

Jessica is a sculptor from Los Angeles who spent three months talking her way into this collection. She raised money on the grassroots fund-raising website Kickstarter to fly here and view the trees over the course of several days. She's working her way methodically through the collection, following notes about varieties printed for her by fruit crops farm manager Bill Smrack. "I'm looking for 120 of the best-tasting apples," she tells me, because Smrack agreed to let her ship this many home to her husband, a retired chef who plans to bake them into pastries for a public tasting. For her own work she'll create naturalistic sculptures based on her experience to help educate the public about genetic diversity. "I love plants, fruits and endangered trees. This is my heaven, this orchard," she'd written on her Kickstarter proposal.

Although the USDA runs this preservation program, everything here is very much in the public domain. The National Plant Germplasm System describes itself as "a cooperative effort by public (state and federal) and private organizations to preserve the genetic diversity of plants." It's accessible to ordinary people, but the USDA typically restricts distribution of plant material to those who can make a decent case for good research and breeding purposes (they also usually no longer provide anything that can be acquired from a commercial source). Nevertheless, they work with serious private as well as public collectors; we the people own this orchard. That it's maintained by an overworked, probably underpaid staff makes it seem all the more connected to the rest of the overworked and underpaid horticultural world.

Jessica has already spent two days at this site. She has plenty of information available on computer printouts, so I stop to learn more from her. "Any recommendations you can point me toward?" I ask. Yes, she says, there's an apple growing just a few rows away, which according to her is Bill Smrack's favorite. This is saying something—the curator's favorite fruit among thousands. She tells me he cares about texture above all other qualities, and the flesh of this apple has a particularly fine grain. I thank her, wish her luck with her project, and head off to find this obscure variety.

There's no fanfare surrounding Smrack's tree. Later I'll learn that the USDA database tells us next to nothing about its history. A forgotten treasure, possibly rescued from an old farmstead. Or maybe it was the result of someone's breeding experiments. The records note only that Dr. Susan K. Brown of Cornell donated it in 1992, and that it originated in the state of New York. The apple grows in the middle of a long row, revealing nothing but the same limited information printed on plastic accession sheets at every tree, stapled to identical slabs of pressure-treated wood. This tree itself is younger than most, its four-inch-diameter trunk standing only about eight feet tall. Roughly thirty large fruits dangle from its branches, and nearly that many rot on the ground. If it's true that Smrack loves this apple, he's let much of the ripening fruit drop uncollected. Could this be the right tree?

The variety doesn't even have a name—no Maiden Blush or King Luscious—just a code, E.8, and a plant introduction accession number. I reach down and pick an apple off the ground, take a bite, and walk away. Then turn around, pick the apple up again, take another bite, and set it back down. A few pictures, a few more bites. Truth is, I don't quite love apples the way I love pie cherries, peaches, and pears, but this is an irresistible fruit. Could it be the power of suggestion? Possibly, but this large apple is rich and juicy, with a tender skin, slight crunch, and a perfect balance of sweet and acid flavors. I can't stop eating it.

E.8 isn't the only apple that captures my imagination. The variety of textures, flavors, colors, shapes, and sizes on display here is astonishing. It doesn't take long to completely lose my capacity to taste and experience new flavors, but some manage to stand out regardless. I take note of the best for my future plantings, even though this quick tour only scratches the surface. Such a short visit provides just a snapshot, and not only because there's too much ground to cover. Every apple has slightly different ripening times and uses, so fruit that hits its peak after a couple of months of storage, or summer apples, or those that make the best cider or pies aren't going to get my attention. Not like the dessert fruit that's ripened by chance at exactly this moment.

So much history and information lies dormant in this orchard, either forgotten or neglected. One of the first trees I come across after leaving the Kazakh collection is the Black Oxford. It was, according to USDA records, donated from Maryland, and "grown before 1790." No other information available. Fine, they got the date right, but let's set the record straight—this is a Maine apple! Why no mention of its origins in central Maine in the town of Paris, or its agricultural history? This may not matter to a plant breeder, but it's news around northern New England. Black Oxford is making a strong comeback. This is a visually striking fruit, with reddish stars on a deep purple background. It's a great all-purpose apple—good for cider, excellent for baking and storage, and at its peak for fresh eating in midwinter.

Another excellent variety is called Sweet McIntosh, which to its credit looks and tastes nothing like McIntosh. It's hard to understand why Macs, disease-susceptible, mushy apples with mediocre flavor, became such a ubiquitous part of the New England landscape. The USDA's Agricultural Research Service description does Sweet McIntosh a disservice, in my opinion. It's a far cry from a chef's menu selection, and hardly a siren call. "Skin 90% red, striped, scarfskin, heavy bloom; shape oblate, symmetrical; flesh semifirm, nearly white; flavor sweet, aromatic, does not resemble McIntosh; eating quality good." Eating quality "good"? Again, this apple is impossible to put down. "Does not resemble McIntosh"—and does not taste like McIntosh, let's be absolutely clear. Cornell developed this variety, but since its donation to the USDA collection in 1985 it seems to have gone nowhere. I've looked for it in the years since, and despite acquiring a tree for my own collection, haven't found Sweet Mac available anywhere in the commercial trade.

Although clearly we're not going to resurrect thousands of apples in the foreseeable future, this visit reminds me that many culinary gems wait to be rediscovered. While walking back to my car, last month's Ark of Taste meeting comes to mind, because it concerned itself above all with bringing genetic diversity to a wider audience. I wonder not only what might lie hidden in a collection of this kind, but how these foods can find new life. What complement to Harrison cider apples might we find among the wild Kazakh trees, and who might use them to develop new businesses? What chefs would jump at the chance to cook with some of these historic baking apples? Imagine farmers' markets filled with fruit like this.

My three-hour tour of the Geneva USDA collections offers the briefest glimpse into something rich and expansive. Much of the potential of these foods remains untapped and unknown. All too often available records tell us little about how they taste, how they were used, who developed them, and why. I feel like an urban dweller seeing mountains and forests for the first time. On the drive back to Syracuse, it's clear to me that the only way I'll come to know more about these foods is to greatly expand my own collections, and discover new purpose in growing them. I've got work to do.

Three

SWELTERING IN THE FIELD:
WORKING FARMS AND GARDENS

*A*s the Ark of Taste committee gathers at the Black Trumpet Bistro to sample rare foods, it's easy to see why this kind of activity at times gets Slow Food into trouble. Flying buckets of fruit by FedEx halfway across the country, meeting in a high-end restaurant to discuss the flavor of watermelon rind, sampling jellies made from the fruits of wild hawthorns—this is the sort of thing that riles people. It flies against American populist instincts and smacks of the worst kind of gastronomic elitism. The people are hungry? Let them eat Long Pie pumpkin.

And yet the foods before the committee originated in the gardens, orchards, farms, and kitchens of ordinary people—they're not the creation of some fashionable elite. Most of the Ark's members sit squarely in the producer camp, working hard to raise and prepare rare foods, and get the message out in a hands-on way about culinary richness and diversity. The fruits, vegetables, and meats listed on the Ark of Taste celebrate deep-rooted traditions, common experiences of the land, and cultural history. Can we distinguish pride in southwestern tribal traditions from efforts to preserve endangered chile peppers?

Here in the United States our perspective is largely revealed by our shopping habits—we're a nation of consumers, distanced from the needs of producers and the realities of farming. If low prices seem to guarantee access and security in our daily food choices, the costs to farm communities, rural workers, and the environment are invisible to us. Market pressures force small and midsized farmers off the land, and competition from huge subsidized operations leads others to abandon biodiversity in their fields. Never mind that independent family farmers struggle to make a living; those pursuing alternative paths, like small-scale organic farmers (and the customers willing to support them), are painted as elitists. Standardization in the supermarket democratizes. Who's in control of this conversation?

To counter this view of good food as somehow "elitist," it's useful to step back to share some perspectives on farmwork, as well as experiences gardening in places that lack access to high-quality seeds and genetic diversity. The time I've spent working with my hands has been at once rewarding, offering the satisfaction of tangible work and a job well done, but also difficult. Often it was hard to say what drove me to continue, working typically for very low wages. The answer was probably some mix of stubbornness, an ideal of living lightly on the land, and unhappiness with environmental degradation. Today I've largely found a balance and a purpose that allow me to enjoy my work, but it hasn't always been this way.

On a hot summer morning in Washington State, July 1993, I pull my truck up to the edge of an alfalfa field. Already by 6 AM shadows from the adjacent hills are retreating to the far edge of this twenty-acre field, and sprinklers running in two sets of irrigation lines reflect the early-morning sunlight. I'm working for a small neighboring ranch, spending several hours a day in the fields watering alfalfa and pastures for the cattle and horses. The ranch uses hand lines, a somewhat dated way to irrigate that most farmers have replaced with larger automated systems. In these small, scattered fields, however, hand lines remain useful and effective, if labor-intensive.

In marked contrast with the near-rain-forest climate ninety miles to the west, where the North Cascade Mountains wring moisture from the air as it rises, the landscape here is open and semi-arid. This field is located near the end of a long mountain valley that gets only about fourteen inches of precipitation annually, which arrives primarily as snow during the long, cold winter. From April to October the sun rises most days in a cloudless sky. Summers are hot, short, and intense, with dry winds that turn the hills varying shades of brown by the middle of June. Irrigation isn't optional for any home garden or commercial farm.

Water comes either from wells, or from ditches that have been in place since the early twentieth century, covering the valley floor in distribution systems linked to the nearby river. This network carries snowmelt from higher elevations in the nearby Cascades down to the farm fields. The ditch that runs through a grove of ponderosa pines by my house is good for swimming, because it's open and free flowing, six to eight feet wide and two feet deep, cold and exceptionally clean. It seems more like a mountain stream than a constructed ditch, yet every cubic foot of water that passes through the system is closely regulated and monitored. Water usage is bought and sold with property rights, and jealously guarded.

Although it's all too easy to leave out the details of this kind of tedious work, they help explain what agricultural workers deal with on a daily basis. Irrigation shares allow the ranch to run forty sprinklers in this twenty-acre field at any one time. A surface-mounted pump draws water from the ditch and feeds it into a four-inch aluminum line that's permanently positioned down the middle of the field. My job is to move two sets of smaller hand lines—sections of portable aluminum pipe that branch off perpendicularly from the main line—marching them steadily down the field day after day. The system is sized so that when hand lines move twice a day, once in the morning and once in the evening, every part of the field receives water over the course of a week.

With a few turns of a hand crank I shut down the main water valve at the first set of lines, immediately stopping twenty sprinkler heads from running. Then I walk out into the field and look around. Knee-high, deep green alfalfa seems all the more intensely colored against the backdrop of brown hills, which are covered in bunchgrass, knapweed, bitterbrush, and sage. Pockets of pine, fir, and aspen follow the hills' contours in the draws and on the valley floor—wherever there's enough moisture to sustain them. Trees and dense shrubs line the edges of the nearby irrigation ditch, quickly giving way to grasses and low shrubs beyond the water's flow.

With the pressure gone from the system, I pick up the first of the hand lines and carry it to its next position, thirty feet down the field and parallel to its first set. Then I connect it to the main line and open the valve. As water shoots from the first pipe, I walk back as quickly as possible to grab the next section, nearly at a running pace. The rancher who's hired me at a minimum wage of $4.50 an hour always pushes me to work faster, comparing my work with that of the high school football players who'd trained in his fields the previous season by running from set to set. Moving quickly is easy enough when the alfalfa is newly cut, but now it's nearly at the top of my rubber boots: heavy, wet, and tangled. Irrigating three hours in the morning and then again three hours in the evening (in addition to working in my own gardens and at a local nursery) has quickly gotten me into shape.

I don't mind as my jeans and T-shirt get wet, because already by 7 AM the temperature is rising into the eighties. It takes a moment to steady each thirty-foot-long pipe section before dropping its end into the cascade of water shooting from the coupling end of the adjacent pipe. If things go right the pipe drops into place, latches securely, and fills with water. The weight of the flowing water stabilizes the line and prevents it from tipping over. If the latch doesn't click into place as the pipe fills, there's no way to maneuver it back into place. The lines aren't especially heavy when empty, particularly the two-inch size—three-inch pipes down the road take some getting used to—but once the end cap is in place and the line fills, it's much too heavy to move. If any section doesn't connect properly, the whole line must be drained and reset.

I get through the first field quickly and without mishap, then head to my truck and drive a couple of miles down the road to the horse and cattle pastures. These are irrigated even as the animals graze. Parking by the barn, I head first to the Charolais cattle pens, which can be difficult to work because the bulls often mess up the lines. The pipes here are bent and buckled, and the animals sometimes snap off the sprinkler heads with their careless steps. When this happens it will be clear from a distance by the gushing water, a fountain often twenty feet high, and the limp look of all the other sprinklers that hardly flow due to the low pressure. If a pipe snaps I have to stop by the workshop to get a hacksaw blade, wrenches, and a replacement. I leave the alfalfa field beside the rancher's house for last. It has only about ten sprinklers, but this is the most unpleasant job of the day because the line generally gives me a strong shock. I stash a pair of rubber gloves in my truck and pull them on before approaching the pump. After hitting the power switch on a nearby pole to shut off the water, I connect the first pipe and restore the power to start setting the line. It doesn't always deliver a shock, and it's this unpredictability that makes it even more aggravating. Every time the aluminum connects the entire line can become electrified.

This to me is serious, and not just because it's unpleasant and a little scary. Just a month ago a malfunctioning pump killed another irrigator at a neighbor's field a few hundred yards down the road. She was electrocuted and died on the spot, as did her dog when he came over to see why she wasn't moving. I've told the rancher here that his pump also doesn't seem properly grounded, and he responded by saying he's thoroughly checked all connections. "It's fine," he said, implying there was nothing else to be done and that I should quit complaining.

Okay, but the line is still sending out hard shocks and this seems to contradict him. I chase him down to say as much, and he's clearly annoyed. Maybe he's frustrated with the finicky pump rather than with me, but whichever it is, he's in a bad mood about it. We walk briskly from the horse barn over to the field, and he checks the pump connections. "See, the ground is solid," he tells me, showing how a copper wire connects the pump casing to a buried grounding rod. This is a surface-mounted pump, open to the elements, but the electrical connections seem clean and tight. He's sure he's right. But so am I. At last, to prove his point definitively he sticks one finger in the housing, another in the ground, and tells me to hit the switch. Nothing. No shock. Get over it.

It's hard to explain why I'm doing this. The work is hard, and the money almost irrelevant because there's so little of it. Taking this job is probably my way of feeling some kind of solidarity with farmworkers like the Sandovals living downvalley. Spending a full day on a picking ladder heaving apples around, or standing ten hours in a cold packing shed sorting fruit, now that's work. Strapping on a respirator and Tyvek protective suit to spray in ninety-degree heat, or bending low all day to prune or thin grapes at knee height, that's work. This is as close as I'm ever likely to get to the brutal world of commercial agricultural labor, and it's more than enough for me. Irrigating is tiring and repetitious, but this is a small ranch and six or seven hours a day in its fields leaves room for variety elsewhere. My job is only a taste of what workers downvalley encounter in commercial fields and orchards, where the same tasks repeat day in, day out.

As the summer progresses I start having health problems. I'm chronically tired and dizzy, suffering from headaches and feeling run-down, despite eating well and getting enough sleep. Something is clearly wrong. One day, while driving back over the North Cascades from a trip to Seattle, my condition worsens, to the point that I need to stop and lie down on the side of the road. Upon reaching the valley floor I head for the nearest friend's house and ask for a ride to the hospital. It's a forty-minute drive out of the Cascade foothills to the Okanogan Valley to find medical help, and they generously drop what they're doing to offer me a ride. We head directly to a one-story clinic and wait until a nurse can see me.

It takes her about two minutes to figure out my problem. "Okay, lie down flat and I'll check your pulse," she tells me. Then she asks me to sit up and checks it again. Her verdict? Severe dehydration. She can tell from the reaction in my blood pressure and heartbeat when my position changes. The symptoms are immediately recognizable to her, because she sees this same problem all the time among farmworkers. Anyone laboring in fields around here has to deal with intensely hot, dry conditions. The nurse puts me on an IV, gives me two liters of saline solution, and after a couple of hours sends me home.

My friend Jeanne is a nurse practitioner at this clinic. She has plenty of stories about the problems the largely Latino workers face. Some are self-inflicted, like the troubles of a mutual friend who rolled and totaled his truck after a night of drinking. Others are likely occupational, like the chronic respiratory distress that afflicts one of her good friends. He's only forty-eight, but he's been working all his life in the orchards handling pesticide spray rigs. All of her stories share a common thread—hard work, poverty, a marginal and often transient existence. I can go home, find an alternative to low-paid farmwork, and rest until my strength comes back. What are their options?

Thanks in part to experiences like these, it's hard for me to agree with those who believe that food should be even cheaper than it is, or that efforts to improve pricing on behalf of farmers and workers are somehow "elitist." As Philip Martin, professor of agricultural economics at the University of California–Davis, pointed out in 2009 (based on data from the US Department of Labor), the average American family spends more on alcohol than on fruits and vegetables combined, and nearly six times as much on entertainment. Less than 1 percent of our average annual expenditures goes toward the purchase of fresh produce, and less than 10 percent of that small amount makes its way into the pockets of farmworkers. If we were to spend a little more at the farmers' market, maybe we could stop paying nearly seven times as much annually for health care as we do for fresh fruits and vegetables. Americans spend a smaller percentage of their incomes on food than anyone else in the world, and anyone before them in history.

My single two-hour visit to that medical clinic to treat dehydration cost nearly a month's wages for irrigation work. And this is just the briefest glimpse into the lives of most farmworkers. Some of the most impoverished people in this country aren't only consumers—they're producers, the farmers and field hands who bring us cheap meats, fruits, and vegetables. Seen through their eyes, it's low prices for industrial foods in the supermarket that bring reduced wages, hunger, and poverty. If those of us who can afford to spend a little more would buy locally adapted apples that require fewer sprays, or heirloom tomatoes that help keep diversity alive, in the process we could help raise wages and ensure better health for those laboring in the field.

By all means let's support consumers who can't afford to eat well, but let's also get our stories straight. All too often cheap food comes at the expense of workers and the environment, and chasing bargains sends everyone on a downward spiral as workers in turn can't afford to eat anything of better quality. A relentless march to the bottom in food prices has far-reaching consequences that are invisible to many of us. Paying a little more to support farmers, farmworkers, and the environment can help bring about better working conditions, more jobs, higher wages, and the preservation of farmland and biodiversity.

If past experiences have given me a natural sympathy for farmworkers and a desire to see better wages for producers of all kinds, others have made me aware how fragile agricultural diversity can be, and why it matters to anyone trying to grow good, healthy food. Time I spent in Argentina several years ago building a school garden for the children of recently displaced, landless campesinos clearly showed the challenge of raising food without ready access to quality seeds and plants, and how easily we here in North America take such things for granted. My trip provided a glimpse into another world, where out-of-work farm laborers squatted on vacant land and even the simplest gardening activity—buying a packet of tomato seeds, or borrowing a wheelbarrow—posed serious obstacles.

Nearly fifteen years after leaving Washington State and moving back to the East Coast, in January 2008, I arrive at the outskirts of Garin, a city roughly thirty miles north of downtown Buenos Aires, Argentina. It's early summer in the Southern Hemisphere and the 103-degree heat feels like an assault in the midday sun. I stand in the middle of a small, treeless, one-acre lot, kicking at plastic bottles embedded in the ground and trying to figure out what the soil is like. The land is parched and brown. Only the most tenacious weeds grow here: chicory, dandelion, purslane, pigweed, mint. It's interesting to see the same mix of plants one would find in weedy, disturbed ground at home in Maine. Their presence reminds me of similar waste areas I've helped turn into growing spaces over the past few years: a community garden in an abandoned alleyway in Lawrence, Massachusetts; an orchard near a busy arterial road in downtown Portland, Maine; and one of my current gardens, previously used as a composting area, which had once been heavily compacted by trucks and tractors.

Here in Garin, horses have historically wandered freely and overgrazed this land. Even now, two ponies wander through a gate in the encircling chain-link fence to graze on the sparse grasses. A boy of eight or nine named Mathias sometimes corrals them, leaps onto their backs, and gallops through the schoolyard, switching their flanks with a length of rope. He's barefoot and mischievous, no longer attending school because of behavioral problems. Nevertheless he's a constant presence in the schoolyard next to this lot, always talking, asking questions, and tagging along behind me or sitting in the shade watching me.

The name of the school next door is La Providencia. Providence— that's about right. When its two founders created the school seven years ago, the community was much smaller than today, its educational needs managed by a handful of teachers. That was before a sudden explosion of shantytown construction in the surrounding countryside took everyone by surprise. Suddenly an influx of families with young children overwhelmed the tiny school, and the teachers responded by expanding to a full curriculum from their original emphasis on cooking and sewing. They hired new staff and searched for additional funding to keep everything afloat. This year La Providencia somehow fits a hundred children and twelve teachers into a two-bedroom bungalow with just one barely functioning bathroom.

"This is the only school in the area," Yamile Sagle says as she ducks through a cut in the fence to join me in the adjacent lot. If not for La Providencia, students would need to ride a bus over an hour to reach the nearest public school. It's largely for this reason that Yamile and her sister Maria, the school's founders, take in as many children as they can fit into the building. Funding is tight, so they've enthusiastically welcomed my visit as a volunteer, as well as the cash donation I've brought with me from an American gardening organization. I'm here to help design and construct a new school garden, which will provide a link to the rural lives these students left behind when their families moved to this newly urbanized area. The garden will become a place where they can learn about ecology, agriculture, and healthy eating.

La Providencia has ambitious plans despite its difficulties. A wealthy donor recently purchased this vacant lot and agreed to put up the money needed to construct a new building. The bungalow next door will stay in service as a kindergarten. Yamile and I walk out into the sunlight in the middle of the open space and start pacing off distances. "The school will go here," she tells me excitedly, pointing to the center of the lot, "and the gardens back there." She speaks intensely and rapidly, maybe as a result of living as a single mother in close quarters with two teenage children. We feel our way along conversationally little by little, meeting each other halfway, since her knowledge of English is roughly equivalent to my limited Spanish.

Yamile tells me the land is free of chemicals and safe for growing food. Seems reasonable enough because of its history—there's no industry nearby, only land previously used for agriculture. This lot has been used for grazing for as long as anyone can remember. A first inspection of the ground doesn't reveal anything alarming. There's nothing but domestic trash in sight: diapers, plastic bags, and soda bottles—no oil drums, factory waste, or old tires. The end of a large black plastic bag tears away at ground level. The soil is too compacted to break apart without tools: baked hard and dry, sparsely vegetated. It must have taken years for all this waste to settle into place. Yamile walks the back of the lot, gesturing with her hands and talking about garden designs, and we brainstorm possibilities.

All around La Providencia the land is filled with small shacks and gardens, where children play in the dust and elderly men and women sit in the shade under tin roofs. "Five years ago everything around us was open," Yamile says. Today temporary structures line the edge of the schoolyard—homes erected quickly by smallholding farmers recently relocated from the surrounding countryside, as well as immigrants from neighboring countries. Their buildings are constructed of corrugated steel, cement block, plywood, and any other found and salvaged material the owners could get their hands on.

Most of these houses appear to have rudimentary electricity from lines strung through the trees, and for water there are a couple of hand pumps on shallow wells. Descriptions of the area had led me to expect more crowding and less greenery. The scene has an agreeable feel despite the obvious signs of poverty. The neighbors who see Yamile standing in the field wave to us; they're friendly and welcoming. A few of their homes even have attractive small gardens filled with blooming roses and corn, lettuce, tomatoes, celery, peppers, zucchini, and squashes—remnants of their formerly rural, agricultural lives. It seems like we should have no problem creating a similar garden for the school.

As Yamile and I stand in the field and talk, her brother Najib swings into the yard and pulls up next to us in a '69 AMC Rambler. There are plenty of old cars like this still on the road in Argentina, and I've been a little jealous of them. Sadly the romance fades as I hop into the passenger seat, reach for the nonexistent seat belt, and feel the sweltering heat inside. No air-conditioning. Stiff vinyl seats. Celina Alcaide, another teacher, joins us for the ride, and we head out looking for seeds and tools. "We need a pickaxe," I tell them, *"una piqueta."* And a wheelbarrow; we can't do much without that, either. We share a dictionary to look for words: hoses, watering cans, rakes, hoes. They're starting with almost no tools and don't know where to find them.

Najib drives through a maze of dirt roads and gravel streets, through crowded neighborhoods and dusty, open fields, and pulls up in front of a small shop with farm equipment lined up out front. It's the equivalent of a feed store or small implement dealer, with a few hand tools hanging on the wall, racks of seeds on display, and various power tools and tractor implements. If we were looking for a Fiat tractor or a rototiller, this would be the place. The hand tool selection here, however, is very limited. A couple of turns in the hardpan dirt at La Providencia would destroy any of these cheap, lightweight pickaxes and shovels.

It shouldn't come as a surprise to me that finding good seeds would pose an even greater problem than tools. Twenty years ago I carried a suitcase of vegetable seeds to San Cristóbal de las Casas, a town in Chiapas, Mexico. These were open-pollinated varieties—capable of being saved and replanted to reproduce each year while yielding consistent results—rather than hybrids, which are good for one crop only. (A hybrid is a first-generation cross of two stable parent lines, often sold for seed due to its increased vigor and uniformity, but which hasn't itself been stabilized over multiple generations to stay true to type.) A local agronomist—from the

Netherlands, but living permanently in that picturesque Mexican town—had requested these varieties through the World Seed Fund, which was then maintained by the Abundant Life Seed Foundation in Washington State. He was having a hard time locating anything but seeds for flavorless, hybrid commercial types for the community food program he'd developed in nearby Guatemala. So he turned to an American company for help.

It turns out this isn't unusual in Argentina, either. Many of the gardeners around La Providencia talk about independent American seed companies with some reverence. There's no equivalent here to our High Mowing Seeds or Territorial Seeds, no functional alternative to the mass-produced, often low-quality vegetable varieties on display in this small shop. Everyone asks whether I brought garden seeds with me, and unfortunately the answer is no. This wasn't only because of the difficulty of transporting them across borders, but also because in my opinion it's generally better to encourage the planting of local varieties. This isn't entirely idealistic; Celina has noncommercial organic vegetable seeds a friend sent to her from Brazil, for example. She also talks about an elderly farmer nearby who maintains his own seed collection. With some legwork the teachers might come up with decent local alternatives. Maybe some of the neighbors save their own seeds, and there's a sort of farming collective a few hours north that might be able to help.

Nevertheless, here we are, looking for something to plant this summer before the season gets away from us. Only three weeks remain before my return to the United States, so time is short. A salesman at the feed store walks out from behind the counter and leads us to the seed display, handing me a catalog from the French company Graines de Semences. He shows us liter-sized, sealed cans of vegetable seeds that include varieties developed for large-scale commercial production from the American company Seminis, owned as of 2005 by agribusiness giant Monsanto. In the next aisle we move carefully past shelves crowded with bottles of herbicides and pesticides manufactured in Israel, Brazil, India, and Japan, as well as Argentina. My concern about the potential cultural imperialism of organic American squash seeds suddenly seems overly delicate and a little ridiculous.

We buy nothing at the feed store. Hoping to find seed racks with varieties bred for gardeners, Najib drives to a big-box store called Easy, sort of the Argentinean equivalent of Home Depot. It's a little frightening how familiar this feels to me as we park in a large lot and walk past the huge cement Santa that greets us at the entrance. Easy has a garden section, and although it's very bare-bones, we're able to pick up a few useful things, like some lettuce and bean seeds. These are probably repackaged from the same kind of commercial stock we saw in the farm store, but at least they're sold in garden-sized lots and don't appear to be treated with fungicides. They'll do until something better comes along.

We spend the entire afternoon driving from shop to shop, searching for materials to build and plant the garden. Celina buys a couple of flats of potted herbs from a local nursery, and we spend hours sourcing materials for a pergola. Toward the end of the day Najib finds a tiny hardware store in a busy residential area with a two-hundred-foot roll of black plastic irrigation line displayed out front. It's long enough to carry water from the schoolhouse to the garden, useful even though the school's outdoor faucets won't provide sufficient volume or pressure to run a sprinkler. There in a back room we also find a real pickaxe—not some lightweight facsimile, but a heavy-duty tool that can take a beating. Najib throws everything in the trunk of the Rambler, the roll of black plastic pipe hanging precariously out the back, and returns to the school.

The vast majority of Argentinians are descended from European immigrants, representing many nationalities with diverse foodways. So one might expect some interesting culinary traditions here. The neighborhood I'm staying in has a bakery that looks like it belongs in Bavaria, where bread is made from wheat grown on their organic farm a few hours north. Nearby is a small shop where until last year an elderly Italian man made gelato daily from his own fruits. He used raspberries and strawberries he picked fresh from his garden. The local greengrocer carries some nice enough fruits and vegetables, some of which are unfamiliar to me, like a round summer squash called Zapatillo. Even so, among most people I speak with, garden traditions and knowledge are surprisingly limited. Maybe this is simply because we're in the land of vaqueros and free-range cattle, of pit barbecue and lamb on a spit. I ate dinner last week in an open-air, covered restaurant pavilion, where more than a hundred guests crowded around rows of banked coals as half carcasses of lamb and goat slowly roasted. Other than a small salad, we ate nothing but meat.

It's getting late, nearly dinnertime, and Celina agrees to give me a ride back to the Buenos Aires suburb where I'm staying, half an hour from the school. "Should I drop you off at Vicky and Pablo's house?" she asks. Celina has become my default driver, since she commutes to school almost daily from her home downtown in Buenos Aires. Our destination is San Ysidro, a suburb north of the city, which is only a little out of her way. "Thanks," I tell her. She drives up to the house and I hop out on the curb in busy traffic, in front of an eight-foot-high concrete wall with a heavy wooden door in it. Behind this is a small compound with a papermaking studio and offices, an apartment, and an unfinished house and small swimming pool. I drop my camera and notebook on the bed, change out of my dusty clothes, and head for the pool to cool off.

Even with our recently acquired seeds and tools, constructing this garden over the next three weeks will involve complicated planning to coordinate my transportation and housing, line up helpers, prepare the space, and finalize plantings. At the moment I'm staying with Vicky Sigwald, an Argentinean who spends a month or more every year in New York working as an artist and teacher, and her husband, Pablo. Vicky made the preliminary arrangements for my visit, responding to a request for volunteer opportunities through the American gardening organization Kitchen Gardeners International (based in Maine and run by my friend Roger Doiron). She essentially created this project, acting as intermediary between the school and me. Vicky also found a parent at another nearby school, a man named Luis, willing to act as guide for my three-week visit. He promised to finalize any necessary details with the teachers, organize my housing and transportation, and help source materials we'd need to construct the garden.

When Vicky learned on my arrival that Luis had failed to contact the teachers, and that they weren't expecting me for another month, she reached them during January vacation and straightened things out. When Luis failed to show up to give me a ride on my first day, she found a driver. And after Luis told her he couldn't help with my housing, either, she let me move into an unused room near her studio. In the end, when he simply stopped taking her phone calls and returning her messages, she stepped up and coordinated everything. Vicky doesn't take no for an answer. She gets things done. The morning after our expedition in search of tools, plants, and seeds, I wake up much earlier than usual. Lupe—Vicky and Pablo's giant rottweiler—decides she's lonely and wakes me by crashing suddenly into my room, throwing all her weight against the door latch. Once she's inside, standing beside the bed, she stares at me blankly for a moment, then turns around and walks back into the yard as if to say, *Sorry, wrong room,* or, *Excuse me; didn't mean to terrify you.*

I get up and pull on shorts and a T-shirt. Something is wrong with the water tank, so for the past couple of days the nearest functioning bathroom has been at the neighbors. Reaching it means meandering down a path past Lupe and the chickens, the caged parrots and tarantulas, through a gate in the garden wall and a maze of construction materials, outbuildings, and lush overhanging vegetation, and into a shed attached to the back of the house next door. Vicky hopes the water will come back on soon so I can wash my clothes in the sink and start cooking again in the studio kitchen (a mixed blessing, because after dark this open-air kitchen swarms with giant cockroaches).

With the water still out, the next day Vicky decides it's best for me to move somewhere else. For two days I wind up in a small hotel near the school, working on garden design plans. Another night a software engineer who recently moved home from Texas loans me his empty apartment, where I battle carpenter ants that swarm around the bed. He apologizes the next day and tells me this must have been due to recent construction. I stay two nights in a loft in a teacher's old stucco house, in a narrow room tucked up close to the rafters under a tile roof that lacks insulation. It's airless and sweltering hot, but kneeling in front of a little borrowed air conditioner allows me to cool off enough to sleep.

Vicky's original plan was to let me live for the duration of my stay at the school itself, since the building is sitting empty and has a working kitchen. This would have saved everyone plenty of trouble, but in the end she and the teachers decided it would be too risky to leave me there. As laid-back as the area feels on the surface, there's an undercurrent of violence in the community around the school, and this makes even an apparently simple project like building a school garden much less straightforward than it appears.

To some extent street violence isn't unusual in Argentina, or all of Latin America for that matter. Even in wealthier neighborhoods near Vicky and Pablo's home, high walls surround many houses and sentries stand guard over quiet suburban streets. One night we head to dinner at a private home in a gated community with a polo club, where kids swim in a lighted pool until 2 AM under the palm trees while armed men on motorcycles patrol the nearby fence lines. Vicky tells me gangs used to signal one another from the rooftops around her home, particularly during Argentina's economic troubles several years ago.

Kidnappings in Argentina have on the whole subsided, and the country is generally safe. It's different here in the school's Garin neighborhood, however, due to the transient and unsettled nature of the community and its many displaced, often desperate people. My new friends don't want me traveling with anyone they don't know, or going out on the streets alone. Part of the reason I've been moving around so much is that my hosts have made sometimes elaborate arrangements to protect me. They carefully orchestrate my travel plans, find secure places for me to stay, and even arrange for a local man who knows the underside of the neighborhood to watch out for me. He's let it be known that the overheated American hauling trash out of the school's future garden and digging postholes in the midday sun is under his protection. "If you get kidnapped," Vicky tells me, "he's the one who'll get you released." Very reassuring.

Simply getting to La Providencia for my first visit proves challenging. The driver bringing me to the neighborhood abruptly pulls over at the side of a dirt road and reaches for his cell phone. "I'm not going any farther," he tells me. We're just a couple of miles from our destination, but he's worried because his cab had been hijacked and he'd been robbed nearby the previous year. So he calls the school and waits for one of the kindergarten teachers to drive out to get me. It seems a little ridiculous, but we sit there at the side of the road until she arrives. I pay him and ride off with her in a dusty, beat-up old Toyota, which feels like a pretty good disguise, even if as an outsider you never really know what others see.

One day while working in the field a mid-1960s vintage Chevy sedan pulls through an open gate and starts driving slowly across the scrub. The temperature is in the mid-nineties and I'm fighting off heat exhaustion while swinging my pickaxe at the edge of the garden, trying to break up some particularly compacted soil. The car holds four unfamiliar men, and it weaves through the underbrush heading straight toward me. I'm working alone, not expecting visitors, and the lot is fenced on all sides. It's hard to imagine what business they have here.

I lean on my pickaxe and watch them approach, thinking of all the precautions my hosts have taken to keep me safe. Before I can make up my mind to do anything, however, suddenly the car cuts to the right, drives across the field away from me, and pulls up sharply at the six-foot-high chain-link fence on the far side of the lot. I relax and go back to my digging as two of the men jump out, peel back the chain link, and drive into the yard of a one-room shack constructed of salvaged boards and corrugated steel. They park their car next to one of the prettiest little vegetable gardens in the neighborhood.

On top of all the difficulties the teachers have had arranging a safe place for me to live and finding tools and supplies, preparing the garden is going much more slowly than expected. It's very challenging pickaxe work. Although in the end the garden will be only several hundred square feet of raised beds, the soil is as compacted as an unpaved country road. Every swing of the pickaxe loosens no more than a few square inches of earth, so prepping the space, a task that should take a few hours, requires several days of heavy labor in intense heat. We consider renting equipment, but nothing available fits the budget. Instead we stick with volunteer labor, and when time gets tight hire a day or two of additional help from a worker Celina calls the Viking—a tall, beefy guy, clearly of Nordic descent, with a long blond ponytail.

We build a garden pergola with a chain saw and a couple of dull handsaws, a hammer and nails, working off an old ladder and a couple of oil drums. For days my feet are swollen by fire ant bites—my first encounter with these nasty creatures. Toward the end of the trip I take to leaving my boots at home and wearing running shoes while working, because it's too uncomfortable to lace up my boots. A year later I'll encounter similar ants while building a garden in New Orleans, where my arm swells up so much it requires a visit to the emergency room.

There's some irony in a Yankee flying down here to help build a garden. This is an alien landscape for me, an unfamiliar land full of strange insects and plants. From a casual glance at some of the small gardens planted beside even the humblest homes, it's also clear there's a storehouse of knowledge remaining in this community. What would an outsider from the United States know in comparison about growing food in this climate, or for that matter in the Southern Hemisphere? It seems strange that the teachers are so eager to turn to me for help and advice, and equally odd how foreign gardening seems to many of them. Surrounded by farmers, living on the outskirts of the city near agricultural land, one would think they'd know at least as much about gardening as I do. Before my arrival I'd imagined a sort of working partnership, and instead I find myself running the show.

Of course, much of what's needed in a situation like this is simply the energy to get started. Anyone willing to jump in and get their hands dirty can be the catalyst that brings people together. And because so many people have stepped up to help, with the deadline for my departure approaching the garden is nearly complete, most obstacles overcome. Herbs and vegetable plants fill several hundred square feet of raised beds, which are loosened and fertilized with truckloads of compost. Just a few spaces remain, reserved for flowers the teachers plan to track down on their own. Most of the pergola in the center of the garden is complete, transforming the area into a shaded outdoor classroom large enough for roughly thirty students. One more trip to the lumberyard, a few more nails to drive, and all will be ready by the time the children return from vacation.

The day before I leave, Yamile's mother comes into the garden, dressed in a loose-fitting smock, cotton cap, blue jeans, and Birkenstock sandals. She's in her late sixties, a bit rotund, quiet, and shy—at least around me. With her are two young grandchildren and one of their school friends, all ten to twelve years old. They find an unplanted corner of the garden and talk among themselves, absorbed completely in their task of planting sweet corn. The children gather closely around their grandmother as she drills a hole with her forefinger and drops in a seed. They kneel and follow her example, intently asking questions, laughing and talking as they go.

At the start of the next season I send a package of seeds from a Maine company, Johnny's Selected Seeds, and Celina e-mails photos of the garden, telling me things are going well. After pitching in on a project like this it's hard to know whether it will flourish or revert to weeds and waste ground, so it's gratifying to see the pergola completed and garden beds filled with herbs, flowers, and vegetables. Gardens are fragile things, easily neglected and forgotten, and rebuilding connections takes time and energy. My visit helped start this project with a few plants, seeds that can reproduce true to type, tools, prepped soil, and hard work. From such modest beginnings I hope the teachers and students can create something lasting.

The work this school does is at heart about good food, stable communities, and healthy kids. La Providencia isn't serving an elite. This garden brings everyone together at the table—growers and cooks, children and adults—in shared appreciation for food produced by their own hands. Through direct participation in this garden, children can begin to see through the eyes of producers as well as consumers. They come to learn that you can't understand the world from one perspective alone. Even something as modest as a school garden planted with local corn is a reminder that what has little value in one person's eyes may have great meaning to someone else. This is a lesson worth remembering as we seek to reshape the future of our food.

Four

THE EYE OF THE COLLECTOR: "BECOME A FRUIT EXPLORER"

*I*f ever I've taken access to seed catalogs and quality nurseries for granted, time spent out of the country in places like Argentina searching for decent plants has set me straight. Here in the United States small independent businesses make available a breadth of plants that would be unimaginable in many parts of the world. Their efforts to collect, trial, and breed seeds and nursery stock are indispensable to most small farmers. The young couple at the farmers' market may be heroes of the local food movement, but they create new markets and earn a living wage by working essentially in partnership with regional seed companies and nurseries.

Back in the late 1990s a friend from western Massachusetts, a small organic commercial vegetable grower, told me she bought many of her seeds from a Maine company called Fedco. Gardener friends in Washington had previously told me about Fedco, but I didn't know much about it. Based solely on the name it seemed like some kind of discount retailer. "Sounds like Acme Seeds," I said, imagining Wile E. Coyote ordering deadly nightshade and a Fedco truck dumping mountains of cheap seeds at the doorstep. Where had they gotten this name?

My assumption couldn't have been more wrong, because it turns out Fedco is anything but the dispassionate commercial behemoth its name suggests. The business evolved from a natural foods coop in central Maine where founder C. R. Lawn worked in the late 1970s. He started out repackaging bulk seeds for retail sales in 1978, and from there moved into mail order. The name is a contraction of Federated Cooperative: proudly anti-establishment hippie chic.

Over the years Fedco has expanded into nursery crops, growers' supplies, bulbs, and potatoes, but despite its success the company has stayed close to its roots. It's still a worker-owned cooperative and runs on a shoestring budget out of a small office in Waterville and two nearby warehouses. "Because we do not have an individual owner or beneficiary, profit is not our primary goal," its website explains. The "About Fedco" web page has nothing to say about founders or staff members, and names aren't even listed there. Instead the site emphasizes their cooperative structure: "Consumer and worker members share proportionately in the cooperative's profits through our annual patronage dividends." No job descriptions, contact information, or e-mail addresses appear there, just a post office box and two phone numbers.

Nevertheless, most growers in Maine recognize the key players behind Fedco, especially C. R. Lawn and John Bunker, founder of its subsidiary mail-order nursery, Fedco Trees. Though John's job title is "coordinator," he tends to be known around Maine as "the apple guy." In fact, he's interested in all sorts of fruits and sells a wide variety of ornamental perennials as well as hardy trees and berries through Fedco's catalog. But apples are his passion. Get into a conversation with anyone in Maine about old varieties, and in all likelihood they'll say, "There's this guy in central Maine who knows everything about apples." They've heard of his workshops at the Maine Organic Farmers and Gardeners Association (MOFGA), attended tastings of rare heirlooms at Maine Apple Day, or stumbled on his book *Not Far from the Tree: A Brief History of the Apples and the Orchards of Palermo, Maine, 1804–2004* in local shops. If you want to identify an apple or learn about forgotten fruit varieties, you need to talk with John Bunker.

One summer day in early July 2009, I set out to do just that, seeking his help to find historic foods for Slow Food's Ark of Taste. I've known John for several years, but have never visited his farm in central Maine. So it's hard to imagine exactly what to expect while driving along Route 3, the well-traveled connector linking the state capital of Augusta with the port of Belfast on the shores of Penobscot Bay. John lives twenty miles east of Augusta in the small town of Palermo, between China and Liberty. (What's the most unlikely name for a town in central Maine—Palermo, China, East Peru, Paris, or Mexico?) On the first pass I miss the exit to his farm while flying along a straight stretch of open highway. After turning around in a pullout, I nearly miss the entrance again on the return. His farm lies down a narrow, unpaved road that's very difficult to spot doing fifty-five miles an hour.

The approach to John's farm reminds me of his depiction of local agriculture in his book. While telling the story of apples and orchards in Palermo, he describes a largely self-sufficient farm community where stone walls typically lined narrow dirt roads in the shade of apple trees. Riders on horseback would reach up and pick ripe fruit directly from overhanging branches. Until the middle of the nineteenth century every family grew diverse crops for their own consumption, and every farm had a small orchard filled with different types of fruit, many varieties distinct to this place.

I watch for apple trees in the woods beside the county road and see nothing but encroaching forest. If once there were stone walls at its borders, these were sacrificed long ago to widen the roadbed. It's hard to imagine such heavily forested land cleared for grazing and crops, but at one time most of these ridgelines and higher elevations were open ground. It's easier to imagine this history half a mile down the road at the property of one of John's neighbors, a working farm with an old and somewhat neglected white clapboard house and barn. A crew is manning an ancient logging truck and sawing logs at an outdoor mill on the edge of their horse pasture. Diversified farming lives on at the margins.

John's land is near the bottom of the hill at the end of a long, rutted, unpaved driveway. Its location is a little surprising, because the land is low and appears somewhat damp and dark. Not the most promising place to grow fruit trees or vegetables, and for this reason it was probably never farmed historically. Like many smallholding farmers, he's making do with some difficult soils and microclimates. In his book John describes Palermo farms aligned along a common axis, with buildings, croplands, and orchards high on the ridges, and pastures and woodlots in the valleys. He and his friends who moved here to homestead in the early 1970s apparently cleared their gardens from substantial forest. Today John owns the land and lives here with his wife, Cammy, while seasonal apprentices share the bunkhouse.

I squeeze into a narrow parking space beside the barn and take a look around. John's homestead is a pretty little cluster of wood-butcher houses and outbuildings: back-to-the-land counterculture vernacular. The property weaves vegetable gardens, fruit trees, berries, and native ornamentals around handmade buildings and small ponds. Solar panels line the roof of the main house, and a grapevine-covered arbor shades a long plank table. A new house is visible under construction farther down the hill at the end of the driveway. The ground looks wet in many places—good mosquito habitat. An apprentice stops by to say hello, his face covered by protective netting. It's a gray day but warm, and the rain is holding off for now.

I knock on the door to find John inside, and in greeting hand over a bag of scones and pastries from Portland's legendary Standard Baking. I should have bought fresh strawberries instead, because he places the bag, unopened, on the counter. It's cluttered in the kitchen without much room to sit, so he pulls on his boots and suggests we head outside to a small teahouse, a screened hexagonal structure overlooking the gardens. I think of the pastries a little wistfully as we walk outside. We find seats at a plank table, pull out the Slow Food notes, and start talking about what is and isn't listed on the Ark of Taste.

John begins by telling me about his experiences collecting plants around Maine. "There are dozens, maybe hundreds of rare fruits" and other formerly cultivated foods still to be discovered here, he tells me. It's as though we're surrounded by fragments of a forgotten culture, signs everywhere for those who know where to look: overgrown elderberries behind a garage at the edge of town,

Jerusalem artichokes standing watch over a cellar hole, rows of sweet cherries at the edge of a neglected pasture, suckers sprouted from a long-dead tree. "A crew exploring the state could spend years searching and never find everything," John says.

He describes a vision of abundance that's hard to imagine. It's all too easy to believe the era of plant collecting has passed, and that the only opportunities for new discovery lie somewhere else, far away. Most of us would probably consider forgotten foods to be remnants of dying cultures slowly swallowed by Central American jungles, or pockets of biodiversity in places with living peasant traditions like Albania and Romania. Yet three years ago while researching his book John devoted a harvest season to exploring the apples of the town he's lived in over thirty years, and he found many surprises. These include grafted fruit—deliberately reproduced and cultivated apple varieties, as opposed to wild seedlings—that he still can't identify.

He tells me the cuisine of Palermo, his small town in central Maine, included dozens of kinds of fruit, vegetables, and herbs, as well as a variety of meats and dairy products that would put many of our contemporary farmers' markets to shame. "In 1880 there were 198 households in Palermo; 184 of them had a least one cow; 165 of them had at least one horse; sixty-five had a team of oxen," he writes in his book. "Well over half grew wheat. Practically all grew potatoes, though only four grew as many as three acres. 151 had a small flock of sheep. 104 had at least one pig. Most grew hay and beans and 'Indian corn'; many grew oats; and practically everyone grew apples." Cooks had a comprehensive and sophisticated understanding of the uses of hundreds of foods, and production was primarily for home use rather than the market. By most estimates at least 400 kinds of apples were grown historically throughout Maine, with approximately 150 unique to the state. Any schoolchild back in the 1800s would have known exactly where and when to eat the best fruit right off the tree.

Today there are few if any standing trees of soft fruits like peaches and cherries remaining from that time, in part because they weren't as widely planted as hardier apples and pears, but also because they don't live nearly as long. Part of what draws people like John to apple trees is their longevity, the continuing presence of very old and forgotten fruit in the landscape. Apples and pears can live two hundred years or more in some places, providing a direct, unbroken link to the past. I have a Fedco pear tree growing in my gardens called Endecott, for example, propagated from what's generally considered to be the oldest living cultivated fruit tree in North America. The original tree, still alive as of this writing, was carried from England to the Massachusetts Bay Colony in the 1630s and planted by Governor John Endecott at his home in the town of Danvers.

The Endecott pear has outlasted nearly four hundred years of hurricanes and occasional abuse, including the stripping of its protective topsoil and aggressive vandalism in the 1960s that hacked its trunk back to a six-foot stump. At one time in the nineteenth century it stood eighty feet tall, and now it's a gnarled old survivor you could pick clean with a six-foot stepladder. This tree is a symbol of a forgotten era. Less than two hours from my home in Portland, a few miles from my birthplace of Beverly, Massachusetts, Governor Endecott's historic farm is largely paved over. Strip malls and office parks run the length of Endicott Street (the spelling of the family name changed in the eighteenth century). Today the tree stands next to a parking lot owned by an outpatient branch of Massachusetts General Hospital, protected unceremoniously by a steel fence and surrounding windbreak of arborvitae shrubs. For many years the property was the headquarters of lighting manufacturer Osram Sylvania. It's tempting to see the full sweep of American history in this place, from the earliest days of Puritan colonization and farming, to industrial development, and now health care. The agricultural lives of previous generations seem like another culture entirely, with the Endecott pear the sole connecting thread.

"Why do you think we've abandoned these old foods?" I ask John. He tells me that, in his opinion, the answer is partly because most of us have forgotten how to think and act independently. We follow the rules, settle down, find jobs, and turn agricultural production over to others. Where does an old Maine apple fit into the scheme of things? Food today is above all a tradable commodity, and as such it must adapt to the market, which demands consistency and discourages variety. It's no accident we find limited selection in our grocery stores.

Over the course of the nineteenth century New England farmers largely transitioned from self-sufficiency to commercial production, or left behind their thin, rocky soils to move west. The population of John's town of Palermo reached a high of 1,659 in 1850, declined to 510 a hundred years later, and even now hasn't rebounded to its nineteenth-century level. With such changes livestock breeds disappeared, fruits and vegetables fell out of use, and old homesteads slowly rotted away, forgotten in the woods.

Sometimes the abandonment of traditional food varieties was due to poor quality or neglect, but in other cases it was the product of deliberate design and development of larger, more far-flung markets. John's book *Not Far from the Tree* describes a 1927 "conspiracy of sorts" among extension agents who set out to consolidate the northeastern apple industry and develop more consistent marketing. They created a list of approved varieties they deemed worthy of commercial production, the "New England Seven," and discouraged planting of all other types. The orphaned plants John spends so much time identifying and rescuing are happy exceptions, a testament to stubborn farmers unwilling to cut down productive trees, or to pure good luck.

It's difficult if not impossible in most markets to sell hundreds of varieties of apples, so no matter how worthy were the old varieties growing in early colonial gardens, gradually, one by one, they fell out of use. Even today, despite the tremendous interest in regional foods, diversity thrives best in small plantings. The sheer time and energy required to keep track of divergent horticultural needs, not to mention the challenge of marketing niche fruits, prevents most growers from experimenting widely. It's often the smallholding farmer and homesteader who lead the way. Or, more precisely, independent seed companies and nurseries guide us, fueled by collectors like John Bunker.

John finishes reviewing Slow Food's Ark of Taste lists, and we take a walk around his property to see his plantings. He's lived in this place nearly forty years, since graduating from Colby College in 1971. John is personable but a bit reserved, viewing the world with a perpetual slight squint and inquisitive look. His plant knowledge comes from long-standing direct experience—heading into the field with picking ladders for hours on end, sampling and salvaging fruit, talking with old-timers who know the histories and uses of these trees. He's followed a particular passion and made it work, translating curiosity about something previously obscure and forgotten into a thriving business.

It's easy to imagine that John's land reflects his character—unassuming and modest, a little quirky, hard to appraise. Just as it takes time to get to know him, his land is full of hidden corners and surprises. As we walk behind the house through a large arbor overhung with grapes, we come across a plank table set invisibly below it in deep shade. Beyond is a tiny, shingled shed that looks like it might collapse in the next strong wind, with a hand-painted sign over the door reading SEED SWAP. The path to the barn winds among apple trees, with several varieties grafted on each tree. Near the house native ornamental shrubs intermingled with perennials and annuals ring a small pond. Beds of garlic and small greenhouses surround the apprentice cabin, an outbuilding that looks like it was built entirely from salvaged lumber. John walks over to a thicket of small Asian plums that he says will soon begin to bear. He's planted the trees very close together, on five-foot centers, to ensure pollination for this finicky fruit.

As isolated as this place feels, I'm startled to hear a large, throaty engine around the bend in the driveway while returning to my car to grab my raincoat. John's farmer neighbor, one of the men milling lumber up the road, drives slowly into view on an antique truck loaded with newly sawn boards on the flatbed. That thing moves? I'd caught a glimpse of it on the drive in and assumed it was a relic long ago settled into the corner of a field, useful only for lifting with its rusting boom, if that. A moment later one of his friends pulls up on an ATV and tells me about the truck. "Needs a new engine," he says, "but otherwise works fine."

The boards on this truck bed will nearly complete the sheathing on John and Cammy's new timber-frame home at the end of their driveway. Their neighbors milled this wood from a stand of red oak and white pine trees that blew down nearby in a recent storm. The new house sits beside a recently excavated small pond, surrounded by ground scraped clean of vegetation by a bulldozer. Plantings of native shrubs and blueberries will fill in the disturbed ground over time. John steps carefully over unfinished floors and enters the building, which is beautiful—solidly constructed with pine boards wrapped around a timber frame, no plywood or drywall in sight. Eventually I suppose one gets tired of living in a house cobbled together largely from found materials, charming as that may be to an outsider's eyes. John's wife, Cammy, would probably agree.

During my visit John talks about his work with MOFGA, or the Maine Organic Farmers and Gardeners Association, which besides Fedco is the other strange acronym at the heart of Maine's organic food community. Both date back to the 1970s, and their histories are deeply intertwined. John Bunker recently served as MOFGA's president; Fedco's Organic Growers Supply division began as a MOFGA project; and Fedco founder C. R. Lawn is a long-standing MOFGA board member. Fedco sells organically certified seeds whenever possible, and takes a public stand against genetically modified foods and large corporate interests. Several years ago it stopped carrying many varieties of high-quality vegetable seeds from the wholesaler Seminis, for example—at the time their largest supplier—as a protest against its acquisition by industry giant Monsanto.

I once read an apt description of Maine's love affair with food, explaining that where hippies went, good food followed. This is true even in downtown Portland, a city increasingly known for its restaurant scene. Visit kitchens in Portland's best restaurants after farmers' markets, and you'll find scruffy farmers selling produce harvested a few hours before from MOFGA-certified organic fields. The city's hyperactive restaurant scene owes a great debt to the back-to-the-land curiosity and experimentation of people like John Bunker. Once-marginal groups like Fedco and MOFGA are respected institutions today, welcome even in the halls of the Maine Department of Agriculture. Tolerated, anyway.

John's preservation work is also closely intertwined with MOFGA. In 2001 he planted the first trees in what would become the Maine Heritage Orchard at MOFGA's Common Ground Education Center in Unity, about half an hour north of Palermo. His goal in creating this permanent preservation site is to protect apples bred and named in Maine. (Like all domesticated apples, their parent stock arrived with European settlers, and they descend from wild apples in Central Asia.) The Maine Heritage Orchard takes up roughly half an acre of MOFGA's two-hundred-acre headquarters. This site is the location of MOFGA's annual Common Ground Fair, and it also houses its education center, staff offices, alternative energy arrays, livestock barns, greenhouses, and trial gardens.

Most apples in the Maine Heritage Orchard are relatively unknown, and some are extremely rare. Washington Sweet, Thompson, Winthrop Greening, Sweet Sal, Hayford—you'd be hard-pressed to find many of these apples growing anywhere but in this collection, even in rural Maine orchards. In some cases none of the original mature trees from which these were propagated remain. John Bunker includes a plea for help on MOFGA's website: "Tracking down these old Maine apples is like a treasure hunt. Every year we locate two or three more. Others are out there growing and fruiting, patiently waiting for us to find them. We'd love to have your help. Check your own backyard. Ask your neighbors, knock on strangers' doors, write letters, follow leads, talk to your local Grange or church group or historical society. Become a fruit explorer."

As John recounts it, sometimes his discoveries seem serendipitous, but they're equally the product of patiently researched and carefully orchestrated searches. Several years ago he set out to find an apple called Fletcher Sweet, noted in area records but in all probability extinct. He enlisted the help of two historians near the coastal town of Lincolnville, about an hour from his home, and advertised the search in local papers. In 2002 an old dairy farmer, Clarence Thurlow, came forward and offered to lead him to a tree. Thurlow remembered eating Fletcher Sweet apples as a boy near the base of nearby Moody Mountain, a place once known as Fletchertown. He guided John to the site of an old homestead deep in the woods, where they located the ancient tree and removed a few scions, dormant cuttings of the previous year's growth. John grafted these to new roots, which he transplanted the following spring. A year later both Clarence Thurlow and the original tree were dead, but the variety lives on in the MOFGA orchard.

Within a few years, as newly grafted Fletcher Sweet trees began to bear fruit, John discovered that this variety is much more than a living piece of history—it deserves a place at anyone's table. Today Fedco carries this apple and sells trees to interested growers around the country. "Very white crystalline flesh with a slightly green tinge," John writes about Fletcher Sweet in his catalog. "Refreshing, mild, incredibly juicy and very crisp without being hard. Snaps when you take a bite. The texture reminds me of an Asian pear, a water chestnut, or maybe a perfect radish. The flesh, however, dissolves in your mouth. Makes a light-textured yellow sauce with a hint of blackberry."

How wonderful to rediscover such a high-quality, traditional food and make it available once again! During my visit to John's farm, I ask him if there's anything else he hopes to find in my part of southern Maine. Yes, he tells me, pulling out a copy of MOFGA's 2009 Common Ground Fair poster. Its artwork features one of his paintings of rare Maine apples, with botanically accurate renderings of sixteen types, one originating from each of Maine's counties. Several are familiar to me, like the Black Oxford and Cole's Quince grafted at the edge of my own garden. But the apple that represents my own county is unfamiliar: Blake.

John tells me he's been looking for a Blake tree to graft for the Maine Heritage Orchard, to date without success. At one time this variety was grown throughout the state, but now it's disappeared. Blake is a tart, crisp, yellow apple, a late-fall variety, known for making excellent applesauce and for fresh eating. The variety may not be extinct, but the only probable specimen he's found grows in a private collection in England. "Maybe you'd like to help me find it?" he asks. "I'd love to try," I tell him, despite my uncertainty about how to go about it. He provides a few ideas to get me started, and I jump at the opportunity to learn something about fruit exploring, knowing full well that this might be the beginning of a wild goose chase.

The Blake apple originated a few miles from downtown Portland in the mill town of Westbrook, so John recommends contacting their historical society. I start with a quick survey of their web page, which tells me, "Westbrook has an exceedingly rich and diverse history, richer than most. We don't want any of it to be lost or forgotten." Sounds promising. Although the city has been known primarily for its mills since the nineteenth century, it also has a long agricultural history. An 1886 gazetteer describes thriving farms and gardens serving nearby Portland markets, and geography "beautifully diversified by swells of land rather than hills." Strangely enticing, like a sea of rolling pasture. It's not hilly around here, but it's not exactly flat, either.

Westbrook's historical society is open Tuesday and Saturday mornings, staffed by volunteers. The following weekend accordingly I pull out my notebook and camera, and drive over for a visit. The society shares space with the American Legion on a side street near the Presumpscot River, the original power source for Westbrook's mills. I stop in front of their largely windowless, architecturally undistinguished two-story brick building, and try to figure out where to park. It isn't clear where on the adjacent expanse of unmarked asphalt they want me to leave my car, so I squeeze into a tight space next to the sidewalk.

While climbing stairs to second-floor offices and exhibit space, I daydream about what this visit might uncover to further John's search. Maybe the staff will help us find an original Blake homestead? Or they'll know someone's great-aunt, a descendant of the family living on the outskirts of town? Five elderly volunteers look up when I enter the otherwise unoccupied, cavernous space, seeming a little startled, and eagerly ask what they can do to help. This is promising; among them they must have some useful information to share.

Unfortunately everyone immediately loses interest when they hear about our search for an apple tree. Do they know any old farmers, orchardists, or historians in the area who might have leads or information? No. Do they have agricultural records in their collection that might be helpful? Can't think of any. Could they tell me something about the history of local orchards and farms? No. Is there anyone they recommend visiting? One of the women suggests contacting the owner of a commercial orchard a couple of towns away, while another leads me around the room, hands me old graduation albums, shows off flapper dresses, and talks eagerly about the Rudy Vallee exhibit.

My visit to the historical society turns up nothing about local agriculture. This is a disappointment, but that shouldn't come as much of a surprise. As a culture we simply don't view food as living history and a significant cultural legacy. While celebrating farming for its traditional values, typically we look at food itself as just another disposable commodity without further meaning. As I get back in my car and drive toward home, I think, *We're Americans, we can't help ourselves.*

And yet clearly things are beginning to change. The success of companies like Fedco shows that there's a new way of thinking on the horizon, and that we're coming to appreciate the value of traditional foods. So what's the next step to continue our search? John offers other suggestions, like exploring area maps to look for old farms, particularly those with a Blake family connection, and even going door-to-door asking for information. Maybe chance can lead us to a Blake tree, and, if not, we might stumble across other interesting finds. There's no way to guarantee success. The best approach is to start with a manageable plan and stay flexible and open to whatever turns up.

A couple of months later John calls to say he has another idea. He will be in Portland the following week with Russell Libby, MOFGA's executive director, and they're planning to continue his search for a Blake tree. According to historical records Blake apples hang very late on the branches, into early winter, so with most leaves on the ground we'd have a clear view of remaining fruit. We might spot something if we pick a likely route and simply drive around. Do I want to come along? It's a wonderfully optimistic adventure, and as unlikely as we are to find anything, I tell him yes.

In the intervening time Karla has come up with nineteenth-century maps of the Westbrook area, using her background in environmental science, which includes cartography and geographical information systems. Poring over the tiny print registering houselot owners, however, we've searched for the name Blake and come up short. There was an engineer named Blake working the Westbrook mills, but he lived in Portland on land now subdivided into suburban plots. Another early map shows the location of an eighteenth-century orchard, with no particular Blake connection, which seems to have disappeared under the sprawling S. D. Warren industrial complex, at one point the largest paper mill in the world. If any nearby fruit trees survived, they'd long since been overrun and forgotten.

John, Russell, and I coordinate plans by e-mail, and a few days later meet up in Portland. I wait in Rabelais, my friends' downtown bookstore, while John unloads boxes of fruit for the last of his 2009 Community Supported Agriculture distributions. It's the end of the first year of his Out on a Limb CSA, which shared more than thirty varieties of historic apples with participants over the course of two and a half months. We've eaten apples like Tolman Sweet, Nodhead, and Cox's Orange Pippin, each with a description of best uses and history, as well as personal stories. Every other Wednesday, John carries bags of fruit to Rabelais, and friends gather through the afternoon to see what they'll be eating and cooking that night. It's like having a private historian and apple connoisseur deliver rare fruits to the door.

As John empties the last of his apple crates and heads off to find a legal parking spot, Russell arrives at the store to meet us. He's been involved with MOFGA since its early days in the 1970s, and has led the organization since 1995. Although he lives an hour and a half away on a farm in central Maine, Russell travels constantly around the state, and the Portland food world is familiar territory for him. Today will be a vacation from his endless rounds of legislative lobbying and meetings, travel that keeps him on the road and far from home much of the time.

The three of us walk across the street for lunch at a favorite local hangout called Duckfat. Husband-and-wife chef-owners Rob Evans and Nancy Pugh opened this small restaurant several years ago to offer panini, soups, and salads. It's the casual-dining answer to Hugo's, their white-tablecloth restaurant next door to Rabelais. Rob won this year's 2009 James Beard Award for Best Chef in the Northeast for his work at Hugo's, and in my opinion there couldn't have been a better choice. He's exceptionally talented, and also one of the nicest guys you'll ever meet in the food world, friendly and modest. For lunch we order Nancy's lunchtime specialty, Belgian fries cooked in duck fat, with a garlic aioli dipping sauce on the side, plus corned beef tongue Reuben and pulled pork panini. John orders a milk shake with ice cream from Westbrook's Smiling Hill Farm to complete the rich meal.

Our search for a Blake tree will take us through Westbrook's urban and suburban yards, because there are few large areas of open space preserved in that city and its outskirts. Smiling Hill is one of its last remaining farms. After lunch the three of us hop into Russell's car and head to our first stop, the downtown home of a mutual friend's mother, who's rumored to have fruit trees growing out back. Her daughter runs a diversified organic farm about an hour north of Portland, where she and her husband make cheese, raise small livestock, and produce herbs, fruit, and vegetables. We pull up to her mother's house unannounced, ring the doorbell, and find no one home. From the street we see most of her yard, so we linger for a while and walk up and down the sidewalk looking for trees.

There's no sign here of any apples, only well-established ornamental plantings, including a beautiful old smoke tree John admires. We're about to give up when suddenly a small woman in her eighties pokes her head out of the house across the street to ask what we're doing. "Looking for an apple tree," we tell her, and try to explain. "You've got the wrong house," she tells us—she's the person we're looking for. And yes, she did have two old apple trees growing out back. Both blew down in a windstorm last year. They made good firewood.

We talk for a while about Westbrook and its neighborhoods, and she's happy to tell us what she knows. Charming and curious, like your favorite great-aunt, the one who guards the family secrets, she has a few leads to share. Though as far as she remembers there aren't any old trees in her part of the city, she directs us to a small farm nearby with abandoned trees where she used to pick apples as a child. Much of the property was cleared recently for the construction of a new school, but something might remain beyond reach of the bulldozers.

We drive over to find the school still under construction, its entrance newly paved. Russell parks his car in a lot surrounded by recently seeded lawns segregated from farm field remnants by erosion control fencing. The building, a large, newly consolidated middle school for Westbrook and surrounding towns, dwarfs what's left of the field. At the edge of its graded and engineered landscape we cross into an overgrown meadow filled with goldenrod and surrounded by stone walls.

A few apple trees hang on in the shadows of forested thickets at the edge of the field. Some are bearing fruit, so John ducks into the woods to take a closer look. He comes back shaking his head. "They're all seedlings," he tells us, wild trees sprouted from dropped apples. He can tell by their unpruned shapes and lack of visible graft lines, where branches would have been cut and grafted to other, more desirable varieties. Some have reasonably good fruit, and he can't help but taste each one, but these aren't what we've come for. Together we return to the car through the construction site, past trailers and equipment, while my iPhone eerily tracks our progress through a satellite image of a field that no longer exists.

John teaches me what to look for as we walk. We pass apple trees that seem quite old, but by his estimate were planted no more than seventy-five years ago. We're searching for ancient specimens dating back at least 150 years. These will look very different, shadows of their former selves, with hardly any remaining living branches. Imagine a large, hollowed trunk, most limbs snapped off, a few feeble shoots barely keeping the whole alive. Russell describes them as "suitably dead" trees. It can be a challenge to get scionwood off a tree like that, but John usually finds enough new growth somewhere to take a cutting. Amazing that from the last growth of a tree's 150-year-plus life span we can generate a new tree and begin again.

Out of leads, we return to the car and fall back on our last resort: simply driving around looking for trees. It's hard to imagine this can meet with any success. It must be more gratifying to explore John and Russell's territory in central Maine, where old farm fields continue to reveal their secrets. Down here the world has moved on. At the start of this hunt John admitted that our chance of finding a Blake tree was near zero, and after a couple of hours we settle in for a little sightseeing in good company. This expedition makes me appreciate the element of chance in all of John's exploring.

We stop at an old farm, now the home of a survey company, with several old but not ancient trees in the yard. The nicest specimen, a beautiful apple tree in an open field, John identifies as probably the relatively common heirloom variety Northern Spy. A few minutes later, passing through a wooded section of a small side road, we stumble on a nineteenth-century farmstead with a large planting of overgrown highbush blueberries. These wouldn't be particularly antique varieties, since highbush blueberries are a relatively recent horticultural introduction, dating back less than a hundred years, but nevertheless the plants may be of interest. Perhaps they represent a cultivated variety that's no longer available through the commercial nursery trade. There are foods to discover even in the suburbs if one knows where and how to look.

Today's experience leaves me thinking that the discovery of a Blake apple will depend largely on chance. We've exhausted the obvious strategies, and for now it seems that all I can do is wait. This work isn't for anyone hoping for instant gratification. Patience is a prerequisite in fruit exploring. The rewards are cumulative over many years. A thread that may seem lost and forgotten can suddenly revive with a phone call or a new piece of information like a book, map, or plant list. It's hard to know the next step in looking for Blake, but we're not finished yet.

While John Bunker searches for abandoned fruit trees and berries, others work with foods that would quickly disappear without ongoing care and attention. However obscure Maine apple trees may be, once established they can fend for themselves, waiting for the right person to come along with renewed interest. The same isn't true for root crops, beans, tomatoes, or any other vegetables, the seeds of which typically live no more than a few seasons without replanting. Even more demanding are tubers like potatoes, which must be grown out every year to survive (unless one uses high-tech storage techniques like cryopreservation—freezing in liquid nitrogen—that are unavailable to most private growers). Neglect an old potato variety for a season, and the line could well disappear.

The first time I called plant collector and preservationist Will Bonsall, we talked for half an hour about mutual friends, plant biodiversity, and his work saving seeds on a small farm in central Maine called Khadigar. Then I asked about visiting to learn more about his extensive collection. It was February 2007, farm downtime, and as leader of the Slow Food Portland chapter I'd offered to bring some of the thousands of obscure foods he's collected over the past thirty years to the attention of small farmers and chefs. His answer was short and to the point: "No." I was welcome to come in August for the public tour sponsored by MOFGA. But otherwise, sorry, not interested. He didn't explain, but gave me the impression that his time had been wasted by similar requests before.

That summer I had a conflict and missed the tour. Last year, in 2008, determined to be there, I marked the date on my calendar months ahead, only to discover too late that the time posted online had been incorrect. This year the tour lands on my birthday, and Karla and I have plans to spend the weekend at a perfect little tent site on an isolated stretch of central Maine's Moosehead Lake. We talk things over and she agrees to leave Sunday morning to visit the farm. Somehow she accepts such quirks of mine with a cheerful smile—at least it's *my* birthday we're screwing up.

Getting to Khadigar means packing up early in the morning, rowing two miles back to the car, and driving hurriedly south to the town of Industry for the four-hour farm tour. Wind whips the waves into whitecaps as we load our boats to return to the car in time. Karla paddles a fiberglass kayak that skips easily across the water, all hatches closed tight. I'm a little less secure in my lapstrake wooden rowing skiff, with kayak-sized dimensions and an open cockpit that draws only about four inches. It handles wind and waves like these without taking on water, but setting long sculling oars in a heavy side chop is challenging. At least we remain close to shore where safety isn't such an issue. Rowing a small wooden boat in these conditions is far from one of my worst ideas, like the time I rolled my boat trying to get off a beach in Nova Scotia in breaking surf, or my decision to row alone to Isle au Haut off Maine's Downeast coast with a thunderstorm approaching.

Our landing spot is on an exposed shore, but before I can pull in to lend a hand Karla leaps out of her loaded boat and lifts it to safety. "Why didn't you wait for me to help?" I ask after drawing in closer. It hadn't even occurred to her. All she considered was the pressing need to save her new kayak from the waves pounding on the rocks. I angle in behind her and leap out to steady my boat while she carries my removable sliding seat and oars to dry ground under the fir trees. Together we empty our gear, lift the boats to safety, and paddle across a small pond to reach the car.

The network of rural roads leading from Moosehead Lake to Industry passes patchworks of forests and previously cleared farmland, a landscape familiar to anyone who's driven through northern New England. Woodlands open onto pastures and fields that reveal the best soils, especially in river floodplains. Most of the cultivated ground is planted in corn, but if you imagine these fields supplying corn on the cob for summer picnics on Cape Cod, you'd be disappointed. This isn't sweet corn, or even feed grain— the plants are used primarily for biomass, silage for winter cattle feed. Farmers cut the plants to the ground in late summer and collect stalks as well as cobs and kernels, chopping and fermenting everything in large piles to render the whole digestible as a feed supplement for dairy cows.

Corn, even in its pre-industrial forms, is an extremely versatile plant. Back when I lived in Washington State in the early 1990s, my friends the Sandovals grew a variety of Miztec field corn they'd brought with them from Mexico. The variety was very different from corn typically grown here in Maine, and it had multiple uses. Its ears could be eaten fresh, but the kernels were best dried and ground into flour, or cooked in tamales. The plants grew very tall, over eight feet, and just before the ears ripened their stalks developed a sweet core. Sometimes Miguel would cut green stalks with his machete and peel back the outer layers, offering sections to the children like sugarcane as a treat. They'd chew on them to draw out the sweet juice. I've tried this with other varieties and haven't yet found one to match it.

In most central Maine fields corn plants are planted very closely together, producing a tremendous amount of biomass, even outcompeting many weeds. That's a good part of the reason you see little else under cultivation. The road to Industry passes only a handful of other crops and field plantings. We see a few small orchards and farm stands, plus a couple of ambitious vegetable gardens. Two homes have large freestanding cages out front—framed structures about twenty feet wide and thirty feet long, covered with screen netting to a height of about eight feet. Maybe they once protected raspberries or highbush blueberries from ravenous birds, but more likely they kept predators away from someone's laying hens or game birds. Now they appear to be standing empty and unused.

In contrast with the uniformity of the surrounding agricultural landscape, Will Bonsall's Scatterseed Project functions like a sort of alternative citizens' genebank, a back-to-the-land collection of curiosities. He's modest about his efforts, telling those who gather for the annual tour that the USDA should hold on to all duplicate accessions "until hell freezes over, in case Will screws up, and that sure can happen." And yet for over thirty years he's saved seeds of all kinds, exchanged material with breeders and geneticists around the world, and preserved numerous plant varieties that would otherwise now be extinct. He does all this on a shoestring budget—without cold storage, specialized mechanized equipment, or even a functional greenhouse.

Will guides a group of about twenty visitors around his farm. He walks barefoot, dressed in loose jeans and an oversized pullover, his hair tied back in a ponytail. A long white beard gives him the look of a biblical elder or Tolstoyan count. He talks forcefully and rapidly, and doesn't shy away from sharing strong opinions. "Hybrids aren't vegetable varieties," for example. Calling them that "is an oxymoron, like safe sex, compassionate conservative, or country music." Farmers can't save their own seeds when growing hybrids, because they won't come true to type when replanted, and they're often patent-protected. To Will a hybrid (the first-generation cross between stable parent varieties) is only a first step in the breeding process, not an end in itself.

I first learned about Will's work in the late 1980s through the Seed Savers Exchange. This Iowa-based organization connects backyard gardeners from around the country in a network devoted to the preservation of rare fruits and vegetables. Every year I list some of my vegetable varieties in its yearbook to exchange with other gardeners. Will has always been something of a folk hero to me, because since SSE's early days in the 1970s he has consistently offered larger and more diverse listings than any other member. It's difficult to imagine the complexity involved in maintaining his approximately three thousand vegetable varieties, or the work that goes into his fields as he regenerates large parts of his collection every year to keep it alive.

Will emphasizes root crops that adapt well to cold inland Maine soils. Many of these are biennials that require two seasons to set seed, so they're particularly difficult for home gardeners to save.

Biennials must be stored in a root cellar over the winter, and they need to be isolated or caged with insect protection in their second year to prevent cross-pollination. It should come as no surprise that few gardeners list root crops in the SSE Yearbook, or that contrarian Will Bonsall would find them so appealing. As our group wanders along the edge of his fields we take in row after row of cold-hardy plants like beets and rutabagas. It's like wandering into a forgotten corner of Scandinavia or some remote homestead in Latvia or Lithuania, among subsistence farm fields filled with root crops and plots of small grains and field peas. Some of these plants could be the last specimens standing between preservation and extinction. By his description, his focus on minor crops, those overlooked by genebanks and backyard growers alike, makes him "a big frog in a small puddle." His collection of eighty or so varieties of Jerusalem artichoke, for example, is one of the largest in the world.

Will is also one of SSE's "curators," one of a handful of growers around the country responsible for backing up the organization's permanent collections. He plants hundreds of varieties of potatoes, and since these have to be grown annually there's little margin for error. Potatoes are clones—new plants sprout from one of the previous year's tubers, and all plants within a named line descend from one original plant. The seeds that flowering potato plants occasionally produce won't come true to type (although I've grown plants from seed as an experiment, they're not raised that way for production). Will's potato growouts require a great deal of space as well as carefully planned rotations and sanitation to minimize diseases. If any of his tubers pick up a virus from the soil or another plant, this will pass to the next generation. Most farmers and gardeners buy certified virus-free planting stock from seed companies every year, because inadequate storage facilities and a well-founded fear of disease prevent them from replanting their own.

In the potato fields Will maintains just a few hills of each type, and they look highly variable, even from a distance. Some are scraggly and forlorn, their few stems and leaves yellowing and trailing along the ground. These weaker plants may produce barely enough tubers to replenish the seed stock. Others appear vigorous and productive, bursting with life, vibrantly green and growing as much as two feet tall and wide. This farm is full of distinct person-alities, not the least of which is Bonsall himself.

What's the point of growing so many potatoes? While walking along the edge of the field Will stops and waves his hand toward the plantings. "Over there I'm growing Lumper," he tells us as we look across potato rows growing between poplar windbreaks. "Has anyone here ever eaten or grown it?" The answer is no, and with good reason, because the taste of this variety is generally consid-ered poor. Will maintains Lumper largely out of historical interest, and why would anyone other than a collector care about such a low-quality potato? "It yields well," he tells us. This is apparently its sole virtue. It was also, however, the cause of its leading role in one of the modern world's greatest agricultural disasters, the Irish potato famine. In a good year without disease pressure, Lumper can produce enough calories on an acre to feed a hungry family. All one needs to survive is a spade for planting and harvesting, and a shallow pit to store the crop. But high yield is only one attribute of a successful crop. In a wet, cold year, entire plantings of Lumper can succumb to the late blight fungus. The variety is highly susceptible to this disease.

High yields caused Irish peasants to adopt Lumper in the early part of the nineteenth century, leading the English to call the potato the "lazy root." In the English view, when the Irish abandoned their traditional diverse diet of oats, barley, rye, beans, and vegetables in favor of the potato, it was due to their weak moral character. By the 1840s, farmers forced onto marginal lands abandoned not only traditional staples, but also most of the potato varieties they'd grown for two centuries, in favor of the higher-yielding Lumper. When disease struck and wiped out Irish crops in the late 1840s, they had little or nothing to fall back on. Inadequate British relief efforts, coupled with discrimination and misplaced moralizing, allowed roughly a million people to starve to death.

Lumper is a poster child for the dangers of monocrop agricul-ture, so it's ironic to find it growing here in this field devoted to agricultural biodiversity. A further irony is that, if one goal of a collection like this is to preserve disease-resistant plants, Lumper has already proven itself one of the most fatally disease-susceptible varieties on the planet. Despite a few potentially valuable genetic traits, especially its high yield, you might consider this potato a cursed food. No one sells Lumper commercially in this country, and only genebanks and a handful of private growers like Will Bonsall keep it alive.

This year the dangers of late blight strike particularly close to home, because already by midsummer the disease is sweeping through New England and taking down entire plantings of tomatoes and potatoes. Though it hasn't yet reached Will's relatively remote fields, if it does strike it has the potential to destroy the bulk of his potato collection in a matter of weeks. A few fungicides like copper solutions are available to help protect organic growers, but unless Will applies them before infection, they'll do him no good. Organic fungicides are expensive and have limited effect, and anyway he isn't using them. If disease symptoms start appearing here, his only option will be to remove infected plants from the field and hope for the best.

This disease is new to me. At one time late blight was a recurring problem for potato and tomato growers here in the Northeast (it's equally devastating to both these nightshade plants), but fungicides brought it in check throughout the country by the 1970s. For a number of years it became quite rare, until fungicide-resistant strains began emerging in Mexico in the late 1980s. Over the past twenty years the disease has spread inexorably northward, gradually returning to New England fields and again threatening growers with widespread crop losses. A rainy year like this provides ideal conditions for fungal spores to reproduce and disperse widely on the wind, infecting farms and gardens in epidemic proportions.

Since June agricultural bulletins have been carrying reports of impending doom. Early infestations typically involved plants purchased from big-box stores, which sold tomato plants from giant southern wholesale nurseries. Trucking infected plants northward spread the disease quickly, much earlier in the season than usual. Overcast, windy conditions sent spores flying everywhere, and a long stretch of heavy rain early this season carried them to the leaves of otherwise healthy plants. By the middle of July, *The New York Times* quoted a plant pathologist from Cornell saying he'd never seen an outbreak on such a wide scale. Tomatoes and potatoes all over the Northeast are threatened, and plantings in my own gardens have started to show symptoms. Last week while pruning tomatoes I found black marks on a few stems and leaves, and one plant with a stem fully rotted through. In all likelihood this is just a sample of what's to come.

Late blight may not make it to Will Bonsall's isolated homestead, but its spores are all around the Portland area. In Massachusetts the situation is even worse; their Department of Agriculture may apply for federal disaster relief. Virtually all of the one hundred or so community supported agriculture farms in Massachusetts lost their tomatoes over the past few days. This means many disappointed customers picking up shares of zucchini and chard while dreaming of vine-ripened tomatoes. Slow Food Connecticut canceled its annual heirloom tomato festival because the fruits are so scarce. It's too soon to quantify the damage, but losing a crop so emblematic of summer is a large blow to growers and consumers alike.

Karla and I walk back to our car at the end of Will's garden tour and stop to admire his kitchen gardens, where many types of vegetables flourish. Despite the precariousness of Scatterseed's large, underfunded private collection, it's impossible not to feel a sense of abundance in this place. Will's diversified farm has incredible resilience, and it's the right season to test his faith in biodiversity. If late blight reaches his fields, it's going to create intense selection pressures that may cull weaker plants and demonstrate which of the many potatoes in his collection carry resistance. Of course this would lead to losses, the disappearance of varieties with other worthy traits, but fighting off newly evolving diseases could make the collection on the whole that much stronger.

Asking people like Will Bonsall to carry on alone comes with great risk, however. It jeopardizes the future of these foods. He himself acknowledges this, and includes a plea every year in the Seed Savers Yearbook: "It is not wise to have so many eggs in one basket (and I'm quite capable of dropping that basket)," he writes. "Sample fees and occasional grants are simply not enough to maintain all this diversity on a sustainable basis. When you request varieties, have at least the intention of growing them out to seed for your own use, sharing seeds with friends and, best of all, reoffering them here in the Yearbook." In other words, there must be a better way to distribute risk than to concentrate plant collections in the hands of a few highly motivated collectors. Such foods need to be shared—grown, eaten, and appreciated—to ensure they can be truly preserved for future generations.

There's a postscript to my 2009 visits with plant collectors, and the time spent searching for the Blake apple with John Bunker and Russell Libby. In early December 2011, while driving down a street in one of Portland's outlying neighborhoods, Karla draws my attention to a large old tree growing by the side of the road. Its leaves have long since dropped to the ground, but even now its branches are filled with bright yellow apples. "You should go take a look," she tells me. After leaving her and our dog Tica at a nearby park to meet friends for a walk, I return to the tree and park in the adjacent lot, which is owned by an automotive repair shop.

These apples grow about ten feet from the roadside, overhanging the sidewalk. Although the tree stands only about five hundred feet from the shores of Casco Bay, the ocean isn't visible from here. Surrounding land is primarily industrial, filled with large warehouses, and a highway runs along the water's edge. Nevertheless, stretching behind this tree for two hundred yards is the remnant of an old farm field, which ends at a line of woods. Hundreds of fallen apples cover the ground beneath it, and many more remain on its branches. I pick up a clean fruit and study it. It's large and conical, vividly yellow, with a light russet along the base (a roughening of the skin, with a grayish, darkened color). The flavor is mild and sweet, though clearly well past its prime. I don't dare imagine this could be Blake, but it seems to fit John Bunker's descriptions.

Back at home later that evening, I remember one of the maps Karla uncovered online, which identifies a property owned by a J. H. Blake living in this same Portland neighborhood in 1871. This was coincidentally the only Blake reference we found on any old map. I pull up the link and cross-check the reference against a satellite photo, and suddenly realize the tree we've found could have grown on his land. Blake's name is recorded just a few hundred yards away, closer than anyone else. If he owned property that extended to the water, this would have been his field. I drove the adjacent road two years ago to look for trees, but found nothing but neatly landscaped suburban homes. It hadn't occurred to me to examine what might have been the back edge of a small farm.

I send an e-mail to John Bunker with photos of three representative samples of the fruit. Two weeks later he replies. He's been away in England, touring orchards and visiting collectors, where coincidentally he met with someone growing a variety also called Blake. He thinks this English apple may originally have come from Maine, and it seems to match the fruit in my photo. "Very interesting," he tells me. John asks whether I can send him a few samples, so four days before Christmas I salvage two of the last intact fruits on the ground and drop them in the mail. A cold snap destroyed those not protected by the long grass, freezing them and turning their skins brown, and these are all that remain.

"Thanks very much for sending the two apples," John writes in early January. "Obviously they are not in great shape, but they certainly look like what we're hoping to find." I tell him the tree has the scraggly look of a wild tree, with no visible graft lines, so this may not be the fruit we're after. Could it be a seedling sprouted from a Blake apple, or the remnant of an older, better-tended tree? He promises to take a look on his next visit to Portland. It will be "really important to see the fruit earlier next fall," he writes. We'll find the answer then. If this doesn't turn out to be a Blake, nevertheless we may be close to discovering other remaining trees. Scouring this neighborhood over the next few months, talking with property owners and walking the adjacent woods, might turn up something new. The search goes on.

#

THE PLEASURES OF OUR OWN TABLE:
GROWING GARDENS AND SAVING SEEDS

"Hi David, Happy Day After Election Day!!!" In what year but 2008, the day after Obama's victory, could an e-mail from a young staff member in the Slow Food office begin with such a line? Jenny Trotter, Slow Food's Ark of Taste program manager, is forwarding a note from Sonja Johanson, a gardener living in Maine's western mountains. "I recently obtained the New England Foods at Risk list" (put together by a consortium of preservation groups, including Slow Food and the Seed Savers Exchange), Sonja writes, "and, after some research, think that I may have a patch of Snyder blackberries. This patch has been maintained at my home in Bethel, Maine, for at least 80 years, and fits all the descriptors that I can find over the Internet. Can you recommend any resources for helping me to confirm the identity of this variety?"

We write back to Sonja to suggest she contact John Bunker, and a few days later they exchange notes. "There are many old plantings of blackberries around the state," John tells her. "Some may be named varieties, while others may be excellent local selections that were cultivated and even passed around, but never named. It may be that no one will ever know the true name of your blackberry, but we'll give it a try." He forwards Sonja's information to a cane fruit specialist living in her area, and promises to follow up the next summer if she'll send over samples of the plants and fruit.

The name of this berry seems less significant than its history, however. Even if it isn't Snyder, from her description in all likelihood it represents an equally endangered food, another neglected and forgotten corner of the blackberry genepool. Sonja's notes are compelling enough for me. According to her these blackberries bear "VERY heavily," don't suffer from disease, are quite cold-hardy (which is unusual in a blackberry), and have very good flavor— "not too sweet." She currently "restrains" her patch at twenty-five hundred square feet by mowing off the new growth that sprouts up every year, as far as thirty feet away in surrounding ground. Despite the difficulty of picking from its ten-foot-tall, thorny canes, she harvests thirty to forty gallons of fruit each season and sells most to local shops and inns, or swaps them for produce at a nearby farm. Her children even set up a roadside stand with the surplus. The berries are very delicate and don't keep for more than a day after harvest, so she freezes the remainder.

Sonja agrees to bring me some plants in the spring once the ground thaws. A few months later, in April 2009, a small, unmarked package appears one afternoon on our porch. As promised, she'd delivered two canes from her field, with a plastic bag filled with wet newsprint wrapped tightly around the roots to keep them moist. Inside there's a message and care instructions that include this warning: "Roots must be kept damp AT ALL TIMES. If they dry out even for a minute, the plant will die. Old-timers would tell you to plant only at dawn or dusk, when sunlight won't touch the roots."

Or stand over them and plant quickly in your shadow, with the sun blazing high in the sky. The next afternoon I choose a patch of good garden soil near one of my peach trees and set the two canes about three feet apart. The location is a bit risky, because offshoots will spread quickly and, without care, could become deeply intertwined with the tree's roots. Sonja describes her soil as poor but well drained, and writes, "I've not improved the soil at all (I'm afraid that I might get more berries . . .)." Who knows what kind of chaos these plants might be capable of unleashing in my warmer climate and fertile soil. This growing space is isolated from the rest of the garden, however, with good sun exposure. So I go ahead and plant, resolving to keep a close watch to prevent them from spreading in unwanted directions.

Sonja and I exchange notes about other varieties she maintains. She's a Master Gardener (trained by Maine's Cooperative Extension Service to teach other gardeners) and seed saver, and she lives part-time in Massachusetts, where she manages a garden in the suburbs south of Boston for second- and third-grade students at a public elementary school. The children grow heritage foods like Green Mountain potatoes from Vermont, native fox grapes, and the rare New England heirloom Canada Crookneck squash. Students eat "snack foods" like strawberries and peas directly from the garden. They taste watermelons (with seeds!) and cherry tomatoes, and harvest and prepare their "Rocky Woods Feast" in the fall. Extra produce goes to senior housing and the town food cupboard. Even scraps like carrot tops don't go to waste; these are donated to "bunnies and guinea pigs at the town shelter."

Having recently spent a year managing a small farm for a nonprofit—working with high school students to produce food for low-income seniors—I can imagine what her days are like. She tells me she's been running this garden for about five years, and that she's "finally beginning to get the hang of gardening with lots of kids and few volunteers." Her school has between four and five hundred students in the two grades that participate in her project. This may sound like a lot of helping hands, until you consider the reality of trying to supervise small children and teaching them new tasks like weeding (around) the lettuce.

While driving home from planting Sonja's blackberries I think with some relief about the year ahead of me, because my gardens are scaled back to a third of an acre, about fifteen thousand square feet, on a corner of the land I managed last year in the 2008 season. Working even this much space and a seventy-five-foot greenhouse may sound like a lot, but it's a welcome relief after last year's hectic farm and volunteer management. The best way to appreciate a third-of-an-acre garden is to begin with two acres. Even though we didn't sell most of the foods we grew last year (the organization I

worked with donated it to those in need, and staff and student helpers did much of the harvesting), growing two acres of vegetables
in fields previously choked with weeds kept me running more
than sixty hours a week (imagine what commercial growers face,
because harvesting and selling produce is at least half the work
on most farms). Downshifting this season leaves time to write and
focus on new directions.

After moving to Maine and taking a few years off from gardening to concentrate on environmental restoration work, several years
ago I began borrowing space at this site and planting again. From
this modest beginning in 2005, initially just a few rows of beans
and tomatoes, it wasn't long before my gardens expanded to nearly
a quarter acre in other available space near the city. Within two
years I'd built up a collection of seeds and plants, and caught the
growing bug enough to leap in full-time. Last year, however, was
a little too much time in the field for me. So I'm cutting back this
season, looking for a better work–life balance and searching for a
new purpose to justify my collecting habit.

What am I out to accomplish this year? Planning my garden
brings up some lingering questions. I'm not running a genebank
or a seed company, so I have to be realistic about the time, energy,
and space available to do this kind of work. And as gratifying as
it feels to call my garden a conservation project, setting goals to
accomplish this isn't as straightforward as it seems. If a food isn't
in immediate danger of extinction, for example, is it better to focus
on others at greater risk? It isn't easy to figure out what's truly rare,
however, and stay a step ahead of the seed trade. Plus I wouldn't
want to ditch a promising variety just because others find it appealing. What would I tell Karla? "Sure, that was a delicious snap bean,
but I'm not going to grow it anymore because Fedco picked it up."
Where's the happy middle?

So what to grow, and why? Some of the foods in my collection
are well known and widely available, while others are extremely
obscure. Take two of the varieties I'll plant this season: Tall Telephone, a New England heirloom shell pea dating back to the 1870s,
and a variety of kale called Portuguese Dairyman, acquired from
a home gardener through the Seed Savers Exchange. Is it more

valuable to grow one of these foods than the other? Tall Telephone is commercially available, even if the number of catalogs carrying it has declined by half since 1981. In contrast, Portuguese Dairyman kale is unavailable in this country except through my source, an American who named it for the farmer in the Azores who gave it to him. It's possible that this kale grows under a different name in every garden in the Azores, but here it's extremely rare.

You could argue that despite its commercial availability it would be best to focus on Tall Telephone, since it originated in New England and has a rich local history. But kale grows well in Maine, and there doesn't seem to be any reason to exclude something so perfectly adapted to our climate simply because it's a recent introduction. My goal isn't to create a period garden, and after all nearly every vegetable we eat arrived here as seeds in someone's pocket at one point or another. Is a nineteenth-century New England food inherently more interesting than another carried here by immigrants four generations later? As much as I'd like to emphasize preserving varieties with a long regional history, I have no intention of stopping there.

How about dropping the peas and growing only obscure foods like Portuguese Dairyman? My garden could blossom with oddly colored heirloom tomatoes, forgotten Native American pole beans, commercially unavailable midcoast Maine rutabagas, and some of the huge, flavorful *Maxima* squashes few take the trouble to grow and cook anymore. And I do grow these foods. But the more time I spend in the garden, the less concerned I become about distinctions between the rare and the not quite so rare. In practice my gardens are pretty inclusive. These days even a few hybrid plants make it into the mix, particularly for foods like melons that struggle in Maine's cold soils. Since hybrids are often bred for increased vigor, among some crops they can outperform their open-pollinated cousins (in which pollination is left to natural means rather than artificially managed by hybridizing).

At the risk of sounding like a crank, I'm starting to come to the conclusion that the purpose of my collection is simply *to collect*. Or, more to the point, what grows in my garden is maybe less important than the act of saving garden seeds itself, or planting uncommon fruits and berries. In Tall Telephone's case, although it's possible to order new seed packets each season, that doesn't mean: (a) that these seeds will be identical in quality and character to those with the same name from another source; (b) that over time, seeds from my own garden won't evolve their own distinct characteristics; and (c) that seed companies will continue to list this variety indefinitely. Every year plants come and go from the trade. Something that seems common can fade little by little, and then quietly disappear. If enough of us build reserve collections of these foods, however, then the opposite can occur: Diversity and richness can increase.

So I begin the new season with a broad selection of plants, whatever has a good story and interests me. By the middle of April 2009, everything is set in motion. Cool-weather crops like Tall Telephone peas germinate in the garden, while vegetables requiring a longer growing season sprout in a sunny window of our house, with the heat in the room cranked to seventy degrees to speed germination. Indoor seedlings get direct light through most of the morning, a few hours a day—enough for everything but the onions and leeks that seem to crawl out of their trays to get closer to the sun. I hang a four-foot fluorescent light over the seed flats to help them along. Soon all my limited shelf space fills to overflowing, with beautiful bluish green French heirloom leeks; various sweet and hot peppers like Fish, a Chesapeake Bay heirloom; and tomatoes like Mankin Plum and Berkshire Polish, little-known varieties with New England roots.

I sort through seeds stored in salvaged glass jars in our dining room cupboard. Large jars hold colorful beans and spiky beet seeds. Tiny seeds like those of kale, arugula, basil, and mustard surround them. My Microsoft Access database stores information about each variety—when it was last grown, how well it grew, and what it tastes like. This database also records information about varietal names and sources, like the seed preservation program at a school in Maine's midcoast that sent me a rare, commercially unavailable rutabaga, and the friend of a friend from New Jersey who shared five heirloom tomato varieties from her husband's Italian family. Her tomatoes are the equivalent of a full set of family china, passed from hand to hand for generations to meet every culinary necessity: slicing tomato, oxheart, plum, paste. Growing these foods is like participating in an ongoing conversation. They're living connections to other growers: those who came before us, and those who'll inherit these seeds one day.

My collection of about three hundred fruit and vegetable varieties has come together slowly over the past few years. Many of the most interesting foods originated with other growers through the Seed Savers Exchange network. Every winter SSE publishes a yearbook with descriptions of heirloom varieties for exchange, an astonishing list that runs to over twenty thousand distinct varieties. This includes approximately three thousand varieties of tomatoes alone, and how many of us have tasted or grown more than a handful? It's ironic that although as a whole humanity has lost as much as 90 percent of the genetic diversity of its food crops over the past hundred years, as individuals we have access to greater variety than ever before. And yet so few of us take advantage of all that remains.

Several years ago I ordered a packet of tomato seeds from a company in Pennsylvania called Amishland Heirloom Seeds, a sole proprietorship with one employee, owner Lisa Von Saunder, who produces all the seeds she sells herself. This tomato is called Amazon Chocolate, and at the time Amishland was its only source in the United States. The packet she sent contained just fifteen seeds, but they germinated well and provided plenty of material for replanting the following season. Since then I've collected and saved seeds every year in an effort to adapt the variety to Maine.

I grow Amazon Chocolate because, like a gifted student with behavioral problems, it's at once challenging and highly rewarding. It has serious disease problems—the fruits tend to rot on the vine, if the vine doesn't rot first, thanks to our relatively chilly, wet climate (gardening zone 5b, according to the 2009 USDA Plant Hardiness Zone Map, meaning minimum temperatures in our area reach fifteen below Fahrenheit). And yet those fruits that ripen fully are among the best tomatoes we've ever eaten. It's easy to understand why the Ukrainian who brought this variety to the United States in the mid-1990s went to the trouble. Dark and smoky, wine red, with a perfect balance of sweetness and acidity, Amazon Chocolate resembles other tomatoes from his homeland, like Black from Tula (a Russian city two hundred miles north of Ukraine) and Black Krim. The latter two often score highest in taste tests at our farmers' markets. My hope is that someday, through persistence and selection, Amazon Chocolate can adapt as well to Maine's cool soil. In the meantime it's worth a gamble for even a handful of these delicious tomatoes.

Gardeners in New England who persist in saving seeds for Tall Telephone peas or Amazon Chocolate tomatoes not only preserve lines that might otherwise disappear, but also help develop and maintain adaptation to imperfect growing conditions. By carefully selecting and saving seeds from those plants that thrive best, over time we help transform them into more consistent producers in any given place. This is one reason seed saving will always be valuable, even for commonly available varieties. Because it's no longer a given that someone else will do this work for us. Pea seed sold by New England retailers, for example, is unlikely to be grown commercially here in the Northeast. Bean and pea seeds are typically raised in mass quantities by farmers in eastern Oregon, where conditions are ideal for minimizing disease and producing quality seeds with high germination rates. These are sold in bulk even to the most independent of retailers, who repackage them for catalog sales.

Look closely at the apparent cornucopia of gardening catalogs and you'll find some disturbing trends. Raising seed and nursery crops is a tough business on a small scale, in part because the return on labor and space is very low, and also because some regions are much better suited to specialized production than others. Most seed companies outsource production to a rapidly consolidating wholesale trade, and very few venture into the difficult world of production by contracting directly with farmers or growing for themselves. Spend time reading through seed catalogs and you'll come across many of the same varieties, which in all likelihood derive from the same wholesale sources. The Amishland Heirloom Seeds of the world are highly unusual in producing all their own stock.

In the case of beans or peas, outsourcing production to favorable regions makes sense on many levels. It ensures better germination rates and prevents the spread of fungal diseases. But over time it also means that unless planting stock used by western farmers is periodically grown here on the East Coast, as a handful of conscientious companies like Vermont's High Mowing Seeds do, plants will gradually adjust to more forgiving environments. If no one breeds and selects individual plants that thrive in our cold soils and relatively damp climate, this can lead in the garden to diminished resistance to pests and diseases, and increased reliance on chemical pesticides and fungicides. In other words, even if genebanks could guarantee perpetual conservation for every food we know, and seed companies could include everything in their catalogs, backyard growers would still have a role to play. Saving seeds at the local level ensures a broad genetic base, helping us face ever-changing conditions in the field.

By early June it's clear that the 2009 season will be one of those years that test the resilience of our gardens and planting choices. This has been one of the coldest and wettest springs in anyone's memory. On a typically rainy morning, I pull into the driveway at my garden site and quickly decide not to head into the fields. Nearly two inches of rain have fallen in the last few hours, and the ground is saturated. Instead I drive a couple of miles to the seashore, park in an empty lot in Cape Elizabeth's Kettle Cove, and start unloading empty buckets from the back of my station wagon in order to collect seaweed for fertilizer and mulch. Lobster boats swing against the wind and disappear into the mist. Their moorings lie a few hundred feet off this small beach, well protected by nearby Richmond Island and an old stone breakwater less than a mile away. Most of the view is invisible today, however; all I can see from the beach are the closest boats and the first line of vegetation, blooming rugosa roses and bayberry shrubs.

Abundant seaweed grows along the protected shore, and retreating tides leave it scattered across the sand. I pull on my rain gear, grab my buckets and a pitchfork, and walk down to the beach. Heavy rains have washed away the salt residues, so it's an ideal time to gather seaweed for the garden. Working quickly in the downpour, it takes less than ten minutes to fill several buckets and carry them back to the car. I rinse my hands in the stream of warm water that cascades off the asphalt and drive back to the farm.

Before spreading this seaweed as mulch I take a few minutes to take stock of the gardens, wandering down what probably look to visitors like randomly arranged paths. Last year at the start of the season I carted a wheelbarrow through my fields from the barn and other access points, marking lines in the dirt along heavily traveled routes. These became permanent walkways, with planting beds radiating outward along the land's contours. Arranging beds by usage rather than symmetry shortens walking distances and makes the field more interesting to my eye. There's no need to plant here in the straight, wide rows dictated by a tractor or rototiller, since I use these infrequently. Although I borrow equipment to till in cover crops, most of my time in the garden is spent on my feet, hoeing from a standing position or digging with a pitchfork. Working so much space by hand might seem a little crazy, but it has clear advantages. It's peaceful and quiet. It minimizes soil compaction, improves attention to detail, and provides plenty of good aerobic exercise. A day spent working with a pitchfork feels much healthier than rattling around on a tractor and breathing diesel fumes.

I've never been very good with mechanical equipment. My most vivid memory of the 1946 Ford tractor I owned in Washington State is of driving it down my town's main street with a set of disks—steel tilling implements shaped like cymbals, and about as loud—clanging on the pavement. It must have been low on hydraulic fluid, because the hitch wouldn't quite lift the heavy disks off the ground. They banged along, making a huge racket and sending loose chunks of asphalt flying. I hid my face, made it through town fast in the highest gear, and ditched the tractor out of sight in the nearest field. Then started walking home to get my truck. Not a minute too soon, because the county sheriff appeared around the next corner. "Hey, did you see a guy go by here on a tractor?" he asked. "No," I replied in all honesty.

My gardens are a discouraging sight today. The rush of May planting is over, and as seedlings emerge and transplanted vegetables like tomatoes and onions take root, I feel a kind of helplessness in the face of heavy pest pressure. Despite nearly two months of planting and replanting, from a distance the gardens look relatively empty. Whether one bite of the cutworm, which nips young seedlings just above ground level, killing them, or a thousand cuts of the cucumber beetles, the results are the same: heavy plant losses and gaps in the rows. You have to get up close to see the young seedlings that remain, and find reassurance that the gardens will bounce back. It's all too easy to focus on the losses.

According to our local paper, the *Portland Press Herald*, many farmers describe this unusually cold, wet spring as one of the toughest early growing seasons in memory. Tomato plants are turning black and starting to rot at a friend's farm. Carrots and beans are failing to sprout, and strawberries are in danger of rotting. My gardens received three times the average rainfall in the past three weeks, and there's no sign of a break in the weather.

I went out last week to reseed cucumbers, thinking they'd failed to sprout, and found germination at last after a two-week delay. In four nearby rows all the lettuce has disappeared, and this baffles me because nothing disturbed lettuce plants last year in nearby areas. I rotate plantings to avoid growing the same crops year after year in the same place, which helps to foil pests, reduce disease, and maintain fertility (since different plants require different nutrients, and some bind nitrogen from the air into the soil). Moving lettuce a few beds away from last year's growing site provides no benefit this season, though. My best guess is that snails and slugs are eating everything to the ground, because the plants are too small for larger predators. There have never been so many snails in my gardens, and this is the reason for my seaweed harvest—another local farmer suggests that when used as mulch it will repel them. If nothing else, spreading it restores my illusion of control. Plus it's good fertilizer.

Other unknown pests mowed down the lettuce in my greenhouse (most likely the two pet rabbits left at the farm by the previous tenants). The plants bounced back once covered by spun polyester row cover, but now it's a struggle to stay ahead of the caterpillars nestling in the leaves. I crush them between my fingers. Woodchucks have been feasting on microgreen salads of radicchio, baby onions, scallions, and dill sprigs. I've been meaning to grind a little pepper onto the remaining seedlings for them, or spray the leaves with sriracha chili sauce. Instead I transplant and replant, cover the most vulnerable plants, root around bases of young seedlings to find and crush cutworms, and place rings made from paper Dixie cups around remaining vulnerable plants to protect them. Maybe things aren't really so bad, it always feels a bit this way early in the season, but nevertheless, all that nice lettuce . . .

Back in April, standing on my porch looking down at the tomato starts I'd managed to drop upside down after hooking a sleeve on the doorknob, the feeling of loss had been the same. These included two of my most endangered varieties, and all of the seedlings were either destroyed by the fall or hopelessly confused with other varieties. I filled new flats with potting soil and started the seeds again, and by early June they'd nearly caught up with the others. Problem solved; life in the garden went on. Cutworms destroyed some of the replacements, but enough remain to replenish the seed stock if they can make it to maturity. It's not too late for the garden as a whole to recover.

There isn't much that can be done about the cold, wet weather, but maybe it's possible to do something about the woodchucks. They wander freely, eating the largest pumpkins, sampling one bite from each cucumber, mowing down greens and carrot tops. With few exceptions they'll go for just about anything uncovered, sometimes taking down entire plantings. Catching them in a Havahart trap hasn't worked. Usually I live with the problem and resign myself to their foraging, but it's hard not to fight back when facing many losses this year. So I put the useless trap away and borrow a .22 rifle from our friend Amanda (she transports deer she shoots with higher-caliber guns on the roof of her Toyota Prius).

One July morning at five thirty I throw the rifle in a banjo case, hoping no one on my Portland street will notice the protruding barrel, and drive out to the farm with grim determination. The police have cleared this and confirmed that shooting farm pests is within the scope of the law. Seems like they don't want to know about it: "Just do it" was the impression they conveyed. "No, you don't need to notify the neighbors," they told me, "that would only worry them." I stopped by the new house next door to fill them in on my plans, but no one was around and it seemed prudent to stay silent. At least I'll be largely out of sight, unlike the local farmer who carries a loaded rifle with him and shoots woodchucks from the seat of his tractor. I'll try not to shoot in the direction of anyone's early-morning coffee.

This doesn't seem like a good idea in the Portland suburbs. Nevertheless I load up the clip, release the safety at the car, and quietly creep toward the garden. Yesterday I set up a "woodchuck blind" (how pitiful is that?) beside one of the electric fences. It's basically a pile of tarps overflowing from a tall workbench. I take up position behind it and start reading *The Atlantic,* cradling the gun lazily in the crook of my arm. The sun is rising, maybe too high already. What time do these creatures eat? They're rarely visible, and then only as a blur moving at high speed at the periphery of the field. Not a good omen for hunting success. It also doesn't help that I've never shot this gun before, because no place in this field is discreet enough to set up a target. Everything depends on getting as close as possible, or waiting patiently for the animal to approach me.

Which never happens. I stand for a while with the gun propped on my carefully positioned bench, sighting down the barrel at a well-worn corridor leading from a nearby woodchuck burrow to the pumpkin patch. An eight-foot-tall stand of parsnips going to seed partially screens the view. After about half an hour, nearing six thirty, tension rapidly de-escalates as I acknowledge how low the odds are that any woodchuck will wander in front of my gun barrel. Then a car door slams behind me and it's over—two friends have arrived from Portland to feed their pigs and goats. "What's up?" they ask. This is a little embarrassing.

Maybe the Havahart trap is worth another try. It isn't much fun releasing the skunks that usually wander into it, but friends offer suggestions for better woodchuck bait. One successfully catches them with broccoli and rigs up an elaborate asphyxiation device involving surgical tubing, duct tape, heavy-duty trash bags, and car exhaust. His wife and I smile carefully and nod as he describes this to us. Not my style. On the other hand, the alternatives aren't very good: dropping the poor animal off in the deep woods to fend for itself, or leaving it at someone else's property. Not without cruelty, either—maybe carbon monoxide is the most humane approach after all. Probably best to shoot it in the trap for the quickest and, hopefully, most painless solution. Does that void the Havahart warranty?

I dislike killing animals and leave it as a last resort after fences and other repellents fail. Actually I probably wait too long, losing much of the best produce in the garden as a result of not throwing smoke bombs down a woodchuck hole or shooting rabbits. It isn't easy to draw the line between sharing the bounty with other creatures and letting them have full sway of the garden for a free lunch. Losing a few plantings is tolerable, because there's usually more than enough to go around, but something more like genteel suburban habit than principle is probably at work here. As Missouri farmer Blake Hurst wrote recently, "Farming has always been messy and painful, and bloody and dirty. It still is." Producing food may not always be the Darwinian struggle that it is this season, but it's never quite the Eden many of us imagine, either. More like a constant effort to balance nature and human desire.

The challenges of the early 2009 season drive this point home. By the time Karla and I visit Will Bonsall's Scatterseed project in early August, it's clear this is one of the worst growing seasons anyone can remember. Heavy rain, cold temperatures, pests, and the arrival of late blight are putting relentless pressure on local growers. Those who farm heavy clay soils that drain slowly, or rely on mechanical tillage instead of handwork or chemicals, are having great trouble controlling weeds. Tractors and tillers bog down in saturated soil, and when the ground isn't dry enough many weeds easily re-root after cultivation. It's lucky that my soils drain quickly and I'm accustomed to working with a hoe, so this hasn't been a problem for me.

Late blight, the fungal disease that kills tomato and potato plants, is taking a heavy toll in my fields. A couple of days ago nearly half the plants of a potato variety called Anna Cheeka's Ozette suddenly died back, despite looking healthy last week. I cut away their withered stalks, bagged them, and took them home for disposal. Unlike highly susceptible potatoes like Will Bonsall's Lumper, Ozette is a survivor, one of the oldest potato varieties in the Northern Hemisphere. I'd hoped it would show at least some resistance to the disease. Maybe it's just been lucky, however, in where it's been planted. Farmers of the Makah Nation have grown this variety since the late 1700s in remote Neah Bay, on the western shore of the Olympic Peninsula in Washington State. In all likelihood they rarely if ever encountered late blight in such an isolated location.

I've bagged infected plants to prevent the disease spores from spreading farther. Two of my tomato varieties are particularly affected, requiring removal first of the withered leaves and then entire plants as they succumb. Can the spores just as readily infect plants in the greenhouse? As of the middle of July these hoophouse tomatoes are holding up well, with few signs of damage, offering a glimmer of hope. We won't lack for other vegetables—despite the challenging start to the season, there will be plenty of things to eat in the gardens one way or another—but turnips are no substitute for all the tomatoes still green on the vine. My tomato seed harvest may also be lost because it depends on outdoor plantings.

What to do with my rapidly accumulating pile of diseased, rotting tomato and potato plants? They can't stay in the field, because as disease spores mature they'll continue to spread the blight. Cooperative Extension bulletins advise suffocating plants in black plastic bags in direct sunlight and throwing them in the trash, but it's hard to bring myself to toss a dozen or more large plastic garbage bags of plant matter in a landfill. They could split open and spread the disease regardless. Advice to larger growers is to burn them, but that also doesn't sound like a particularly good option. How do you ignite piles of wet, rotting vegetation? Douse them in kerosene and drop a match? There must be other safe and environmentally benign disposal options away from productive fields and gardens.

How about burying them in the woods? On a detour south for a visit with my sister in Connecticut, I come up with a plan to ditch the contents of a few bags on a remote section of the Massachusetts Turnpike behind a McDonald's. So I pull in, drive to the back of the lot, and look for breaks in the chain-link fence. Several guys watch from the cabs of their idling eighteen-wheelers as I drive past with a carload of heavy trash bags. It's immediately clear how much unwanted attention this would draw, and what a foolish idea it is. I decide not to stop and head straight for the exit instead.

In the end I dig a trench behind my parents' house in Massachusetts, line it with infected plants, and cover everything with a thick layer of brush and leaves. The nearest gardens are at least a quarter mile away, and late blight spores are everywhere anyway. My conscience is clear, or good enough on balance, all things considered. Other than the extra bag whose contents I dumped unceremoniously in the woods in Connecticut, twenty minutes before boarding a train. Without acting quickly dozens of rotting tomato plants would have baked for three days in my car in an urban parking lot in ninety-degree heat. Sometimes, something has to give.

A couple of weeks later, in early August, our weather suddenly turns. The heavy, consistent rains and cold weather that have plagued us since planting season began in May break at last, bringing a long stretch of hot, humid weather. Organic potato farmer and seedsman Jim Gerritsen writes from his farm in far northern Aroostook County to say they've experienced more heat in the first two weeks of August than they'll typically encounter in an entire summer. Despite the poor growing season, thanks to this change his spring wheat is ready for harvest, nearly on schedule. Here in southern Maine the heat is just as welcome. I fill baskets with summer produce and bring home large quantities of heat-loving crops like basil, peppers, eggplant, summer squash, and cucumbers.

Commercial organic farmers continue to struggle. At the height of the summer season heirloom tomatoes are selling in Massachusetts for as much as $6.99 a pound, twice their usual price. Most local growers have lost their crops to blight. Only in my greenhouse are tomato plants producing; after nearly a month of infection nearly all my plants in the field are a complete loss. Since we have no available second-quality tomatoes to substitute, Karla and I boil five gallons of beautiful greenhouse tomatoes into sauce. My five-gallon bucket probably weighs about thirty pounds, and this cooks down into five quarts of thick, rich sauce. We try not to think about what these blemish-free fruits would fetch in the market.

My greenhouse is producing excellent tomatoes with no use of sprays, organic or otherwise. Missouri Pink Love Apple tomatoes are particularly beautiful: huge, flawless, and delicious. This relatively unknown and commercially unavailable variety grows outdoors here with mixed results, so their high quality in the greenhouse comes as something of a surprise. Not only do they appear to be fairly blight-resistant, but their production is consistent and heavy. The variety traces back to a Civil War–era gardener who believed tomatoes were inedible, so he grew them as ornamentals. We prove him wrong at every opportunity.

Every day the gardens yield buckets of summer produce: Czech Black peppers, La Ratte potatoes, Cinnamon basil, and perfectly ripe Chateau Rose tomatoes, sweeter in the greenhouse heat than any I've ever grown. I harvest hardneck garlic and hang it to cure beneath the rafters of the barn. Karla helps put up foods for storage as fast as we can, blanching and freezing beans, canning sauces, making zucchini bread, freezing pesto into serving-sized blocks in ice cube trays.

We eat as many speckled Rattlesnake beans as possible, blanching and then freezing the surplus. The variety is large and meaty, incredibly flavorful, easy to prepare. We harvest wild arugula and Black Winter mustard from patches where they volunteered and reseeded themselves. These sprout wherever seedpods shattered in the fall, creating mats of tiny seedlings. You can almost taste them in the pungent aroma that fills the air when turning soil or inadvertently crushing them underfoot. Their rich flavors are in marked contrast with increasingly bland commercial varieties, which lose more of their appeal to me with each passing season.

It's amazing to see what an intensively managed garden can produce, even in such a challenging season. Staying ahead of fast-ripening fruits, vegetables, and seeds is a scramble. Despite losses to pests and diseases, in the end most of my plants survive to maturity and produce heavily. Diversification pays off. High yields for some vegetables offset losses elsewhere—one food thrives while another struggles. This is also where good seed saving practices come in, the selection of plants for a wide range of traits to ensure balance in the garden from year to year. Plants that suffer in one year's cold and rain may be the best performers in the next summer's heat wave. Everything can change from one season to the next. Plants essentially encode memories in their seeds of experiences in the field, and the gardener's job is to preserve these memories.

One morning toward the end of August I grab my wheelbarrow and walk over to a large patch of cucumbers. From this vantage point in the garden I look down into a marshy area overgrown with shrubs like honeysuckle and rose, and across fields screened from neighboring homes by a wooded border. Despite its suburban location it feels very private, secluded, and rural. At one time a wealthy landowner on the adjacent property tried to buy this farm from its now elderly owner, concerned that it would be developed. The offer was refused, and it's ironic that in the end the opposite occurred. Heirs to the property next door subdivided it into small residential lots years ago, while the Cape Elizabeth Land Trust now holds full conservation easements on this land.

I start collecting cucumbers, pulling plants and dropping two fruits from each in a bucket for harvesting seed. The vines have nearly finished producing for the season and we've had more than enough to eat, so the rest go in the wheelbarrow and over to the compost pile. The variety, Early Russian, has been something of a disappointment. On the whole its fruits have been thick-skinned and largely flavorless. Unfortunately they're the only cucumbers in the garden this year, because otherwise they would cross with other types like Boothby's Blonde. Bagging flowers and pollinating by hand can keep the lines true when growing multiple varieties, but it's difficult to coordinate when living off-site. Keeping varieties isolated in space or time is a much easier option.

Early Russian's shortcomings may be due in part to the difficult season, or it could explain why the variety is favored for pickling. On the other hand, though, I might have picked up some inferior seeds. My sense is the variety may vary considerably in quality, reflecting a tangled history. It goes by many names—according to a University of North Carolina list, it's also called Borowskian, Early Russian Gherkin, Extra Early Russian, Improved Early Russian, Muromian, Muromian Gherkin, Russian, Russian Gherkin, Russian Shortish Green, Russian Early Pickling, and Small Early Russian. It's anyone's guess exactly what this strain growing in my fields might be.

To save cucumber seeds I choose the largest and best-looking fruits from each vine, letting them go a little past the fresh eating stage until they're starting to soften. Back at our house I slice them and squeeze the seeds and pulp into a jar. Much like tomatoes, ripe cucumbers contain mature seeds, so harvesting isn't difficult. The main challenge is to remove the gelatinous case around each seed so they won't stick together when dry. This is easily accomplished with a brief fermentation, leaving seeds and pulp to sit in a warm place for two to three days. As Suzanne Ashworth writes in her excellent guide *Seed to Seed*, "During this period, the aromas from the bowl will be less than pleasing." Once mold forms on the surface, running the seeds under tap water rinses away hollow seeds and debris. Dump them out to dry in a paper coffee filter, store them in a cool, dry place, and they'll remain viable for up to ten years (each kind of vegetable seed has different longevity).

Maintaining vegetables through their full life cycles, from planting to seed harvest, is a bit like solving an elaborate puzzle. Every kind of vegetable has different requirements to stay true to type and ensure good germination. Collecting tomatoes, for example, is relatively easy—cross-pollination is minimal, and the seeds keep for years. Biennials like parsnips, on the other hand, demand constant attention to stay viable and true. They produce seed in their second year that survives little more than a season, and they cross in the wind. To keep track of all this I keep careful records of my plantings and seed saving on the computer, and take notes in the field on printouts stored in the car during the season.

It isn't hard to collect cucumber and tomato seeds, but other plants have tight harvest windows. Leave dried seedpods on the Waldoboro Greenneck rutabagas a day too long, for example, and they'll shatter to the ground. Thousands of little rutabagas will germinate at that spot the next year, transforming themselves into weeds of a sort. This is one reason few farmers and gardeners save their own seeds. Here are a few others: Harvesting seeds demands attention during a busy time and reduces marketable yields, as the finest specimens are left to reproduce; cleaning takes care and can be tedious; preventing crossing and managing disease requires knowledge and planning; and essential skills have been forgotten. Perhaps the most important, and logical, is that it's relatively inexpensive and effective to purchase clean seed each year instead.

Our growing season in southern Maine begins to wind down a little in September. By the middle of the month there's a chill in the air that sends me digging through piles of tarps and raincoats to find a sweater in the backseat of my Subaru. Every day begins with a sweep through the gardens to note ripening seeds and plants, check for disease, and remove the odd weed from cover-cropped beds of clover or rye. Despite the onset of fall weather and cooler temperatures, my gardens continue to thrive and produce heavily. Gradually summer produce like tomatoes slows down, but vivid orange Habanero peppers, early-ripening Canada Crookneck winter squash, and root vegetables like carrots, onions, and beets come on in their place.

A few of the maples start to turn and I stop to look around at the fields, so beautiful in the clear fall light. A quick pass with a wheel hoe and rake prepares garden beds for cover crops after vegetables stop producing. Seeding out mats of sweet white clover or winter rye helps protect the soil from erosion, and builds organic matter and fertility. Gradually the ratio of still-producing vegetable beds to cover crops begins to shift. By the end of September clover stands nearly a foot tall in rows that once held plants like garlic, harvested in early August. It's a pleasure to watch slower-growing purslane weeds disappear under waves of thriving clover, drowning in it. It seems almost too good to be true that sweet clover also introduces nitrogen to the soil for next year's strawberry planting.

This point in the season provides plenty of time to stop and reflect. Growing food by hand is a lot of work, of course, and I'm not advocating that everyone do it. Large farms gain from all kinds of efficiencies, from higher levels of mechanization to more organized labor. The relative advantages of home gardens and small farms can be harder to quantify: productive use of marginal land, ecological diversity, fresher and generally better-quality food, and often a relatively low input of chemicals and fossil fuels. That said, in my opinion the foods I choose to raise and my approach to growing isn't a form of nostalgia. This kind of small-scale organic gardening and farming reflects a particular worldview—that it's better over the long run to work with nature, find subtle ways to adapt to it, than force it to bend to our will.

So much of our contemporary agriculture depends on manipulation of conditions in the field: heavy irrigation, artificial fertilizers, soil fumigation, and pesticide use. Farmers control field conditions to grow plants within a narrow genetic range. If lettuces in the produce section typically look and taste the same, they may in fact be nearly genetically identical. In some cases a modern lettuce strain can descend from just one plant—an unblemished, long-storing field specimen reproduced on an industrial scale. Growing these foods works in part because they're entirely predictable: consistent in their horticultural requirements, harvest times, storage, taste, and appearance. It also works because we don't typically grow them commercially in challenging places like New England. We count instead on long-distance shipping and favorable conditions elsewhere.

In contrast, most of the foods growing in my fields vary a little, even among plants of the same variety. They show slightly different colors and textures, sizes, tastes, and, most critically, adaptation to imperfect growing conditions. The ideal I'm striving for is a regionalized, ecological agriculture that builds soil and fertility through plant growth, and matches the right plants to the right place. From the conventional grower's point of view this lack of uniformity is a weakness, because it doesn't maximize production under any one given set of conditions. Seen from a more ecological perspective, however, it means the garden continues to evolve, to change with the seasons and shifting weather patterns. The world isn't static, and neither should be our approach to producing food. Growing these plants and saving seeds is like participating in a breeding project that never ends, that evolves with each passing season into something new.

Six

BREEDING IN THE FARMER SPIRIT:
THE NEXT "HEIRLOOMS"

The Snyder blackberry, the possible match to Sonja Johanson's Bethel, Maine, variety, is first on a list of over 350 rare, place-based New England foods compiled by a working group called RAFT, short for Renewing America's Food Traditions. Like Sonja, I often consult RAFT publications to learn about regional New England foods. Every year my search for new flavors and plants that thrive in this relatively cool, wet climate sends me on a treasure hunt, and RAFT's listings of rare and endangered varieties help guide me. Nevertheless, identifying and tracking down these foods is a tremendous challenge. Web searches turn up little. Instant gratification this is not. Many of the listed RAFT foods aren't available commercially, and like the Blake apple some may have disappeared from cultivation. Where would one locate a "functionally extinct" Souhegan raspberry? How about highly obscure Evelyn persimmons or Slaybaugh Special peaches? It's hard to know even where to begin.

The now defunct RAFT alliance was a collaborative effort of several like-minded organizations, including, among others, the Seed Savers Exchange, Slow Food, and the American Livestock Breeds

Conservancy. Conservation biologist Gary Nabhan, the author of more than twenty books on ethnobotany, seed saving, and local foods, and the recipient of a MacArthur "Genius" award, led the way. He developed the alliance, arranged funding, organized research groups around the country, and published the results. I was fortunate to participate in one of his workshops in Vermont in the summer of 2007. For several hours we met with roughly twenty farmers, fishermen, foragers, conservationists, historians, and chefs to share knowledge about regional foodways. It was a little like Ben Watson's Ark of Taste meeting, minus the hands-on eating and drinking.

One food that came up during this Vermont meeting particularly intrigued me, and would come to have an indirect but profound effect on the way I view biodiversity. This was George IV, a peach that traces its history back to 1821 in New York City, and that is widely considered to be one of the oldest named peach varieties in the country. Despite its rich pedigree, however, George IV is now largely forgotten. The variety is slightly less obscure than many foods on the RAFT lists—a couple of nurseries even carry it commercially—but nevertheless it's rarely grown. After the meeting I remember wondering what happened to it, why a peach beloved by many would fall out of favor and disappear. Some of the answers I've found have helped change my thinking about heritage foods of all kinds, as well as contemporary plant breeding.

When I started growing food twenty years ago, reading about gardening gave me the impression that on one side lay heritage varieties, a collection of names from the past, and on the other were their modern counterparts. Heritage foods were essentially unchanging and fixed, the product of forgotten eras, while plant breeding had broken from the past. As I've learned more about old plant varieties and modern breeding, however, many of these assumptions have been turned on their heads. A closer look has opened the door to a freer, more dynamic and flexible way of seeing plants and agriculture.

A year and a half after our Vermont RAFT meeting, in the winter of 2009, I sit down at my computer to research fruit trees and come across an online description of the George IV peach. "Melting, juicy, aromatic, richly flavored flesh. One of the three best white-fleshed peaches of all time," reads the website of a small, independent mail-order nursery. It quotes Andrew Jackson Downing, celebrated landscape designer and nineteenth-century horticultural authority. "Remarkable rich luscious flavor," he wrote, "no garden should be without it." Downing knew his fruit trees, and as far as I know had no commercial stake in the sale of this variety. I'm reminded at once of the RAFT meeting, and decide it's time to order a tree. Who could resist such a peach?

A few months later, however, I stumble across a piece of directly contradictory information. In 1917 the New York Agricultural Experiment Station, located on the grounds of today's Cornell and USDA's facilities in Geneva, New York, published a large-format, illustrated guide called *The Peaches of New York*. The book's frontispiece includes a full-page portrait of Andrew Jackson Downing, and it cites him frequently throughout. But flip to the George IV description on page 218, and you'll find this: "Once one of the mainstays of American peach growing, George IV is now of but historical interest. [This peach] is not worth planting now and is illustrated and described in *The Peaches of New York* only that fruit growers may note progress in the development of peaches . . . We doubt if it now deserves to be recommended on any list of fruits."

Why? Because the New York Experiment Station researchers disliked peaches that dripped aromatic juice down their chins? Did Victorian writing about luscious fruit flesh embarrass them? Maybe 1917 marked a high point of American fruit growing, a plateau from which they could look down and sneer at the best of an earlier generation? I find this puzzling, a mystery, and set out to learn more.

The history of George IV is better documented than most fruits, but still elusive. *The Peaches of New York* acknowledges that it's been confused with many others over the years, most often another type called Morris Red. According to the text, however, "the variety rapidly grew in favor and within a few years was everywhere grown in eastern America." So George IV was widely recognized and commonly available, known to a broad public. Commercial plantings remained in Europe as late as 1917, where it continued to be popular. Apparently Europeans wouldn't have known good peaches if they'd hit them on the head.

George IV originated from a chance seedling in the backyard of a man named Gill on Broad Street in New York City in 1821. I assume trees bearing the name would have been bud-grafted from that point forward, as most peaches are today. Bud-grafting involves inserting a newly formed bud, taken from a desirable variety, into the bark of a young seedling, creating a tree with fruit identical to its bud-donor parent. It seems to me that, unlike vegetables, which can change over time depending on their handling, Downing's George IV peaches would have been genetically identical to those grown at the Geneva Experiment Station. It shouldn't matter that Downing died in the explosion of a steamer sixty-five years before the publication of *The Peaches of New York*. He lived in Newburgh, New York, where he would have had many opportunities to taste and know this fruit. Since his home was less than three hundred miles from the experiment station in Geneva, variations in climate probably wouldn't account for such widely differing opinions. So, are my assumptions correct?

A little more research turns up other marginally relevant but entertaining information. King George IV was known as a glutton and a hedonist. He was soft and round, extravagant, lazy, but bright and devoted to the arts. Is that why Gill commemorated his 1821 coronation by naming a peach after him? *The Times* of London wrote after King George's death that "there never was an individual less regretted by his fellow-creatures than this deceased king. What eye has wept for him? What heart has heaved one throb of unmercenary sorrow?" It also wrote he'd always prefer "a girl and a bottle to politics and a sermon." Exactly the sort of pleasure you'd want from a good peach.

In early June 2009 I take time to look over my own trees. It's hard to admit with the promise of the season ahead of me, but no one really lusts after a Maine peach. As Maine's Fedco Trees nursery catalog gamely writes about Reliance, generally considered one of the hardiest northern varieties, "Flavor usually considered fair, but those who grow it in Maine love it." Even when trees survive winter ice and cold, and blossoms escape spring frosts to form new fruit, cold summers can hold back its sweetness. I'm managing several peach trees, ranging in age from three to about ten years. They're mostly Madisons and Red Havens, only one Reliance, and they taste pretty good. But love? Maybe our relationship will deepen over time.

It's a bright, sunny day, a break from this year's heavy rain, and the air is crisp and refreshing. I've come to the garden to thin fruit and avoid repeating last season's excess production. Last year a surplus of young peaches on my trees forced me to prop branches with spare strapping lumber. They couldn't hold themselves up under the weight of so much fruit, and without support the branches slowly sagged and broke to the ground. It was disturbing to watch the trees deconstruct themselves, like chickens that can't stand because of overbreeding or racehorses performing at the limit of their long, delicate legs.

This year I remove most of the newly formed peaches on the youngest trees, and nearly half those on the older trees, and try to look on the bright side. Overproduction not only damages trees, it leads to smaller and less flavorful fruit. Removing excess peaches allows the tree to put more energy into those that remain. Nevertheless, every dropped peach feels like a lost opportunity, and I watch them fall wistfully. What's the point of all this fruitfulness and fertility if you have to pick it off and throw it on the ground? Reluctantly I sacrifice the little ones so the rest will grow large and sweet.

Later in the morning I return to the computer to discover a strange coincidence—an offhand reference to George IV. The note is a request from Jenny Trotter at the Slow Food office to Ark of Taste committee chair Ben Watson in New Hampshire, asking him to "tell the George IV peach story" during a panel we'll share at the New York Botanical Garden in August. What story? Already there are such sharply differing opinions; will Ben shine new light on this mystery?

It turns out Ben plans to nominate George IV to the Ark of Taste in the fall. He's eaten it, and in his opinion objections in *The Peaches of New York* have nothing to do with quality. He tells us the flavor is very good. The fruit is a little on the small size—that could be part of the problem—and by 1917 there'd been plenty of advances that improved rival peach lines. Politics may have played a role, too: Did some experiment station plant breeder have it in for this old-time peach?

The Peaches of New York generally seems evenhanded and fair, though. Its editors point out the good and bad even with varieties they condemn, like the Heath Cling. In the case of that old variety, although "antiquity constitutes about its only claim to recognition" (it was "unquestionably the oldest named American Peach now under cultivation"), nevertheless they considered it "the best of all peaches to preserve or pickle whole." Pickled peaches! Sounds like a good use for Maine fruit. The book describes another variety, Gold Drop, as "doubtfully worth planting in New York as a peach of commerce," due its small size, "but should find a place in every home orchard" for its appearance and distinctive flavor. Doesn't George IV deserve as much?

Ben brings nurseryman and historian Tom Burford into the conversation, and at first his response to my questions bewilders me. He'd always assumed that flavor variability for many old peaches is explained not by soil or climate, but because of "the brutal fact" that they were often propagated from seeds rather than grafted. Tom's grandfather grew varieties like Oldmixon Cling from seed. He writes that in the nineteenth and early twentieth centuries, in addition to grafting, "there were millions upon millions of pits planted" for direct propagation of peaches.

How can this be? Tom's comments throw all my assumptions about named varieties out the window. If the fruit isn't grafted, how can there be a true line? Apples grown from seeds, for example, show all kinds of traits distinct from their parents. I respond to Ben, saying this is an entirely different way of thinking about plant selection and breeding from my own—much more malleable—and it's hard then to understand what defines a named peach. Trees we know as George IV have the genes of Gill's original seedling, but might also have any number of other variations, depending on cross-pollination?

And then it hits me. As Ben and Tom know, peaches don't require a second variety for pollination; they're largely self-fertile. Unlike most apples, which need another variety to set fruit and therefore create a hybrid every time a flower is pollinated, peaches are unlikely to cross. A chance seedling like the one Gill found in 1821 would generally come true to type from seed. The line would largely stabilize, but variations would emerge over time through occasional crossing with other varieties. Like a hall of mirrors it would be impossible to track these changes without genetic testing. Growing conditions and climate could amplify even minor differences—when spring frosts damage early-blooming trees, for example—providing a reasonable explanation for the variety of opinion.

I've since learned that even grafted fruit may change over time, because chance mutations within trees can alter their genetics. What we know as a McIntosh apple, for example, may differ some-what from older plantings, or those descended from another tree the next town over. When breeders release new fruit today, some-times they go to great lengths to control propagation and preserve desired traits, licensing only approved nurseries to sell patented fruit. Whether Downing's peaches were grafted or pit-propagated, therefore, we can't know how closely they matched those at the experiment station, or how either would compare with the George IV peach that I've ordered this season for my own garden (which will need three or four years to begin bearing fruit).

Still, this changes everything. It's a vision into a world much less fussy and defined than our own, where plants were propagated, named, and exchanged freely, and allowed to cross, evolve, and adapt to local conditions. It's a far cry from contemporary fields filled with hybridized, patented varieties, or large-scale seed monocultures tested for consistency and trueness to type. Over the past couple of seasons I've been learning this same lesson by work-ing with vegetables like Tall Telephone peas, but sorting through contradictions behind George IV takes everything a step farther. Even grafted fruit isn't necessarily consistent from tree to tree. So what do any of the names on the RAFT list really mean?

As a collector of heritage foods I've often felt torn between maintaining lines as close to their present form as possible, and engaging creatively with them. What happens by accident is one thing, but few growers deliberately take the latter approach, jug-gling selection for new traits with genetic preservation. And yet this is exactly how these plants were grown historically. Actively pursuing novelty and breeding new lines is very much within the traditional spirit of these foods. In other words, as much as we need to conserve a wide range of genetic traits to maintain a healthy, stable agricultural system, if we don't equally embrace heritage foods as raw materials to develop, then we lose touch with something vital. How can I discover the right balance between preserving the past and looking ahead to the future?

Soon after my conversations with Jenny Trotter and Ben Watson, Slow Food asks me to join their Ark of Taste committee, and requests a food nomination for its annual meeting at the Black Trumpet Bistro in Portsmouth, New Hampshire, in September. They suggest Maine's Boothby's Blonde cucumber, so I start researching its history. By late summer a few phone calls lead to a retired agronomist living in Bangor, Maine, who certifies organic farms for MOFGA. His name is Charles Boothby, and he's directly descended from the Maine family that gave this yellow cucumber its name. "I never saw a green cucumber until I left home as an adult," his sister, Willie Irish, told me when I reached her a few days before. Imagine knowing cucumbers only through the family garden! What a contrast with the schoolkids who visit farm fields around Portland, many of whom wouldn't recognize a cucumber of any color growing on the vine.

Cucumbers have never been especially interesting to me—at best they're a vehicle for salt and vinegar, or something to add crunch to a sandwich—but Boothby's Blonde is something of an exception. Its pleasing greenish flesh doesn't turn bitter as the fruits mature, and its pale skin deepens over time to an attractive shade of lemon yellow. Although it has a few disease problems, it yields well and the fruits are a good, consistent midrange size. Thanks to its pleasant, mild flavor and interesting regional history, Boothby's Blonde has become increasingly available at Maine farmers' markets.

The nomination form for the Ark of Taste requires background notes, so Charles Boothby provides additional historical information. Seed catalogs typically write that this cucumber originated in Livermore, a town in south-central rural Maine half an hour north of the city of Lewiston, where it was grown for generations in his family. Stories like these become established fact through repetition. One source copies another, until it becomes difficult if not impossible to sort truth from fiction. Charles largely confirms Boothby's Blonde's lineage, but tells me his aunt and grandmother brought the cucumber with them from the nearby town of Wayne, where it was commonly grown.

His uncle Leslie turned it over to a breeder. How long ago? "Twenty, thirty years, at least," he tells me. Nevertheless their cucumber didn't make it into commercial seed catalogs until 1994, and during our tour of the Scatterseed Project in July, Will Bonsall tells me it was he who introduced Boothby's to the trade, through Fedco Seeds. Since these modest beginnings in the mid-1990s, every year more seed companies have picked it up, and Slow Food has been working with farmers and chefs to promote it with taste events around New England.

Cucumbers are ancient vegetables that date back thousands of years in North Africa, India, and Asia. A variety unique to Maine might seem a little incongruous for a food enjoyed by Egyptian pharaohs, but this vegetable was widely distributed historically around the world. The English grew cucumbers in the Middle Ages, and by 1494 Columbus had introduced cucumbers to the island of Hispaniola (occupied by present-day Haiti and the Dominican Republic). American colonists grew them in their gardens, even on Maine's frontier, and shared seeds with native peoples like the Mandan and Abenaki. A rich history, to be sure, but there's no easy way to trace the stories of foods so freely traded—our knowledge of varieties growing in isolated places like Wayne and Livermore is extremely limited, their origins quickly fading into obscurity.

If the history of these plants is murky, so, too, is our understanding of how they were grown and what constitutes a named line. An open-pollinated cucumber (a category that includes all heirloom and some modern varieties, as opposed to hybrids) is inherently somewhat unstable in terms of its genetics. We might look back and imagine a named variety like Boothby's had the same kind of defined character as a hybrid, and find instead that, despite its long history in this region, it remains something of a work in progress. Saved over many generations, Boothby's Blonde has gradually adapted to this place while maintaining some frustrating limitations and inconsistencies. The variety is susceptible to powdery mildew, for example, a disease common in Maine. In this genetic variability, however, also lies its promise.

Researching Boothby's background brings me full-circle to some of the same questions raised by the George IV peach. If our goal is to preserve the past, how do we deal with unstable lines and natural variation? When planting trees or saving vegetable seeds, to what extent should we acknowledge and accept change, even work with it? It seems safe to say that the first rule of garden biodiversity is to avoid throwing out the old, the tried-and-true, but it's equally important to continue to evolve and explore, to embrace natural changes in the plants we choose to grow.

Old standbys like Boothby's Blonde have evolved through selection, chance pollination, and experimentation. Every seed saver makes fundamental decisions that determine the future of the line, like whether to discard mutations or preserve new traits that appear in the field. Should one save seeds from that cucumber with the lighter color, or throw away the fruits? What to keep, and what to abandon? Select too few plants and cucumbers will "run down" and become inbred, but keep too many with divergent traits and the population can become large and unrecognizable as a single variety after a few generations.

When we look at plants this way, quickly a few artificial distinctions begin to blur. The old isn't better simply because it's stood the test of time, and the new isn't necessarily different in kind or quality simply because it came from a modern breeding program. The closer you look, the more the boundaries between old and new can become murky and indistinct. Everything depends on the underlying philosophy and goals of the seed saver and the plant breeder. The story of Boothby's Blonde, past and present, is a textbook example.

At Cornell University breeders working to improve vegetable production for organic growers have increased resistance to powdery mildew in Boothby's Blonde. Should we call their intentional crosses "new" cucumbers, or revised takes on old favorites? If by accident a patch of Boothby's in a grower's field were to pick up stray pollen from another variety with better disease resistance, they might continue to list it as the same variety. But if breeders were to perform the identical cross, the result would be a new line. What's the difference?

Some of Cornell's breeding work is connected to a project called the Organic Seed Partnership, a network of universities, nonprofits, government agencies, growers, and seed companies that was launched in 2005. The OSP's purpose is to "create a robust national network of organic vegetable breeders working with each other and regional growers to benefit the organic community." It does this with "improved vegetable varieties that are adapted to organic systems combined with disease resistance, nutritional and flavor quality, and contemporary productivity traits crucial to modern markets." That about says it all.

Plant breeder Michael Glos, the contact person for farmers participating in the OSP effort, is coincidentally one of the two Cornell researchers working on improvements to the Boothby's Blonde cucumber. His multiyear project to breed disease resistance into Boothby's has included collaboration with more than a dozen conventional and organic farmers, as well as other Cornell researchers and breeders working under program director Dr. Molly Jahn. From this collaboration has come several promising new cucumber varieties. Some closely resemble the original, while others show entirely new traits and tastes. In my opinion, Cornell's work with the OSP falls squarely within the spirit of traditional plant breeding, embracing the best of the past while looking ahead to the future.

Plant breeding conducted by researchers like Michael Glos takes seed saving in gardens like mine to its next logical step. He and others at Cornell are developing what my friend Jim Gerritsen—Maine potato farmer, seedsman, and activist—calls "heirlooms of the future." Jim participates in Organic Seed Partnership breeding projects and leads a related project called the Organic Seed Alliance. He knows everyone in the field, so one day in the early fall of 2009 I call him for a reference. He puts me in touch with the Cornell office. "Sure, I'd be happy to show you around," Michael Glos tells me over the phone a few days later. He's willing to talk about his organic breeding work, the Organic Seed Partnership, and Boothby's Blonde cucumbers. We set a time to meet two days after my tour of the USDA collections in Geneva, New York.

A couple of weeks later, in October, I leave Karla to her thesis work in Syracuse and drive south through low hills and open fields along Highway 81 toward Ithaca and Cornell. The highway follows dead-flat farmland between narrow ridgelines that run on a roughly north–south axis, the product of glacial retreat eleven thousand years ago. Amid spells of heavy rain, I drive slowly through the fog and mist that have settled deep into the valleys. Sovereignty and independence are on my mind as I pass the Onondaga Nation a few miles from downtown Syracuse. The Onondagas are one of the five tribes of the Haudenosaunee, or Iroquois Confederacy. They trace their land jurisdiction to a 1794 treaty with the US government that acknowledged their right to an independent homeland. Nothing more than a highway sign distinguishes their territory from any other rural highway exit, but their continued (and determined) existence as an independent nation has resonance for me.

That's in part because the Onondaga helped formulate one of the guiding principles of the modern environmental movement. The Great Law of the Haudenosaunee taught land stewardship and governance with an eye to future generations and long-term stability. "In every deliberation," the law states, "we must consider the impact on the seventh generation . . . even if it requires having skin as thick as the bark of a pine." What a wonderful qualification—doesn't it belong on the label of Seventh Generation brand paper towels?

Who speaks for this kind of long-term public welfare in food and agriculture these days? Along with a nationwide decline of public-spirited breeding programs like Cornell's, funding for agricultural research focusing on areas other than major production centers like California's Central Valley has become increasingly scarce. As farms become marginalized, technology and research dollars move elsewhere, adding to the pressure on independent regional producers. Relying too much on large commercial interests to determine breeding priorities leads to a vicious circle. The return on breeding a cucumber with resistance to powdery mildew, for example—a disease prevalent in New England fields—is negligible when most cucumbers are grown in places where the problem is relatively rare.

Driving near Syracuse by old barns, abandoned locks from the Erie Canal, and dilapidated Greek Revival farmhouses, I think of the invisible hand of Onondaga farming. Agriculture here dates back hundreds of years. Many of these fields once supported diverse native crops of corn, squash, and dry beans, the sophisticated polyculture known as the Three Sisters. Beans fix nitrogen in the soil to help meet fertility needs; broad-leaved squash suppresses weeds and retains soil moisture; and corn creates a natural trellis enabling beans to climb into the sunlight. Three Sisters plantings are a mutually beneficial, elegant cropping system. They're so well adapted to this land and climate that they can sustain soil fertility for decades without additional inputs (though eventually the Onondaga allowed tired land to revert to forest to restore its fertility). These plants also have the added benefit of nutritional balance for a complete diet.

Modern expanses of single-species plantings may appear equally robust, but will our farming approach withstand the test of time? In a *New York Times* article earlier this summer devoted to the ongoing late blight epidemic, chef and restaurant owner Dan Barber described the danger of "tight coupling" in agricultural uniformity. He explained the tendency of highly orchestrated systems to unravel with unnerving speed. Was he thinking of line cooks as he wrote this? Food industry consolidation allows failures in the system to multiply rapidly and spread widely. Examples of broad breakdowns include recent outbreaks of antibiotic-resistant strains of *E. coli* bacteria, as well as the spread of late blight from wholesale nurseries to farms throughout New England.

As much as uniformity creates vulnerability, Barber argues that the answer isn't only to be found in old varieties and a return to forgotten and neglected foods. He writes that it's time to resurrect regional plant breeding programs: "In our feverish pursuit of what's old, we can marginalize the development of what could be new." In his view the disappearance of breeding programs like Cornell's has two contributing factors: "a food movement wary of science" and "an industrial food chain that eschews differentiation in favor of uniformity."

Maybe the two are at heart inseparable: The public is mistrustful of scientific research that's excessively in the service of large-scale, highly specialized production. If that's the case, researchers at institutions like Cornell suggest a compromise and a way forward. Their focus on regional plant breeding, and especially on participatory programs that enlist farmers and seed companies to address the needs of alternative growers, has the potential to steer contemporary agriculture in new directions. I'm here to look for common ground.

My route into Cornell passes a bewildering array of greenhouses, poultry experiment stations, academic quads, playing fields, and concert halls. At the heart of the campus the road passes Weill Hall, architect Richard Meier's $162 million, 263,000-square-foot life sciences building, named for its principal donor, financier Sanford Weill. Dedicated last year, Weill Hall is described by the university as one of the most ambitious facilities projects in its history. Open floor plans encourage interdisciplinary collaboration; professors from the Institute for Cell and Molecular Biology mingle with grad students from the Department of Biomedical Engineering, and underground tunnels connect with the Biotechnology and Plant Sciences buildings. Designed as a model of environmental design, this new building earned a gold rating from the US Green Building's Council of Leadership in Energy and Environmental Design program (LEED).

A Cornell development website describes their new research facility's gestalt: "More than 15,000 gleaming white panels cover the outside, announcing confidence and purpose." Funding for the structure is only a small component of a larger goal, a $650 million investment in biological sciences, described as "the biggest academic initiative in Cornell's history. At stake are insights into the basic functions of life, as well as breakthroughs for human and animal health, the world's food supply, the environment, and the ethical and social aspects of science." Weill Hall is a sort of latter-day cathedral of scientific ambition, a place gunning for the big ideas.

I pass through this part of campus and a few blocks away pull up behind a plant breeding lab. The research facility where Michael Glos works is a world apart. There's no underground tunnel connecting to nearby bioengineering and genetics departments, or to Weill Hall. This lab is housed in a modest concrete-block building, constructed in the 1960s and originally intended as a temporary structure. Lavish budgets for cutting-edge facilities haven't reached this part of Cornell, or this discipline. Michael Glos divides his time between plant breeding and running a small, diversified organic farm with his wife, Karma.

Michael and I meet in the parking lot and stop to talk with a field worker cleaning an old combine harvester beside a steel-sided utility barn. The technician is perched on the engine block, using his fingers to remove bits of cornhusk stuck in the housing. The cold summer delayed their harvest, and field corn hasn't dried down enough to process well. Plants with too much moisture jam in the machine, he tells us. Wooden harvest bins filled with squash line the edge of a nearby lab building. Michael gives me a couple and I slip them in my pocket. They're like "personal-sized" servings for a new generation, perfect for the microwave. Farm fields, greenhouses, and experimental orchards surround us. This is where science meets the gritty reality of the barnyard.

Cornell publishes an online newsletter called *Plant Breeding News,* sponsored by the UN's Food and Agriculture Organization. In an article published six years ago titled "The Future of Plant Breeding," contributor Jonathan Knight wrote, "All over the world, conventional plant breeding has fallen on hard times, and is seen as the unfashionable older cousin of genetic engineering." He went on to say that plant breeders are retiring, and are being replaced with molecular geneticists. Government funding for traditional research has "all but dried up" in the United States and Europe, even for conventional breeding programs like the nonprofit International Maize and Wheat Improvement Center, where Norman Borlaug launched the Green Revolution in the 1940s and '50s. For the first time since its founding in 1943 the center has been forced to cut back on breeding trials due to lack of funding. This is surprising to me, particularly because Nobel Prize winner Borlaug was named *Time* magazine's "Person of the Year" on his death last month at the age of ninety-five, with a tribute by Bill Gates.

Michael and I head into the plant breeding building and stop by a small, windowless storage room on the way to his office. It looks like the back room of a retail warehouse, filled with shelving and boxes. Several assistants are cleaning and evaluating squashes, collecting seeds, and recording results. Each squash on the table is similar to the two in my pocket, but with slight variations in size, color, and shape. They look like half-sized butternuts with mottled splashes of green over a dull orange base. Posters on the walls outside advertise recent breeding successes, varieties from Cornell that have entered the seed trade and reached our tables: Harlequin squash, Marketmore cucumbers, Hannah's Choice melons.

Michael is one of a handful of breeders in this country who focus on organic production. He looks every bit the part of the organic farmer: dressed for field work, suntanned, kept trim by years of hoeing, his long hair tied back in a ponytail. Karla and I bought chorizo sausage from his friendly wife, Karma, at the Ithaca farmers' market a couple of days ago. Although she generally handles the sales end of the business, the farmers' market community seems as much Michael's element as hers. Located in an open pavilion at a former steamboat landing in a park at the tip of Cayuga Lake, it's filled with products ranging from sweet apple wines to Khmer Angkor Cambodian spicy chicken. The market pavilion is styled after a thirteenth-century European cathedral, arguably the organic farming community's answer to Cornell's Weill Hall up the hill.

Michael describes his surprise visiting organic farms ten years ago and seeing some of the plants growers were raising. He often found disease-susceptible varieties that produced poorly and failed to live up to their potential. A squash or cucumber that succumbs early to disease won't develop full flavor and nutrient content (could this be part of the reason Boothby's Blonde cucumbers failed to board the Ark of Taste last month?). Growers were forced to choose between conventional varieties bred for the mass market and heirlooms that were all too often run down by years of poor selection and neglect. And yet Cornell had on its shelves improved varieties that weren't of interest to large growers for minor reasons, like squashes that didn't develop full color until they were ready to eat. Marketers typically want vegetables that look ripe even when they're immature in order to boost sales and extend shelf life. Clearly this isn't in the best interest of the consumer. Here was an opportunity for small-scale, direct-marketing organic producers to leap ahead, by focusing on flavor and high quality.

Michael's work is classic plant breeding, not far removed from the farm-based breeding that brought us most of the foods we know today. He describes some of his projects as relatively straight-forward cross-pollination and selection, such as the development of powdery mildew resistance in Boothby's Blonde. He crossed Boothby's with Marketmore, one of Cornell's resistant varieties, and after several years selected two of the most promising lines for commercial release. He tells me he can't disclose the names yet, but then quietly lets me in on the secret.

Why has this sort of practical, relatively affordable research become so uncommon? Maybe plant breeders would become fashionable again if Richard Meier designed them a new lab, or Sanford Weill threw some money at organic agriculture? There's no inherent reason we can't apply technology to improve regional production, and breed better pest- and disease-resistant crops for the marketplace. Yet most agricultural research goes in other directions, toward products like herbicide-resistant corn and so-called Terminator seeds that can't reproduce themselves when saved and replanted the following year. Politics and the economics of seed sales rather than ecology and good farming drive too many of these decisions. It's ironic that as local, organic agriculture enjoys increasing public support, the vast majority of research dollars go elsewhere.

Some technologies can be particularly useful for organic production. A breeding method called marker-assisted selection, for example, can help researchers identify traits genetically and track desirable lines in the field. This may sound like genetic engineering, frightening a public wary of science, but MAS is simply a form of mapping that offers better management of traditional breeding approaches. It's especially useful when dealing with invisible characteristics like drought tolerance, or looking for multiple traits like disease resistance in fruit of a certain size and color. Lab tests can stand in for laborious and time-consuming trials as breeders assess which crosses are worth saving.

Organic and other "low-external-input" approaches that focus on traits like natural disease resistance often yield as well as or better than conventional farming, but they're up against a larger reality. Take plant breeding out of the public realm, turn it into a business, and it has to answer to powerful economic interests. The result may or may not also prioritize the needs of farmers and consumers. Cornell's squashes didn't fail to enter the seed trade in the 1990s because they yielded poorly or fell short agriculturally, for example, but because they didn't meet the marketing requirements of seed companies, commercial wholesalers, or supermarkets.

By bringing plant breeders and local growers together, in a sense the Organic Seed Partnership is trying to return to something that's been nearly forgotten. Historically legions of farmers in this country essentially conducted democratic experiments for free by scattering seedling fruit trees in tiny orchards throughout the countryside, or adapting vegetables like Boothby's Blonde to pest and diseases pressures. Trial-and-error plant breeding and seed saving, the hallmarks of subsistence growers the world over, have fallen by the wayside in our farm system. The OSP is working to bring that spirit back.

Every year the OSP puts out a call to farmers asking them to share the labor and benefits of plant trials. Growers step forward because the extra work of evaluating new strains can repay their efforts in the future, with access to improved plants. Breeders participate because including farmers and seed companies helps field-test new crosses, and reduces costs for expensive trials. Small seed companies benefit with access to raw material, trained expertise, and crop evaluation data. It's a win–win all around. This is the message of the Organic Seed Partnership: that in the absence of adequate funding, the burden of selection for plant diversity and regional adaptation depends on broad participation.

History has pushed us in the other direction, however. The trend toward uniformity has been a long time in the making, concentrating innovation into ever fewer and more specialized hands. As John Bunker noted in his book *Not Far from the Tree,* for example, back in the 1920s extension agents in the Northeast discouraged planting of all but seven of the most commercially acceptable apples. Their goal was to reduce orchard diversity and standardize fruit quality, production, and marketing. For this they chose a few very old apples like Rhode Island Greening and Gravenstein, plus newer discoveries like Wealthy and Golden Delicious. Some were selected for production potential, others for eating quality, but each offered yield and market appeal designed to guarantee consistent profits. A handful of winners would replace the hundreds of varieties then in common use.

What's wrong with this approach? Within a few years the first signs of trouble appeared. One of their selections, Baldwin, would prove disastrous for growers. Baldwin is good for fresh eating, stores well, cooks into excellent sauce, and makes a fine single-variety hard cider. It was a favorite dating back to 1740 in Massachusetts. Despite many good attributes, however, it has a crippling weakness. It isn't particularly cold-hardy, especially when the trees are stressed by pushing them to produce heavy yields. Several years after farmers began turning land over to the "New England Seven," one of the hardest winters on record struck. The deep freeze that settled over orchards in 1934 killed roughly two-thirds of all apple trees in Maine, and destroyed most of the Baldwins in New England. This marked the end of regional commercial production for the variety, and dealt a substantial blow to the northern apple industry right in the middle of the Great Depression.

You could argue that Baldwin was simply the wrong selection. That's true, but part of the beauty of old plantings was the recognition that no single fruit can meet every need, and that every fruit has its strengths and weaknesses. Cold-hardy apples like Duchess of Oldenburg thrive in northern Maine, in places where most varieties can't survive or produce. Astringent (bittersweet or bittersharp) apples that blend into the best hard ciders aren't good for fresh eating. Sweet summer apples without acidity taste strange to modern palates, but make excellent sauce and pies. Apples serve many purposes beyond fresh eating. They can be boiled to make sauce, fruit butter, and a molasses-like sweetener; pressed for juice, hard cider, and vinegar; distilled into brandy; dried for long-term storage; baked into pies. Relying on a handful of standardized varieties to deal with every culinary purpose, and to meet endless subtle variations in climate and growing conditions, is a diminished and precarious way to raise food.

After visiting Michael Glos at Cornell, I'm curious to learn whether other public breeding projects use different models, and what the comparative benefits and drawbacks of participatory breeding might be. Take apples, for example. Can we really expect farmers to share the labor and capital-intensive costs of breeding fruit? Investments in manpower and technology pay out over a very long time frame for fruit trees, with no guarantee of success. For every new release, hundreds of thousands of hand-pollinated apple seeds will be germinated, grafted, grown to fruiting size, tested for flavor and productivity, and ultimately discarded.

At the end of my conversation with Charles Boothby, he changed the subject from cucumbers to fruit trees and told me, "I'd trade every old apple variety for Honeycrisp." As an agronomist he probably didn't mean this literally, but he's not alone in his high praise. In 2003 *The New York Times* called Honeycrisp one of the best eating apples available. Nearly twenty years after its release, the variety remains extremely popular, and for good reason. It's sweet and tangy, juicy, equally good for fresh eating or cooking. This is a great apple, a contemporary answer to the market's demand for all-purpose fruit. It's also highly profitable for growers, often returning twice the price per bushel of other standard varieties.

The University of Minnesota made the original cross that resulted in Honeycrisp in 1960, the year of John F. Kennedy's election. Thirty-one years and six presidents later, halfway through the term of George H. W. Bush in 1991, it released Honeycrisp to the trade. This puts a fruit breeder's career in perspective! Twenty-five to thirty years is a typical time span for the development of a new apple, and it hints at the tremendous amount of work involved. It also raises interesting questions about the respective roles of researchers and farmers. Could growers in a cooperative project have this kind of generations-long dedication, without any direct financial reward?

The Minnesota horticulture program that developed Honeycrisp shares common roots and many of the same goals as Cornell. Both trace back to the land grant colleges of the nineteenth century, established in part to teach practical agriculture to regional farmers. They retain a sense of mission to support agriculture in cold northern climates. It's no surprise that Cornell should pursue participatory farmer breeding, or that Minnesota would release high-quality fruit that prioritizes the needs of farmers and consumers. Minnesota is justifiably proud of its tradition of breeding apples. Many of its releases are among my favorites, like Haralson, Keepsake, Sweet Sixteen, and Chestnut Crab. No Red Delicious there.

And yet fundamental differences distinguish these two programs. To use an analogy from the computer world, if Cornell's work with Boothby's Blonde represents "open-source" breeding, Minnesota follows a more proprietary model. Due to the high cost of breeding fruit, maybe it's inevitable that the University of Minnesota would adopt patenting and licensing techniques more often associated with private agribusiness. During the twenty-year span of Honeycrisp's patent, from 1988 to 2008, any reproduction, sale, and use depended on approval from the university. Nurserymen couldn't reproduce trees without acquiring licenses, and growers couldn't plant them without paying a fee to the school.

In many cases plant patenting can have the effect of dampening research by restricting access to genetic material. In this case, however, it had several advantages:

- In the right hands, plant patenting can prevent, or at least delay, undesirable changes in the fruit, keeping a line from running down through lower-quality mutations.
- Commercial orchardists welcomed Honeycrisp patent protection because it ensured a high level of quality control, and consistency in the marketplace.
- Consumers knew exactly what they were getting when buying Honeycrisp.
- Patenting provided much-needed revenue for a program working in the public interest.

To date Minnesota's revenue has amounted to over $10 million, divided equally among the school, Honeycrisp's breeders, and a fund for ongoing projects. This influx of cash has been critical for sustaining the Minnesota horticulture program, particularly since budget shortfalls forced state funding cuts several years ago.

The need to recoup costs also explains some of the hyped-up marketing behind this apple. Trade organizations, websites, and a dedicated Wikipedia page heap lavish praise on Honeycrisp, and a 2006 vote of the Minnesota state legislature designated it their official state fruit (take that, Keepsake and Haralson!). Honeycrisp was "the best, most exciting apple we've ever introduced," according to Minnesota horticulture professor Jim Luby. "Explosively crisp!" writes their website. Even the name Honeycrisp has the ring of an advertising slogan to me, and it's easy to feel nostalgic for others that hold something back, particularly if they hint at a rich history: Rhode Island Greening, Northern Spy, Roxbury Russet, or even the humble Baldwin. Honeycrisp sounds like something you might order at the Dunkin' Donuts drive-thru, or the name of a breakfast cereal. Not quite worthy of a high-quality new fruit, but never mind . . .

Public-minded programs at Cornell and Minnesota need to find innovative ways to stay afloat in challenging financial times. As appealing as Cornell's open-source sharing may be, there are advantages as well in Minnesota's willingness to borrow strategies from the business world. And yet we need to guard against complacency. By creating commercial incentives to market new fruit aggressively, patenting can work against diversity and overshadow other deserving fruit. Is Honeycrisp really the perfect apple that can supplant all others? Older Minnesota releases like Sweet Sixteen are also outstanding, deserving a place at the table. Would Charles Boothby really trade every ancient Gravenstein and Ashmead's Kernel for this relatively new release?

The Baldwin's story should give us pause. Narrowing the range of fruits in the field has risks, today as much as in the past. According to an Integrated Pest Management bulletin sponsored by Cornell University, West Virginia University, the USDA, and the National Science Foundation, "Over the last decade, consumer and market demands have forced major changes in horticultural practices" for orchard fruits. When it comes to a highly contagious and damaging disease like fireblight, for example, these changes have "not only increased chances for infection but the level of damage/infection likely to occur." What are the implications for Honeycrisp?

Fireblight is a particular concern here in the Northeast. This is a bacterial infection that infects numerous plants, and it shares hosts ranging from raspberries to hawthorns to roses. Epidemics are hard to predict. When temperature and humidity conditions are right the disease can erupt with great speed, destroying blossoms, leaves, and branches. Although frequent antibiotic spraying offers preventive control for conventional growers, applications are expensive, and bacteria can evolve in turn. Planting resistant varieties and following good horticultural practices, like burning infected vegetation and diversifying plantings, is the best line of defense. High-density orchards planted on dwarf rootstocks, which are bred to bear fruit quickly, substantially increase the risk of fireblight, as does the planting of susceptible varieties. According to the report these include such popular cultivars as Gala, Fuji, Jonagold, and Braeburn. And Honeycrisp.

That roster sounds like my entire supermarket apple aisle, Red and Golden Delicious aside. Other reports are mixed on the subject of Honeycrisp's vulnerability, giving it ratings from good to mediocre. The University of Minnesota itself takes the middle ground, saying Honeycrisp's resistance to fireblight "depends on age, rootstock and disease pressure. Vigorous young trees on susceptible rootstock may show serious infection in severe fireblight years. Older trees under normal conditions show moderate to good resistance." So we only really need to worry about susceptibility during a disease outbreak. Hmmm.

It's the same old story. Planting too much of any one thing, whether in an organic vegetable field or apple orchard, brings greater vulnerability to pests and disease. When every apple is susceptible to a devastating disease like fireblight, the entire orchard puts itself at risk. Whatever our approach to breeding new plants, therefore, maintaining diversity counts. The time has passed for thinking any one variety can supplant all others. We need the old, the new, and the ever-changing to maintain a healthy agricultural system.

A few last notes about Honeycrisp raise some tantalizing questions about the distinction between modern varieties and heirlooms. As of this writing Honeycrisp.org, a promotional website sponsored by a group called All About Apples (whose goal is to serve as "the premier Internet site for the apple industry"), continues to describe Honeycrisp as a straightforward cross between two celebrated parents: Macoun and Honeygold. Sounds like traditional plant breeding at its best. Take two varieties with desirable traits, cross them, evaluate the results for several generations, and select a promising new strain. In essence this is exactly what farmers have always done when propagating fruit from seeds, only now the process is carefully managed and controlled in a research setting.

Except, as it turns out, that's not exactly true. A few years ago DNA tests at the University of Minnesota revealed that Honeycrisp's real parents are the 1978 release Keepsake and an as yet unidentified tree, probably an unnamed seedling from another experiment. Honeycrisp isn't related to either of its previously claimed parents (those listed on its patent application). In fact it's an accidental cross, an heir to the random farm breeding of millennia. Macoun and Honeygold are something more like the respectable middle-aged couple that adopts an abandoned child, and this Minnesota apple is more in the spirit of traditional breeding than anyone ever imagined.

There's a message in this for people like me, working outside academia. The odds of discovering the next George IV peach, Boothby's Blonde cucumber, or Honeycrisp apple are long, but you can't know the potential of a seed until you plant it and taste the results. Whether using high-tech screening like marker-assisted selection, selecting among thousands of crosses in a controlled setting, or growing by trial and error in the field, curiosity counts. A vibrant regional cuisine depends as much on broad participation, on openness to chance discoveries by professionals and enthusiastic amateurs alike, as it does on continued funding for university programs and enlightened breeding projects. If a cross as successful as Honeycrisp can occur by chance, then engagement and effort count.

Seven

SMALL FARMS
IN THE CITY, THE COUNTRY,
AND EVERYWHERE IN BETWEEN

"*D*idn't think you'd make it," my friend Jeremy Oldfield says as I come rushing through the New Haven, Connecticut, train station. He's standing near the platform with an overnight bag, scanning the crowd. "Already got our tickets, though," he tells me. We walk through the station to the nearest car and find seats a couple of minutes before the train pulls out. Still sweating and breathing hard after running half a mile in August heat from the nearest parking lot, I take a moment to decompress before settling in for the hour-and-a-half trip to New York's Penn Station.

Jeremy and his girlfriend, Emily, worked as apprentices two years ago in the summer of 2007 for Eliot Coleman (Maine vegetable farmer, organic agriculture guru, and author of *The New Organic Grower*). Now they live in Berkeley, California, where they've started a business designing and building residential vegetable gardens. He and Emily are back on the East Coast for a brief visit. She's looking into graduate work at Yale's School of Forestry, and he wants to catch up with friends. We're headed to New York to meet up with Cerise Mayo, a mutual friend I know through Slow Food. Cerise apprenticed at Coleman's Four Season Farm with Jeremy and Emily, then returned to Park Slope, Brooklyn, the following winter. There she's tending bees and working with a variety of food and agriculture groups. It's hard to imagine a better guide for the Brooklyn food scene than Cerise.

Many of Jeremy's peers live very different lives in New York. He's a recent graduate of elite Williams College in northwestern Massachusetts, and his girlfriend Emily went to Yale. Both grew up in cities and weren't raised to be farmers, not by a long shot. This is a lifestyle choice for them. Jeremy has the close-cropped beard and longish hair of a new farming generation, but he's too open and engaging, too California-friendly and warm, to fit in exactly with the hipster Brooklyn crowd. He favors Carhartt pants and T-shirts over skinny jeans and a fedora.

"Tell me about Chez Panisse," I ask him. Building gardens by day, he's been waiting tables at Alice Waters's famed Berkeley restaurant by night. "It's amazing," he says, to be in the center of such a vibrant food world. How did he wind up with a shift there? Isn't it all but impossible to get in the door? "Working with Eliot helped," he tells me. You couldn't ask for stronger farming credentials than Coleman's, and this matters at Chez Panisse, the restaurant that launched America's love affair with local food. It also doesn't hurt that Jeremy and Emily are a photogenic couple. I often stumble across shots of him in unexpected places, like gardening websites and the glossy pages of seed catalogs, digging carrots and demonstrating farming techniques.

As much as I'm anxious to see Cerise and visit with Jeremy, my primary reason for traveling to Brooklyn during the height of the growing season is to check out some pioneering urban agriculture projects. With Slow Food headquartered near the East River, and countless food and farming start-ups, Brooklyn is one of the epicenters of the local food movement. Around every corner in Williamsburg, Green Point, Red Hook, you'll find shops devoted to creative fermentation, baking, brewing, and butchering. Working with food is a kind of contemporary art form here. Urban gardens spring up in all sorts of unused space: schoolyards, vacant lots, playgrounds. Beekeepers like Cerise place hives on rooftops, carry honey extractors around by bicycle, and store comb in home freezers to keep the wax from melting in intense summer heat.

I'm drawn to Brooklyn's vibrant food scene and find parallels in Maine. There's much the same spirit in both places, with small businesses building on one another's energy to create something new. Which comes first, the local foods diner or the organic microfarm, the apiary or the mead maker? Each goes hand in hand, bootstrapping their way to success. Most farmers and food entrepreneurs around here aren't exactly making a fortune, but they're supportive of one another and share a sense of mission that justifies, arguably, their hard work.

My interest in Brooklyn's food revival reflects a transformation in my thinking over the past couple of years. Until recently it seemed to me that the best place for conservation projects was in the nonprofit realm. The bottom line of business thinking seemed inherently at odds with preservation goals, like stewardship of plants and animals left behind by industrial agriculture. Looking around in Maine and New York, however, something new is clearly at work. Vibrant small food businesses are driving the most exciting changes, often with altruistic goals.

Can a conservation project tap into this energy? To use plant patenting at the University of Minnesota as an example, what useful lessons might business models hold for public-spirited enterprises? Although there can be drawbacks to the commercial approach, the nonprofit world has its constraints, too. Every project needs sustainable funding, and compromise is part of the game, whether relying on donations and grants, or sales and marketing. In my experience the nonprofit world can at times lack accountability, and overhype achievements to draw donors. Friends who run food businesses like bakeries, wineries, and market gardens engage in a fair exchange of valuable products with appreciative customers. There's integrity in that. The allure of creating a small business based on high-quality heritage foods is becoming increasingly irresistible to me. I'm heading to Brooklyn to look for alternative food and farming models, and a few answers to help me understand the for-profit/nonprofit divide more clearly.

Jeremy and I switch to the subway in Manhattan and reach Park Slope by late afternoon. We meet Cerise and her boyfriend Adam, drop our bags at their apartment, and hop in their car to head to nearby Greenpoint. A car in New York—this is unexpected. It's one of the legacies of her time in Maine. Cerise and Adam don't use it much, preferring bicycles and the subway, but we're in a hurry. By driving we can squeeze in a quick visit before dinner to a micro-farm about fifteen minutes away.

Our destination is a market garden in a highly unlikely location: Greenpoint. Not only is this neighborhood intensely urban, with little available land for gardening, but it's also home to multiple superfund sites. Hidden beneath its streets are toxic plumes of chemicals and oil released over the course of 150 years from refineries, ruptured storage tanks, and pipelines. It's estimated that over time Greenpoint's industry released into subsurface waters as much as three times the oil lost in the wreck of the *Exxon Valdez*. That everyone expects toxicity here may account in part for relatively limited media coverage and lapsed public memory of these spills.

The secret of farming in places like this is to keep plants as far from contaminated soil as possible. I've constructed gardens in urban ground poisoned with high lead levels, building stone walls to hold raised beds and trucking in clean soil from the countryside. This Greenpoint microfarm takes everything a step farther, however. Its vegetables grow on a six-thousand-square-foot patch of earth dumped on the rooftop of a four-story industrial building. Like refugees from a flood escaping to higher ground, they rise above contamination and chemical vapors in search of clean soil, water, and a fresh breeze.

A frenetic young guy in cutoff shorts, work boots, and a T-shirt runs out the door, then stops to say hello as he catches sight of Cerise. He's Ben Flanner, co-owner of Rooftop Farms. "I'm in a hurry to deliver veggies," he tells us, showing us the basket he's carrying and pointing to his bicycle. A local restaurant is counting on him to help supply their dinner rush. "Do you have a minute to show my friends the garden?" Cerise asks. It's hard to say no to her—she's too good-natured, always willing to do favors herself, like touring around with Jeremy and me. So Ben unlocks the door and we head inside.

We climb through a darkened stairwell and pass through empty hallways and a storage room before emerging onto the rooftop. Ben tells us that beneath our feet are soundstages and theater sets where production crews shoot commercials, television segments, and MTV videos. There are no signs of life on this roof—animal, vegetable, or insect. But as we climb another flight of stairs to the highest level we encounter an incongruous sight. Here we're surrounded by vegetables of all kinds—herbs, greens, peppers, zucchini, cabbage, tomatoes—and before us lies the East River and an unimpeded view of the Manhattan skyline. Rows of bamboo stakes support climbing plants in the exposed, windy location, and plastic drip tape provides steady irrigation. The ambitious range of plants surprises me, because I'd expected mostly microgreens that don't require much space. This is Ben's first season, so it's hard to say whether the choice is visionary or a little misguided.

"Getting the soil up here was a challenge," Ben tells us. They used a lightweight mix of expanded shale, loam, and compost, hauled it up by crane, and dumped it directly onto the existing rubber membrane. He and his farming partner, Annie Novak, kept things simple when setting up the garden. There aren't any planter boxes here, no engineered structural support, no subsurface drainage systems. Salvaged boards hold the soil back at the building's edge. There's not even a railing to prevent a fall—the fifty-foot drop at the end of the zucchini patch is reminder enough to stay on the path. Within its border the garden's layout is as straightforward as any kitchen garden. Sixteen 4-foot-wide raised beds follow a simple grid pattern, with mulched pathways. If not for the sweeping views of the city and surrounding rooftops it would be easy to imagine this garden in any residential neighborhood.

Before getting carried away by this scene, I have to acknowledge that growing on a city rooftop is difficult, a little like trying to produce food in the desert. In the absence of shade from surrounding buildings and trees, relentless sunshine and wind quickly desiccate shallow soils. Urban heat islands, which often raise temperatures in cities several degrees above outlying suburbs, further intensify the growing environment. The challenge for rooftop gardeners is to create a soil mix that balances moisture retention with drainage.

Ben and Annie first had to figure out where to buy clean topsoil and transport it to this fourth-story roof in the heart of New York. Then they had to develop a lightweight mix that ensured good plant nutrition without becoming too heavy, particularly when saturated with water after a rainstorm. Rule number one: Provide enough depth for plants to root deeply. Rule number two: Don't collapse the roof.

"Adam won't eat anything coming from Rooftop Farms," Cerise admits to me later. She smiles as she says this, though, because she knows that he has, many times, without his knowledge. It's often on the menu at some of their favorite restaurants. So much for knowing your farmer—or putting your faith in local food. Eating these vegetables wouldn't concern me very much, though. Is it simply the incongruous association of Greenpoint with anything edible and nourishing? There may be fallout from urban soot and pollution, but after all, everyone here breathes the same air day in, day out.

While others in the urban farming movement talk and dream of high-tech approaches like greenhouse towers powered by wind turbines, I'll root for people like Ben and Annie. They find scrappy, real-world solutions to growing food in limited urban space, typically without a lot of external support or funding. Thanks to their no-frills approach, start-up costs for Rooftop Farms stayed within a modest budget of $6,000, or $1 per square foot. It's partly this affordability that appeals to me, because the project demonstrates democratic initiative at the grassroots level.

Similar models are springing up around the country, from gardens in vacant lots in downtown Detroit to Will Allen's highly ambitious and successful Growing Power, headquartered in Milwaukee. MyFarm, for example, is a "decentralized urban farm" in San Francisco that produces fruits and vegetables in residential yards. Its crew gets around mostly by bicycle. My friends Jeremy and Emily have launched something similar with backyard gardens in Berkeley. Such businesses help transform the way their communities view food, while making good use of unused spaces within them.

That said, gardening on this rooftop would drive me a little crazy. Maybe if I lived in Brooklyn and felt starved for open space it would seem worthwhile, but carrying produce by basket down several flights of stairs and delivering to restaurants by bicycle sounds like a recipe for burnout. Costs may be relatively low, but so are profits. Clearly it took a lot of time and energy to set up this garden, and in the end the beds cover less than an eighth of an acre, the size of an urban houselot back home in Portland. This is a fun idea, and inspiring for those living here, but given the constraints it's hard to imagine farming rooftops like this as the wave of the future. I wonder what Brooklyn's terrestrial food projects have in store for us.

We say a quick good-bye to Ben as he hops on his bicycle, and then return to the car for the drive to dinner. Cerise leads us to a local bar, and out one of its side doors to a space packed with friends of hers and local foodies. She's brought us to a onetime event, sort of a 1960s-style happening and celebration of late-summer bounty. Five dollars provides admission and an all-you-can-eat dinner served on paper plates. The restaurant, butcher, and specialty shop Prime Meats is behind this generous giveaway, a "summer blow-out" that features fantastic grilled heritage pork belly, apple cobbler, and several side dishes. One of its owners described their business as "pre-industrial revolution tactics with food" a few months ago in *The New York Times*. I'd call it a barbecue.

The next morning Jeremy and I catch a cab to nearby Red Hook to visit Added Value, another ambitious Brooklyn farming project founded on community organizing and hands-on innovation. The car leaves us next to a huge Ikea retail center, in the shadow of abandoned cranes scattered along the waterfront. Aside from the few trees lining the streets and Ikea's landscaping, nearly every square inch of earth here is paved. The growing environment is as inhospitable in its own way as Ben and Annie's warehouse rooftop, and in fact the two sites have much in common. Added Value imported all the soil needed for this microfarm, simply spreading it over the asphalt that runs unbroken across the lot. Field edges taper off at the paths to reveal the pavement beneath, like lath showing through a crumbling plaster wall. This farm is urban to the core. We catch our first glimpse of the operation through a twelve-foot chain-link fence that encloses it on all sides.

Three generations of dockworkers once used this site for round-the-clock pickup games, a place to unwind and share a sense of community. They played football on the paved field, and you can still see yard lines painted directly on the asphalt—a kind of group expression of sadomasochism. The playground was a rail-switching yard before the city converted it to ball fields. Today the New York City Parks Department owns the 2.75-acre lot and leases it to Added Value, which runs as a nonprofit youth development organization as well as a market farm. The baseball backstop holds a compost pile, and an old shipping container serves as an office. This land waited a long time for the return of green fields and fruit trees.

Though it might be unconventional, Added Value's pavement subsurface arguably serves a useful purpose by limiting potential soil contaminants. Co-founder Ian Marvy allays fears of oil leaching out of the asphalt into crops by pointing out that chemical waste typically travels down rather than up, most of the crops they grow have shallow roots, and their plants grow in fifteen inches of clean soil maintained organically. Neatly maintained compost includes manure from the Bronx Zoo. Most of the work here is done by hand, greatly reducing soil compaction and minimizing tillage. The fields are weedy, and I've heard management can be a little chaotic, but to me this demonstrates close kinship with the majority of other small organic farms. Look beyond the weeds and the site seems productive enough.

One of the workers in the field tells us this farm is the only viable option for fresh produce for many local residents. The last remaining neighborhood supermarket closed eight years ago, and the average income for a family of four is $14,000. Many locals lack the time, money, or access to transportation required to buy groceries, so Added Value's twice-weekly farmers' markets, which include fruit, vegetables, and dairy products from Long Island and upstate New York farms, provide for many the best access to good nutrition. The organization pays stipends to local youth, teaches them how to grow good food, and makes produce accessible to those in need.

While walking around, I begin to feel this work is replicable in every abandoned or underused paved lot I've ever driven by and tried to block from my peripheral vision. Dreams of superstore parking spaces growing fresh green beans and tomatoes temporarily fog my brain. The Ikea next door is already designed for herding, so why not fill it with dairy cows? Here's a post-apocalyptic vision of a fallen paradise. Maybe one day urban farms will spread into the surrounding suburbs, gobbling up the malls with cornfields and vineyards. Sounds like an idea for a children's book.

My search for growing space around Portland has been difficult, so I can only imagine what it took to get this project off the ground and persuade the city to turn a playground into a small farm. Nevertheless, in the absence of clean fields and garden soil, Added Value's approach seems workable and relatively affordable. It reminds me of an operation run by a guy named Ken Dunn in downtown Chicago, which farms vacant land with temporary leases and trucks soil and compost from lot to lot as needed. That's a radical approach, but so is growing on pavement. If anything, an asphalt barrier separating clean from contaminated soils would make mobile operations more manageable. Next year they could scoop up the farm and drive it to Maine.

It's worth remembering how productive small gardens and farms like this can be. At the height of the Second World War home Victory Gardens produced roughly 40 percent of the vegetables consumed in this country. This shows what's possible, at least when someone is shooting at us. Today the challenges are different, and persuading people to put down the remote and head outside to weed can be a tough sell. We're facing a combination of inertia, at least a generation's distance from the land, limited access to good gardening space, alienation from anything involving physical activity and food production, and a lack of information and time. Brooklyn's Added Value and Rooftop Farms point to some radical ways forward for those of us willing to pick up a shovel.

These projects also remind us the extent to which our American view of food has changed in recent years. Until recently vegetable gardening carried a bit of the stigma of your great-aunt's pickle relish. That you now think that's cool and search her closets for the recipe says a lot about how far we've come. Blame it on Brooklyn, or Berkeley, or people like Jeremy and Emily. I may not be able to apply many of the tactics used in Brooklyn's dense urban environment directly to very different circumstances in Maine, but this energy is infectious. It makes me wonder what I might be missing closer to home.

On my way back from a visit with my sister and her family in Connecticut the following spring, I stop to see a friend, Dominic Palumbo, at his Moon in the Pond Farm in Sheffield, Massachusetts. Dom and I met several years ago through Slow Food—he leads the western Massachusetts chapter, as I once led the chapter in Portland. A transplanted New Yorker who constructed rooftop gardens for wealthy clients in Manhattan before moving to this old hill farm, he's a bit of an anomaly. Gregarious and warm, he looks like someone more at home at the dinner table with friends than alone in a field herding livestock. I hope to catch him with dirt on his hands.

I pull off Route 7 in southwestern Massachusetts soon after entering the state from Connecticut. Here paved roads quickly turn to gravel and streams of tourist traffic give way to beat-up pickups and farm machinery. Surrounding cornfields remain cultivated thanks to a fortunate combination of fertile river-bottom soils and stubborn Yankee farmers. It's unusual to see so much land still farmed in New England, where profit margins are slim. The road here opens onto broad vistas that look like snapshots of forgotten farms from an old photo album. After a few miles of driving through tree-lined fields and pastures beside the Housatonic River, looking out at the Berkshire Hills, it's easy to forget the clamor of nearby shopping areas.

I park by the barn at Moon in the Pond and track down an apprentice cleaning stalls. "Dom's off in the field out back," he tells me, getting the ground ready for planting. He gives me walking directions, and as I head outside dozens of ducks, chickens, and Horned Dorset sheep swarm around me in greeting. Highland cattle watch from fifty feet away, recognizable immediately thanks to their shaggy coats and horns like water buffalo. A dozen young goats line the edge of their electric fence, angling for a photo. Beehives in the small orchard hum in the unseasonable ninety-degree late-April heat. Coppiced mulberry trees, an outdoor pigeon roost, espaliered Seckel pears—this is the idealized farm of a fairy tale.

If it's easier to imagine Dom cradling a glass of wine than a pitchfork (thanks to his New York City background), his passion for rare livestock breeds and heritage fruits and vegetables is grounded in the unglamorous daily routine of small-scale commercial farming. The Highland cattle graze steep hillsides and heritage Large Black pigs forage in the woods near the pond. To see Dom among them is to appreciate him in an entirely different light. Keeping up with chores on this farm must be quite a challenge, and it's beautifully maintained.

This old farm has held on for nearly 250 years in more or less the same state, probably always a bit lonely and out of the way, making do with hillside pastures and a few level fields. The oldest living space is a one-room shack built in the mid-eighteenth century, now sandwiched between the back of the main house and a timber-frame storage building. Most structures date back at least two hundred years, and like many such colonial buildings, the house is set only a few feet from the road. Unlike most other houses of its era, however, it remains in a tranquil spot. The road is unpaved and very lightly traveled.

I think about the layout of this old farm, how well it works and what secrets it holds, while walking around looking for Dom. To most eyes everything here—house, barn, paddocks, gardens— would probably look relatively straightforward, easy enough to understand, the product of a simpler time. But how simple is it, really? What lessons does it hold about agricultural design, the threads that interweave plants, animals, soils, and climate to sustain us? Living here, making this place work—these are challenges foreign to most of us. Where would one start? We can't really know the functional from the merely picturesque until we spend a season or two herding cows into a milking parlor, feeding a herd of goats, and harvesting hay.

A hardscrabble New England farm is an expression of endless trial and error as well as a complex mix of traditional knowledge and individual inspiration. Generations of previous farmers adapted to the realities of this landscape, keeping what worked and tossing aside what didn't. Pastures on Dom's farm fan out around the nearby barn, following the land's contours in a way that saves walking and encourages efficient movement of animals to avoid overgrazing. Soil types are invisible to our eyes, but it's a good bet the placement of pastures, fruit trees, tilled fields, and woodlots mirrors life below the ground. Dom's recent additions also show good instincts, like placing a small plastic hoophouse on a sunny hillside next to the chicken house. Both are easily accessible from the back door of the farmhouse.

I've learned the hard way that clean, simple design isn't as easy as it looks. While living in Washington State in the late 1980s and early 1990s I built a tiny house of about two hundred square feet in a beautiful spot, a dramatic overlook with sweeping views of the North Cascade Mountains. It was perched on a small knoll near the bottom of a steep hillside, invisible to anyone passing by, no other house or road in sight. Friends warned of potential drawbacks, but I was young and ignored what in retrospect were clear signs of danger. Like the boulders scattered all around, some of which were nearly the size of the house. *Well, they didn't roll any farther,* went my reasoning. In other words they'd been coming off the hillside above for ages, but most had lost their momentum before reaching this spot. How much damage could they do?

One morning I arrived home to find a refrigerator-sized boulder in the kitchen, the door blown out, and my cat freaked out on the bed. The next day I started building an inverted V-shaped berm in the hill above to deflect the next rolling rock, using excavated dirt from a large root cellar to build the sides up to nearly six feet. The site was too steep for a wheelbarrow or heavy equipment, so I had to dig with a pickaxe and shovel and haul dirt around in five-gallon buckets. I don't recommend this. In the end my cellar worked for storing root vegetables, but it was in the wrong place—out of the way and hard to access, particularly in heavy snow. Once I'd made that first fateful decision to build at this site, it pulled me in farther and farther.

Sometimes my valley in central Washington received a great deal of snow. The year after my departure it piled up eleven feet deep on the thousand-foot hill behind the house, and the berm around the cellar wasn't enough to deflect a large avalanche that slid one night. My friends who were caretaking had mercifully left for the weekend, so no one had to dig them out from their bed, which, along with most of the little house, was engulfed in heavy, compacted snow. The slide blew out the same door the boulder had smashed, this time shattering it to pieces against the far wall. Snow filled the little place like ice cream fills a cone.

My Mexican friends the Sandovals were right—devils were out to get me. Or maybe I was my own worst enemy. Despite attending good schools and thinking I knew a thing or two, here was my education in the real world. It's hard to argue with an avalanche; my choice of building site had been poor. Here in Massachusetts the challenges are subtler, but nature still teaches hard lessons. You wouldn't plant potatoes on a steep hillside, for example, or in a waterlogged depression. Or you might once, but not again after the first heavy rains either washed away the soil or turned the potato patch into a frog pond. And as for apple trees, the variety that tasted so good on a trip to New Hampshire last fall might not sweeten up as well in this warmer location, or develop the same rich flavor in these soils.

This sense of agricultural design begins to get at the essence of the French idea of *terroir:* that a successful farm matches the particularity of its landscape with thoughtful selection of crops and animals. Fruit trees may thrive best on a southern or northern exposure, for example, depending on the climate and the variety: southern to warm up earlier in the springtime and extend the season, or northern to delay blossoming and avoid losing the crop to a late-spring frost. And each site can influence the flavors of the foods we eat. Sometimes choices like these come down to a roll of the dice, but more often they're the result of trial and error. Over time our forebears gained intimate knowledge of what did and didn't work in their particular microclimates, a hard-earned balance of risk and reward. Then came the great anticlimactic moment: We all moved away and forgot.

After a few minutes of following the sound of a tractor I find Dom out back in the vegetable fields, working with an apprentice to turn in a cover crop of rye. They're using an old Farmall tractor rigged up for the market garden with chisel plows and a harrow. Dom grins as he runs it down the edge of the field. His apprentice follows with a hoe, turning in whatever cover crop the tractor missed. Working with this old equipment rather than a rototiller is a good approach, trading ease of use for less disturbance of the soil structure, and fewer weed seeds carried to the surface. Even if the result isn't as gratifying as beds smoothed by the blades of a tiller, a little handwork at the beginning of the year pays off as the pace of the season accelerates.

This kind of small organic farm has become familiar to many Americans, particularly with the growth of farmers' markets. Buy a piece of land, maybe rent a bit more if the cost is too high, pick up some old machinery, and bring in apprentices for a cheap labor pool. It works, sort of, though profit margins are very slim. Thanks to an apprenticeship at a farm near Dom's the summer after my college graduation, I know something about farming this way. At that point I'd never really held a tool in my hands, and didn't understand the first thing about gardening. I showed up in June and found myself knee-deep in weeds, swinging a heavy hoe and learning to scythe. A friend of the farmer used to stop by with helpful advice, like "Let the tool do the work." The others liked to point out that he never did any work himself.

That year I rented a room in the barn at nearby Indian Line Farm, owned by Robyn Van En. Robyn is widely credited for introducing the idea of Community Supported Agriculture to this country in the 1980s. (CSAs distribute farm products in exchange for the purchase of shares at the start of a season.) Her CSA was one of the first, though she'd temporarily suspended it during the year of my stay. She spoke of various difficulties during our dinners with her son David. An ongoing struggle with the farmer who'd worked her land the previous season was especially troubling to her. He insisted it was his right to strip the top foot of soil from her fields and truck it to his new farm, because he'd improved it with biodynamic amendments. I never heard how she resolved this, though the soil stayed.

The owner of the farm I worked wasn't interested in Community Supported Agriculture. He was, and still is, a very hardworking market gardener, selling to local shops and restaurants. Unknown to me, though, he had a sideline that boosted his profits. Call it his farm subsidy. Growing an extra illicit crop in the woods worked well enough until someone tipped off the local police a couple of years later, and then it nearly proved his undoing. He stayed afloat by moving to a new farm and reinventing the business.

In 2008 Dominic Palumbo joked about the economics of farming while addressing the American delegation at Slow Food's Terra Madre, a worldwide gathering of farmers and activists in Turin,

Italy. "I only began farming a short eighteen years ago," he told the crowd. "I thought, I could make some money. So you know, straight up, I'm not too bright." In his case, highly diversified operations sustain Moon in the Pond. He sells heirloom vegetables, pickles, duck and chicken eggs, and a wide range of meats at farmers' markets and restaurants, and to visitors like me who stop by the farm.

"Need anything to bring home with you?" Dom asks. We walk back to the barn and step into the walk-in freezer to select meats he processed last fall. I spend a couple of minutes looking over the wide variety of cuts, then quickly step back outside. He keeps the freezer set at ten below zero Fahrenheit. It's unbearably cold. Before returning to the car we fill my bag with sage breakfast sausages, lamb cuts, half a dozen duck eggs, and a jar of horseradish root pickled in vinegar. Dom makes change for me from a self-service area on the porch and we throw everything in a cooler, placing it in the back of my station wagon for the ride home.

Stopping by a farm to pick out high-quality meats and produce feels like a kind of foraging, or at least a throwback to earlier days before supermarkets. Filling my car with good food produced by a friend touches something deep, an instinct to gather and provide. It also strengthens community bonds. As appealing as Moon in the Pond looks from the outside, however, I know this is a difficult way to make a living. Running a small farm in the country can be very isolating, and my experience has been that the hours are long, the work hard, and the returns modest at best. The most capable farmers in our Portland area make a living of sorts, even supporting families, but they do this by working day and night, rarely taking a break, and sometimes destroying their health in the bargain. I'm willing to work, and interested in scaling my own project up to something more, but I'm searching for a different approach.

Back in southern Maine, near our home in Portland, farmers contend with high land prices and limited availability of tillable ground. In return for living here, however, they gain access to thriving markets and a supportive urban food scene. Theirs is a kind of suburban farming, falling somewhere between rural Moon in the Pond Farm and urban gardens in Brooklyn.

Part of Portland's appeal to prospective growers is that it's a city on the rise, well on the way from a picturesque, somewhat down-and-out industrial port to a vibrant center for the arts, small business, and great food. In its newest incarnation Portland has become unabashedly a town obsessed with eating. Chefs head home to continue cooking in their off hours, trying to top one another in "death match" bacchanals with themes like *Grow! Kill! Forage!* Seasonal tourist migrations fill restaurants like a decidedly un-hip converted car ferry floating at a downtown wharf, while locals flock to intimate spaces like Caiola's, one of our favorite hangouts. Only San Francisco has more restaurants per capita in this country than Portland, Maine.

Around the corner from my first home in town was a tiny store-front that housed a succession of failed businesses, from a gallery to a pizza shop. They came and went so fast the landlord should have posted a warning sign on the lease: NO ONE SHOPS HERE. The space seemed suitable only for a business that could attract its own subculture clientele, like a tattoo parlor or a pawnshop. So it was a surprise a couple of years ago when a Japanese chef named Masa Miyake arrived from Manhattan to open a restaurant there.

Karla and I can hardly keep up with the influx of new restaurants in Portland. They show up in unexpected places, from old gas stations to abandoned churches, and carry with them a steady stream of innovative culinary talent. It's somewhat misleading to call Miyake a sushi chef, for example, in part because he trained in New York under renowned French chef Daniel Boulud. His level of experience isn't unusual here, and he isn't alone in his appreciation for quality ingredients. Many local chefs value their suppliers so highly that they list farmers, fishermen, and foragers on their menus. Their restaurants create a restless market for culinary experiences, a taste for different foods, and awareness of the people and stories behind them. As in Brooklyn, Portland's local food energy builds upon itself and moves in sometimes surprising directions.

Less than a quarter mile from my garden in suburban Cape Elizabeth, a young couple recently tilled an acre of ground in the backyard of a private seven-acre estate. Mary Ellen and Austin Chadd grow vegetables and cut flowers for the farmers' market, and sell to restaurants around town. They're leasing space from owner Rodney Voisine, a practicing anesthesiologist with a background in pharmacy. Rodney also runs a weight-loss health clinic and sells a line of nutritional supplements. The Chadds are working his land and selling under his Old Ocean House Farms label.

I've met Rodney a couple of times. When I ran the educational farm next door last year, he generously suggested that he'd make his land available if ever we needed more space. This was hard to imagine. The property is striking: a large old farmhouse with a columned portico, perched in an imposing location on a hill overlooking the road. Its grounds include formal gardens laid out with parterres, elaborate perennial flower beds, fountains, a garden house, and espaliered fruit trees. Would Rodney really want a working farm in the middle of this pristine backyard?

Apparently, yes. As I walk into the field Mary Ellen greets me wearing a heavy respirator and carrying a spray tank on her back. It's an unusual sight in a field maintained organically, but the middle of the summer of 2009 is a difficult time. This season will go down as The Year of No Tomatoes. She's applying an organically approved copper solution to control late blight, and her plants are holding on, though not quite as well as she'd hoped. In any case, this impresses me. I don't even own a spray tank. That's partly because I want to observe the progression of pests and diseases in my fields—and select plants for seed according to their resistance— but also because I've never faced a growing season as challenging as this. Mary Ellen and Austin are ahead of the game.

She stops to give me a tour of their gardens, which lean heavily toward heirloom varieties. This is the Chadds' first year as commercial growers, but they studied sustainable agriculture at Evergreen State College in Washington State and seem very knowledgeable. Clearly they like to experiment. Mary Ellen rattles off names and shows me a few of their trials, like rows of different melons they're testing for viability in Cape Elizabeth's cool summers. Plantings include more than twenty-five varieties of tomatoes and a wide range of vegetables in the brassica family, like cabbage, kale, and turnips.

A chicken wire fence buried several inches below grade surrounds their one-acre vegetable plot, to keep woodchucks away, and a single strand of electric fence runs along the top to discourage deer. While Mary Ellen sprays tomatoes, Austin works with a walk-behind tractor—essentially a large rototiller adaptable to many small farm tasks, from weeding to mowing. The compact maneuverability of this tiller is especially useful as they convert their newly cultivated field to dense rows of vegetables. Until last spring this back part of the property was a meadow filled with grasses and Queen Anne's lace, bindweed, and bittersweet vines, so it's going to take time and effort to reduce weed competition and eliminate sod and perennial roots.

Mary Ellen and Austin have worked hard to prepare the planting beds. You can't start a farm overnight; typically it takes years to build soil and fertility and learn which crops thrive in a given location. Even in a relatively small farm field like this, growing conditions can vary considerably. Some of the ground here is ledgy, filled with small bits of shale, while other areas look clean and easy to work. The field has some fairly steep slopes for growing vegetable row crops, and it drops off into a hollow with a tall line of pine trees along the edge. Heat- and sun-loving plants probably wouldn't do well down there, but lettuce and spinach might.

Young farmers like the Chadds typically have to choose between searching for available (and affordable) farmland well out in the country, thus spending hours driving to and from their markets, or squeezing into limited space closer to home. This site a few miles from Portland is a compromise, exchanging the independence and openness of the countryside for better access to the city. Not yet driven to the rooftops or farming the nearest parking lot, their garden doesn't exactly look like a traditional farm, either. The field seems a little tight for a full-time market garden.

I'm facing similar limitations in my garden nearby, where this 2009 season I'm growing a third of an acre of vegetables for our home use and building up my plant collection. Although soil fertility remains high thanks to cover crops and compost, I don't have enough space to take land out of production during the growing season, and this is starting to lead to trouble. Ragged Jack kale and Vermont heirloom Gilfeather rutabagas are showing signs of black rot infection, for example. This is a bacterial disease common among plants in the brassica family, and it gradually causes them to turn yellow, wither, and die. Now that it's entered my soil, short of fumigating the entire field (which as an organic grower I would never do), fixing the problem requires rotating susceptible plants out of contaminated areas, composting infected leaves, sterilizing seeds for future plantings in hot-water baths, and cover-cropping infected areas. Good sanitation will gradually eliminate the problem, but it's difficult to reduce contamination without sufficient land. If this garden was large enough I'd remove brassicas from infected areas for at least three years.

"You should wash the dirt off your boots before leaving the field," Mary Ellen tells me as we finish our conversation. It turns out some of her plants are also showing signs of black rot. Her cabbages are alive and thriving, but starting to show dieback around the outer leaves. They may not keep much longer or store very well. Since this field was a meadow last year, the problem points to the seeds she purchased, even though these came from reputable companies. Regardless of the source, black rot is particularly challenging because the Chadds depend heavily on brassica sales. Crops like broccoli and turnips thrive in our cool coastal climate, so they're essential to many small local farms.

Maybe I'm simply projecting some of my own restless feelings, but it doesn't seem like an acre is enough ground for a successful market garden. There isn't much room here to maneuver when problems arise. Mary Ellen and Austin can't diversify into livestock, or leave part of their fields in cover crops to help build fertility and reduce pest and disease pressures. I read between the lines, wondering whether they intend to search for their own farm and expand their business, and how long they plan to stay here.

This year I've been putting a lot of thought into how to expand my limited garden space into something larger and more substantial. Many of the small businesses I've read about and visited recently offer inspiring lessons applicable to my own experience and circumstances. Borrowing ideas from each might look something like this: the mobility of Ken Dunn's Chicago vegetable operation; the diversity of products at Dominic Palumbo's Moon in the Pond farm; the creative use of space at Rooftop Farms and Added Value;

and the low overhead and shared resources of Mary Ellen and Austin Chadds' market garden. Somewhere in these ideas must be a business model that can work for me, a way to develop fruit and vegetable collecting into a sustainable business.

The first challenge is simply to find adequate growing space near our home. Urban and suburban ecology, ecology with a human footprint, introduces layers of complexity to growing food that most gardening books ignore. Vegetable gardeners in Portland typically begin with a hunt for land, water, and light, then quickly run into questions of soil contamination and safety. Sometimes this can take a bizarre turn, like when a gas line explosion in our downtown neighborhood two years ago demolished a house and buried the adjacent community garden in rubble. Luckily no one was hurt. It took a full season to clear the debris, replace the contaminated topsoil, and reopen the garden.

In our own urban yard in Portland's West End, renovations uncovered shards of pottery, endless bits of broken glass, old shoes, and chunks of coal. I rented a jackhammer to remove asphalt and concrete paving and for years picked pieces of trash from the soil like stones from a cornfield. Today the ground looks clean and healthy, transformed by plantings of native dogwoods and viburnum, but tests show over six hundred parts per million of lead, twice the level considered safe for food gardens by the EPA and four times the standard set in Europe. Our herb garden depends on nearly two feet of soil imported from the countryside, spread over a one-hundred-square-foot bed excavated and lined with heavy landscaping fabric.

The majority of land in urban areas has been damaged ecologically: poisoned with chemicals, altered with heavy equipment, and overrun with invasive plants. Portland's landscape has been repeatedly torn apart and stitched back together—much like our house, which endured all kinds of abuse in its 150 years. While renovating several years ago I discovered plumbers had cut through structural floor joists to install drain lines; someone removed the load-bearing stairs to the basement, causing the floor to buckle and undermine the foundation; and the roofing framing was so widely spaced it was foolhardy. Previous owners played a game against gravity: How much could they cut away before everything came crashing down? And outside, how much contamination could the land absorb?

It's hard not to look away and pretend all's well, but searching for clean growing space often runs headlong into difficult issues. Whether we inhabit urban, suburban, or rural places, we live with layer upon layer of previous uses, each building upon or disrupting what came before. Ride a mountain bike along Portland's Fore River, between tidal inlets and the train tracks, and you'll come across trees that might be crab apples or the remnants of an old orchard. It's easy to forget that industry once thrived in this quiet space. The Fore River was dredged here in the nineteenth century to serve as the main commercial transportation route between Portland and inland lakes, and brick warehouses on adjacent Thompson's Point housed a polluting cement plant. Paint factories nearby spewed heavy metals. The legacy of such previous use hasn't been erased; this history is simply invisible to us.

The challenge of finding safe, accessible farmland extends even beyond the urban fringe to Portland's suburbs. Trash that used to come to the surface in my borrowed Cape Elizabeth field after tilling always surprised me, for example. Where did it come from? Most likely it was hidden in leaves and yard waste trucked in for composting over the years, but some of the owner's stories suggest other sources. One of the previous tenants was a theater set designer who liked to stage large parties and burn leftover props and materials in the field. Patches of earth near the house are still charred, and who knows what found its way into those fires.

The expansion of my gardens into a business will require accounting for constraints like these while making good use of Portland's opportunities. Success will depend on finding clean, workable land, identifying reliable markets that haven't already been tapped by other growers, and keeping costs low. Above all else, I'll want to stay focused on my primary goals: conserving rare plants, finding pleasurable work, building community, and producing high-quality food. What's this going to look like? And where will I do it? Since I have no idea how to answer either question, all I can do is get started and see what happens.

Eight

SCALING UP THE GARDEN:
THE RELUCTANT "FARMER"

$\mathcal{M}$y search for land begins with FarmLink, a program managed by the Maine Farmland Trust. Since I've used this service before to look for garden space, the FarmLink coordinator writes to thank me for rejoining, and adds enthusiastically that she can't wait to help me search for a farm. FarmLink connects prospective growers with property available for lease or sale, helping people like me find unused space. Its goal is to keep Maine farmland in production and facilitate land transfers between generations. MFT distributes a list of available land periodically to FarmLink subscribers, covering all of the state and every scale of operations, from part-time market garden plots to commercial dairies and potato farms.

My hope is that FarmLink can help uncover more land within a half-hour commute of Portland. Karla and I periodically talk over other options, like buying property and moving out of the city, but to date nothing we've found has seemed right. Karla divides her time working for the state in Portland and the capital city of Augusta, an hour's drive to the north, and although this leaves some flexibility around her commute, like me she wants to minimize time in the car. We moved to Portland in part for its walkable neighborhoods and car-free lifestyle. Only a really exceptional opportunity would convince us to pack up and leave behind our friends and the good life we've made for ourselves here.

My application to FarmLink includes notes about orchards and fruit nurseries. Recently my collecting interests have turned in this direction, in part because there just aren't enough people doing this work. Since it takes several years for a newly planted tree to begin to bear, growing fruit depends on long-term commitments that many gardeners are reluctant to make. Even when we have enough space, knowledge, and time, most of us simply don't set down roots in any one place long enough to grow trees. We're a mobile nation, on average packing up and leaving home every six or seven years. You can cart along bean seeds when moving to a new garden, but your fruit trees stay put.

My circumstances are a little different; I've lived in the same home for several years while my gardens moved around me. Finding growing space has depended on the goodwill of landowners and on temporary arrangements with other growers. Over the past five years my search for land has taken me to a small plot with heavy clay soil next to the Bowdoin College student farm; a neglected quarter-acre kitchen garden at a beautiful old dairy farm west of the city; a large urban garden next to a busy four-lane road in downtown Portland; and a vacant city lot beside a homeless shelter. In the end none of these gardens lasted more than two seasons. Whenever possible I've tended fruit trees and even planned, planted, and maintained an orchard for a community food group. But to date no one has offered a permanent home for more than a handful of our own fruit trees.

The last time I planted an orchard for myself was nearly twenty years ago in Washington State. These trees—a mix of apples, pears, sour cherries, and plums—grew well enough, but didn't survive their first season without me, when I left them in the hands of a teenager who'd recently avoided arrest by swallowing several hundred doses of LSD. After months of recovery in the hospital he'd been released to the care of his girlfriend, his liver and judgment permanently impaired. A mutual friend assured me that tending the orchard would be good for his soul, but every day for three months as he turned on the drip irrigation he neglected to see if any water was coming out. A blown cap on the end of the line meant that little to no water reached the trees. By summer's end they were all dead. None of them ever set any fruit. This time around I'm determined to find a place where newly planted trees can reach maturity.

In her reply to my application, the FarmLink coordinator adds a further note describing a farm for sale in central Maine, which she thinks might interest me. Clicking on the link brings up photos of a stunningly beautiful eighty-four-acre farm located near Augusta. It's for sale through MFT's Buy/Protect/Sell program, in which the trust purchases significant farmland, adds conservation easements to protect it, raises money to subsidize a lower asking price, and resells "to a farmer at farmland (not development) prices." The property she has in mind is prime farmland on a hilltop surrounded by lakes, with panoramic views of distant mountains. Across the road is a private academy that attracts students from around the world—a pretty campus of brick buildings, playing fields, and sports buildings. She's attached the link because this farm is largely set up for orchard production. It includes thirty-four hundred apple trees, as well as "a 2,800-square-foot cold storage building, a workshop, two sizable storage sheds, a bunkhouse for farm workers, and a newly-constructed 6-stall horse stable and outdoor riding ring." Asking price: $305,000. That's very reasonable.

Despite persuading myself of the many advantages of growing in borrowed space, like leaving barn repairs and tractor maintenance to others, the dream of owning land dies hard. There would be security knowing that the property will stay under my control, and the land under my trees won't transfer to new owners who don't want me around. Most of my gardens have been arranged for short-term use, because they either required too much commuting time or were borrowed from other growers. Could this farm persuade us to leave our home in Portland, sell our house, and build something new together? It would shorten Karla's commute to Augusta, and she loves the idea of spending more time outdoors. Would buying an eighty-four-acre farm and orchard be a good idea for me? No, probably not. It's entirely beyond my urban gardening experience, but nevertheless there's something irresistible in it. No harm in taking a look.

The wind is blowing hard as I crest the hill near the orchard and pull into a parking lot beside the packing shed. It's early December 2009, and the trust's land projects coordinator has agreed to meet me on-site for a tour. She drives in a few moments after my arrival as I'm rummaging around searching for gloves and a hat. Nice timing, since we'd both traveled nearly an hour and a half from opposite directions. This visit works out well for both of us because she needs to be in town later today for a public meeting. It's going to be a cold walk, however. Until last week the weather was warm, the ground bare, and it seemed winter might never arrive. But a foot of new snow fell over the weekend—December is capricious in Maine. Already a crust of shimmering ice has formed on the surface, making walking difficult. It hadn't occurred to me that the drifts might be deep enough to require snowshoes.

In contrast with the Greater Portland area there's plenty of land available around here. The road from Augusta passes small farms and orchards, with rolling fields surrounding old clapboard farmhouses, and beautiful views of mountains and lakes with native names like Maranacook and Cobbosseecontee. This part of central Maine is very quiet and pretty. Despite its proximity to Augusta, nearby Readfield is a sleepy little town with a café and a natural food store. The area isn't immune to the pressures of development, though—before MFT stepped in this orchard was on the market for over half a million dollars. Without intervention and conservation easements it most likely would have become a subdivision with multiple suburban houselots.

"Should we start with a walk around, while we're still warm from the drive?" MFT's coordinator asks as she greets me with a friendly smile by the barn. She's carrying a clipboard of information about the trust's conservation work, as well as flyers describing the farm. Wind is whipping across the field and it's cold, below twenty degrees. As usual I'm underdressed, having underestimated the weather, wearing just a windbreaker and vest. We muffle our heads against the wind and start walking across the field, breaking steps through the snowdrifts.

We head first for the horse stable. Inside a genial, elderly man of about seventy, the owner's father, listens to Rush Limbaugh as he mucks out a stall. I ask him about the wind, which is merciless. "You call this wind?" he jokes, and points out there's nothing standing between the farm and Sugarloaf Mountain, visible on the horizon seventy miles to the northwest. We're standing at the crest between Maine's moderate coastal plain and the frigid, mountainous interior, with the land sloped north toward the cold. At first glance this may seem like the wrong place for fruit trees, but the site has excellent soils and a gentle grade of 2 to 4 percent. Its hilltop location ensures a steady breeze that reduces fungal diseases, and surrounding climate-moderating lakes help prevent late-spring frosts. Most of this farm has been in fruit trees for at least a hundred years.

The orchard comes right to the edge of the horse barn. Leaving behind the building's relative warmth, I brace for the cold and walk into the first block of trees. Most are semidwarf, ranging from eight to twelve feet tall. Rows of trees alternate with open pastures in what seem like random patterns. Twenty years ago roughly sixty of these acres were in orchard production, but over the past decade its owners gradually reduced tree plantings by half. They pulled less marketable fruit and unproductive trees, leaving rows of remaining orchard widely spaced. It's hard to get a sense of everything in this dormant state, the trees bare, the ground covered in snow, but MFT's information sheets provide photos of the property in summer. It's a shame we couldn't have timed this visit before snowfall.

In many ways this orchard is a relic, its infrastructure developed thirty or more years ago to serve a very different agricultural market. "This is a dying business," a ninety-year-old retired orchardist told me last fall, when I called in search of information about the Blake apple. It's very difficult for a wholesale New England operation to compete with imported fruit, and the financial breakdown MFT shares confirms this. This orchard has survived thanks to pick-your-own apples, hayrides, cross-country ski trails, and value-added sales at the family's retail shop next door, which is up for sale in a separate listing. Its pickers' bunkhouse is largely unused, relegated to office and storage space, and expensive infrastructure like the cold-storage packing shed stands empty. Last year's net income for fruit production was about $15,000—barely holding on, though in the black at least, if the numbers provided by the owners are accurate.

Part of the problem is that most of these apples are McIntosh, a variety whose productive commercial run has passed. More recent introductions like Fuji and Braeburn have cut deeply into McIntosh's market share, and with good reason. Macs are too common to fetch a good price, and to my palate they're mealy and not very tasty. They're also fussy and difficult to produce without conventional sprays, because they're highly susceptible to scab, a common fungal disease. The majority of these trees were planted in the late 1970s on semidwarf stock. They're reaching the end of their productive life span, which is generally thirty to forty years. These trees are as much a part of the aging infrastructure as the sagging tractor barn—an outdated investment that's more liability than asset. The best I can say about them is that many are small enough to "topwork," by cutting existing branches and grafting different, more marketable and disease-resistant varieties onto them. With well-established root systems, new grafts could start producing within three or four years.

Our tour doesn't last long. Neither of us is fully prepared for the cold, so we duck into the packing shed and stumble around blindly in the windowless space, searching for the light switch. It snaps on to illuminate a largely empty room, with a forklift standing over a puddle of machine oil near a stack of old picking boxes. A quick glance reveals everything; this is an insulated, steel-clad barn with a concrete floor, in good condition. We wander out a side door into an attached three-sided shed where we find a hydraulic cider press. It was idled several years ago when changes in FDA regulations began requiring pasteurization for any cider not sold directly to retail customers (and clearly labeled as a raw product). This forced most producers to either purchase expensive new equipment or shut down operations. By coincidence I came across a commercial posting the other day advertising this press for sale on an equipment list out of Goshen, Indiana. The asking price: $13,000. Like the rest of the farm equipment, it doesn't come with the property.

I pull back the heavy sliding door on one of the barns and start photographing its interior. Two vintage tractors, powerful old workhorses, sit side by side on a stained concrete floor. A tractor-driven spray rig is covered with white chemical residue. The walls are sheathed with something that might be asbestos, but on closer inspection turns out to be Styrofoam insulation, its surface blackened by years of diesel exhaust. Next door two sheds that stored agricultural chemicals stand empty, but everything about them seems to retain a chemical pall. My imagination, maybe.

The look of this place makes me wonder, not for the first time, whether we've reached the nadir for midsized commercial agriculture in this part of the world. Soldiering on with the current orchard model doesn't seem like much of an option, but trying to envision an alternative is a puzzle. On the face of it, transitioning to something new appears simple enough. This is beautiful farmland with excellent deep soil, a sharply reduced price, ready access to markets in Portland and Augusta, and an established business with thousands of productive trees. It looks like a solid foundation to explore all kinds of ideas, like growing diversified vegetable or berry crops for direct sale to local markets, developing niche products such as hard cider and nursery plants, or incorporating educational programming. Teachers at the adjacent school want to involve their students in farm projects. Because this site is located close to the highway, at a crossroads where inland farming regions meet the central I-295 transportation corridor, the large cold-storage building could even become the focal point of a regional food distribution network.

On closer examination, nothing is this straightforward. Yesterday Karla and I learned that friends of ours intent on farming here have already walked away from the table, signing a preliminary agreement and then changing their minds as they dug deeper. Their plan was to let the apples go unsprayed and focus efforts on raising animals beneath the trees. As they uncovered more about the site's residual chemical contamination, however, they worried that pesticides would accumulate to unsafe levels in the bodies of their pigs. Other concerns about the healthfulness of living on this site surfaced as well. Maine Farmland Trust's tests of the well water, for example, found concentrations of arsenic above EPA standards, due either to Maine's high background levels or past spraying of arsenical insecticides. Living here seemed to pose multiple risks for our friends' baby and their own long-term health. Not exactly what you bargain for when dreaming of life as an organic farmer.

Are such concerns about toxic residues real or overblown? Since orchards have historically depended on a wide variety of pesticides, from lead arsenic to DDT, the Maine Farmland Trust has done its homework, compiling detailed chemical analyses of these fields. They forthrightly share this information with me, and back at my computer the next day I start researching known hazards. The largest concern is an organochlorine chemical called dieldrin. This is an insecticide that dates back to the 1940s, and although it's been prohibited for most uses in this country since the 1970s, it bonds tightly with soil and can persist for hundreds of years. Dieldrin is a neurotoxin that can cause kidney damage and a host of other problems, ranging from immune suppression to endocrine disruption. The EPA lists it as a probable carcinogen. Due to its toxicity and longevity, and because concentrations increase as it travels up the food chain, dieldrin is now banned throughout most of the world.

I search online for answers to two very basic questions: Would crops growing in these fields be safe to eat, and what would be the risks to those living on-site? It isn't easy to find good data, but the State of New Jersey mandates cleanup for residential sites if dieldrin in the soil exceeds forty parts per billion. Researchers generally agree that cucurbits in particular—squashes, cucumbers, and melons—shouldn't be grown in contaminated soils, because these concentrate dieldrin in their fruits at a very high rate. An article in the *Journal of Applied Microbiology and Biotechnology* discusses soil remediation by growing squash (which would then need to be disposed of as toxic waste), and another piece in the *Journal of Environmental Science and Health* recommends a safe maximum level of ten parts per billion for growing any cucurbit. Little data is available for other vegetables. Since I'd like to grow cucumbers and squash as well as a wide range of other foods, this is a real concern. And as much as I don't like to be an alarmist, considering the potential cancer risks to those living on site is troubling.

The Maine Farmland Trust works closely with me to sort out the numbers and reach good conclusions about chemical hazards and safety. Their initial test, which combined soil from randomly selected points around the property into one sample, showed relatively high dieldrin levels: 220 parts per billion. Because this was greater than expected, they followed up by dividing the site into eight smaller plots for more detailed analysis. The second round of soil samples showed lower average dieldrin readings of 38 to 120 ppb, with one small parcel around the barns registering little to no contamination. These are more encouraging results, but nevertheless several times higher than known safe maximum concentrations for crops like melon and squash. Lower levels in the second round also raise disturbing questions about where that first 220 ppb average came from. Did they hit a hot spot where concentrations are much higher? Mapping out safe growing areas and locating chemical spills will require much more testing.

The Maine Farmland Trust didn't legally have to do these studies or share their results. Soil chemical analysis and environmental risk assessment are part of the service they provide to prospective farmers and the public. As long as a pesticide was applied legally and in accordance with the regulations of its time, property owners have no legal mandate to disclose known hazards, or clean up the site. A further irony of legacy soil contamination is that it doesn't factor into organic certification, even after tests reveal potential dangers. A farmer could certify plants produced on these soils as organic after three years of rest without further use of conventional chemicals, and sell organic squash even though this crop in particular rapidly accumulates dieldrin in its fruit.

Current regulations make sense from a practical standpoint, in part because residual agricultural chemicals are everywhere: in agricultural fields, lakes and streams, the foods we eat, our own bodies, even breast milk. There's no escaping contamination. High residual levels of banned pesticides like dieldrin have been found in places as diverse as farm fields in Denmark and New Zealand, groundwater in US military bases in the Philippines, vegetable fields in California's Central Valley, and fish consumed by Greenlanders. Organochlorine pesticides were sprayed heavily on a wide range of fruit and vegetable crops, and used for residential termite control. Although these fields are substantially contaminated with a probable carcinogen, they're simply the devil that we know.

How many purchasers of old New England farms follow the Maine Farmland Trust's lead by conducting environmental site assessments and submitting soil samples to analyze residual chemicals? At an intellectual level we know orchards have been heavily sprayed for generations, but the eye sees apparently healthy fields that appeal to something deeper, signifying robust good health. Most of us don't associate chemical contamination and hazards with picturesque meadows and orchards, so the results of these tests would probably come as a surprise even to many local residents. They've rallied around the preservation of this beautiful open space and contributed generously to keep it in farmland. Its prominent setting and history as one of the earliest farms in the area are important to the community. In the nineteenth century this farm supplied the adjacent school, and today students wander over to pick apples after class. It's quite a leap from this pastoral vision to a hard assessment of invisible dangers.

Preliminary research suggests that although this land is safe for tree crops like apples, which won't take dieldrin up from the soil into their fruit, it wouldn't be a good idea to grow vegetables here, particularly if food were destined for the nearby school cafeteria and if students visited these fields to tend educational gardens. Not yet ready to give up on such an appealing farm, however, I scour the Internet for more information and pester a funny and helpful toxicologist at the Maine Board of Pesticides Control. She sends a report from the US Department of Health and Human Services that profiles chemicals likely to be found at Superfund sites, including dieldrin. Her report briefly addresses the toxicity of crops grown in contaminated soils, but information about food safety beyond cucurbits is limited. Instead she wryly suggests sticking a photo of the farm under my pillow to see what kind of dreams result, as someone who'd contacted her with similar concerns had done recently. "Do you have a pyramid?" she jokes.

How about remediation, treating the soil to remove contaminants? Some of my reading uncovers tantalizing possibilities. A type of iron called zero-valent binds with and rapidly degrades organochlorine pesticides, and a company based in Boulder, Colorado, has a proprietary blend of iron dust and biologically active organic matter that can apparently clean up contaminated sites. They spread the mix directly on farm fields, rototill, and irrigate heavily to accelerate biological activity. Sounds like it works relatively quickly and well, so I call for more information. My goal is modest: to clean the least contaminated ground to a depth of one foot, reducing levels from 38 ppb to 10 ppb. After a few days one of their technicians calls back with a quote: the price, materials only, to clean up an acre would be $112,200. Their CEO calls and leaves a voicemail message over the weekend to say that in practice this might cost much less—maybe half—because testing can pinpoint required application rates precisely.

Great, so they could treat the surface of much of these sixty acres for roughly $3.5 million, plus labor and equipment costs. Remediation might make sense when the intention is to build condos in an urban area, but it's never going to fly for working farmland. The most encouraging piece of information I learn is that organic farming can in itself accelerate the degradation of remaining chemicals. A fundamental difference between organic and conventional farming is that building soil with cover crops, manure, compost, and natural soil amendments rather than relying on processed fertilizers creates a biologically active soil. Flourishing native microorganisms not only process nutrients for plants, but also break down chemical contaminants. This is reassuring and even appealing, suggesting an opportunity to clean up a beautiful, compromised piece of farmland, but it's anyone's guess how long the process would take. Should I spend the rest of my life in atonement for someone else's past mistakes, repeatedly cover-cropping contaminated soil in an effort to clean it up for future generations?

Even without residual chemical concerns, however, this orchard is starting to look like the wrong fit. Diversifying tree plantings will require a substantial investment in equipment, nursery stock, and time. Building a small house, repairing the barns, and drilling a well would quickly add over $200,000, raising our stake above half a million. That's a risky debt load for a farm-based business. After making necessary investments we could only resell to another farmer, because the Maine Farmland Trust retains the right to block a sale even if the purchaser has in mind a gentleman's farm or private estate instead of a working farm. The idea behind this is good, that the land should remain in commercial production, but could we pay off our investment one day with such a small pool of potential buyers?

Thinking about purchasing this farm raises interesting questions about appropriate scale. Sixty acres of farmland may look like a lot to someone like me, but it's relatively small even by Maine's modest standards. This site is considerably larger than the average diversified organic market garden, which typically falls in the four- to twenty-acre range, yet it's smaller than most farms growing commodity crops for wholesale markets, like Maine potato farms and dairies. As in too much of contemporary life, it's hazardous to occupy the middle ground. A farm this size would produce too much to eliminate middlemen and sell directly to consumers at farmers' markets, but it would have a tough time competing anywhere else.

Running through numbers and thinking seriously about purchasing farmland is a helpful exercise in clear thinking for those of us who dream of laden fruit trees and misty meadows. Putting aside the high level of risk involved, if Karla and I were to move to this farm to pursue some kind of commercial operation, everything would change dramatically for us. Not having grown much for the market before—my previous experience managing a farm near Portland was for a nonprofit that gave away most of its food—trying to buy a large orchard quickly puts everything in perspective.

I've always bristled a little when people call me a farmer. Not because it's in any way offensive, but because the word seems off the mark, as though gardens have become stand-ins for disappearing family farms. Kitchen garden, market garden, farm, dairy, orchard—these boundaries and meanings have become pretty murky. Maine is experiencing rapid growth in the number of its farms, but many of these are small, labor-intensive start-ups that compete by minimizing cost inputs and avoiding wholesale distributors. Thus the proliferation of farmers' markets and CSA operations, and many "farms" that once would have been known as market gardens for their emphasis on handwork and diversified vegetable plantings. Unless we're all going to drop what we're doing to produce food, we also need the economy of scale of larger farms, and these begin with altogether different premises, an approach based on specialization and mechanization.

The truth is that at heart I'm a plant collector, not a farmer, and I don't want to lose sight of the essential nature of the garden while scaling up to develop a business. Growing for Karla and our friends encourages creative experimentation, whereas the pressures of farming dictate what to grow, weeding out poor sellers and underperformers. Take the commercial prospects of a beet as ugly as Bordo, for example, which in all likelihood you've never seen or eaten. Only a couple of small, obscure seed companies carry it, and I save my own seed by wintering the biennial roots in the cellar. Bordo bristles with stems growing along the top edge of an elongated root, looking a bit like a warthog's snout. How many customers would buy something like that? Nevertheless when a chef friend of mine roasted its roots last year, the rough skin transformed into a caramelized delicacy that contrasted beautifully with the sweet, bicolored flesh. She called it a revelation, her favorite discovery in my fields that season. Who knew?

In the name of efficiency it's all too easy to put finicky varieties like Bordo beets or Amazon Chocolate tomatoes on the back shelf. This is one of the reasons gardeners in places like France and Italy—anywhere people value high-quality food—roll up their sleeves to plant herbs and heirloom vegetables, put up preserves, and ferment their own ciders and wines. They're filling a gap left by commercial producers. Their concern isn't fundamentally about greater efficiency or productivity, but taste, friendship, family, culture, tradition, and identity. Gardening, not farming, is equally my starting point. Deep down I have to admit that I don't belong at this orchard, or any site with so much workable land.

This fall Karla and I have simultaneously explored other options—scanning real estate listings, touring properties, and hopping in the car to visit towns that until recently were only names on a map to us. Searching for land is a little addictive, with corresponding highs and lows. Anyone who's looked for real estate has stories of the perfect-sounding house listing, the one that neglects to mention early-morning blasts at the neighboring gravel pit, or plans to build a new power line through the backyard. Beyond such ordinary letdowns, as we weigh dreams of independence against hidden costs and constraints it feels like we're shopping for something completely anachronistic. Not looking for a three-bedroom colonial on 1.2 acres? How about a sliver of hay field with heavy clay soil, bordered by fifteen acres of forested wetland and ledge? In the end everything we come across seems too isolated, overpriced, ultimately unprofitable, or otherwise unappealing. There must be some other way.

Our search for land has made clear that we may not find everything we're looking for in one place, particularly if we hope to stay close to Portland. On a rural farm all the elements needed for growing and storing food—root cellars, greenhouses, storage sheds, tools, and equipment—can be neatly integrated. But unless we're willing and able to drop everything and move far from the city to find affordable land, that luxury escapes most of us today. Traditional New England farmsteads—timber-frame barns and white clapboard farmhouses, surrounded by woods and meadows—have largely disappeared in Portland's suburbs. Seventy-five years ago farmland spread inland from Portland in every direction, but today it's common to find commercial growers driving up to three hours to reach urban markets from affordable farmland to the west and north.

What opportunities remain in and around Portland? Last year I worked on an assessment of potential tillable land for a local farmer's alliance in nearby Cape Elizabeth, one of Portland's wealthiest suburbs, and with the exception of a handful of large landholdings found mostly garden-sized plots of less than half an acre. It's striking to see older photos of the town, its broad, open vistas contrasting markedly with today's wooded suburbs and seaside mansions. Cape Elizabeth historically supplied crops like lettuce, cabbage, and strawberries to markets throughout Maine and Massachusetts, but long-distance shipping and increased competition made business increasingly unprofitable after the Second World War. Few working farms survive anywhere near the outskirts of Portland today, and those that remain are typically well-established family businesses that go back many generations.

To develop something near the city I'll need to be flexible and adaptive, taking inspiration from others who overcome constraints in creative ways. Like the forty-something African American guy named David I met last year in New Orleans, for example, whose business traveled on the back of his pickup truck. For $60 he sold me a salvaged bicycle for my commute from the Garden District to Carrollton, where I was working on a community garden. Wherever David found space to park he pulled over and worked on the sidewalk, sorting through junk frames piled five deep on his truck until he had enough components to resurrect a bike. He drove around the neighborhood collecting parts, fixing broken bicycles, and selling his finished products.

As Karla and I turn away from the search for our own land and our desire to run a "real" farm, examples like David's seem increasingly appealing. On balance he appeared to get by pretty well. He ran a small, independent business that suited him, using simple resources readily at hand. Could I do something in this same spirit? Even in the absence of an intact, available farm within reach of Portland, in other words, everything I need might be scattered around in one form or another—unused greenhouses, barns, equipment, and small parcels of land. Starting with such resources would give me an opportunity to learn while slowly growing into something larger. The key would be to figure out how to assemble these fragments into a workable whole.

While thinking all this over, little by little it dawns on me that I'm already well on my way, collaborating in ways that suggest a path forward. "I shut the root cellar window last night," Meghan Wakefield tells me in a voicemail message soon after Karla and I put our property search on hold. "Hope that was okay." She rents the farmhouse where I tend my garden, and we exchange small favors like this all the time. With the owner's blessing I walled off a corner of her basement to create space for vegetable storage. Meghan shares this space, and she controls its temperature by opening and closing the window according to the weather. We have much the same arrangement in my greenhouse on the same property; she rolls up its sides and opens the doors on warmer days, and in return I water and tend her early-season plants. On a larger level I've done much the same for years to grow my gardens, exchanging time and labor for access to land and equipment. In such simple interactions have come a sense of community and shared responsibility. Could this be the foundation for something more?

Several years ago a friend of mine named James came to Portland for a weekend visit, and inadvertently reminded me that, despite the constraints of the city, growing space remains all around us. He grew up in the Northeast Kingdom of Vermont near St. Johnsbury, and in that isolated rural place developed a taste for apples growing wild in the back pastures of old homesteads. James never lost the habit of sampling whatever fruit he comes across, even after moving to suburban Massachusetts. As we drove north several years ago to go rowing and kayaking off Cape Breton Island in Nova Scotia, he made me stop to sample every abandoned apple tree along the way. Ten hours into the trip, pitch black outside, we argued as he called out, "Wait, pull over! Go back!"

During his visit to Portland we walked around my urban neighborhood, where he spotted a handful of pears on a gnarled old tree that had previously escaped my attention. It was struggling for light in a narrow alley, squeezed between overgrown lilacs and a maple tree. "Let's try one," he said. He picked one of its bruised fruits off the pavement and brushed it off, and I followed his lead, each of us taking a bite at the same time. For a brief moment we took in the flavor, then simultaneously spat out the highly astringent fruit. The variety was inedible, too bitter to swallow, best left to rot on the ground.

Half an hour later we drove over to South Portland to a favorite breakfast spot to cleanse our palates with coffee and bagels. But James couldn't hold back: First he had to taste an apple lying on the ground nearby. It had fallen from an old standard-sized tree wedged in a few square feet between the sidewalk and a large community college parking lot. The tree was twenty-five feet tall and at least seventy-five years old, possibly the last vestige of a forgotten farm. I hesitated, the taste of the pears still lingering, and let him take the first bite.

This time the fruit was so surprisingly flavorful that I returned the following spring to take cuttings and graft them to new rootstock. John Bunker has since identified the variety as most likely a Fameuse, or Snow Apple, one of the oldest on record. You can trace a line directly from this tree back to eighteenth-century Quebec, and from there to earliest written descriptions of Fameuse in seventeenth-century France. Here in South Portland the solitary Snow apple grows untended and neglected, but its fruit is largely free of disease and insect damage. Local residents know and love this tree; they converge on the spot every fall to glean its fruits.

It's becoming clear to me that my search for farmland has been something of a distraction from my real preservation goals. The truth is that I don't need sixty acres to grow trees, and that it would be much more prudent to expand slowly and collaborate with others than isolate ourselves on some remote homestead. Finding space to run a small nursery might be a better fit, with an acre or so for permanent plantings and trials. Cuttings from an orchard would support further propagation, and unsold stock could go back in the ground for evaluation and production. A nursery would encourage more people to make use of their own neglected spaces to grow rare foods, which would broaden and reinforce my conservation efforts.

One of the positive outcomes of exploring orchard production and searching for land, however, is that it's only strengthened my desire to grow fruit trees and berries. I've spent hours recently poring over my copy of the Seed Savers Exchange *Fruit, Berry and Nut Inventory,* the companion to their *Garden Seed Inventory,* and developing lists of highly desirable fruits. This is a dangerous book for anyone with slightly obsessive tendencies. It describes every mail-order nursery and commercially available fruit in the country—over five hundred varieties of peaches, three thousand apples, thousands of minor fruits like lingonberries and medlars, and on and on. I think back to my visit to the Geneva apple collection, dream about apricots and cherries, and wonder where this interest will lead me.

The *Fruit, Berry and Nut Inventory* describes foods like Clairgeau, a large French pear with a rich orange-yellow skin and melting flesh. It includes fruits like Smokehouse, a tasty nineteenth-century Pennsylvania apple descended from a chance seedling discovered behind the smokehouse of a man named William Gibbons. The name may stem partly from its mottled surface, which in John Bunker's words is "colored with a muted blend of yellows, greens and reddish browns," as though stained by a smoldering fire. It lists sources for Wolf River apples, an old Wisconsin variety with a long history in Maine, much prized for baking when stuffed with mincemeat and hazelnuts. And it describes Green Gage plums, which fruit explorer David Karp—who lives in Southern California and travels the world to taste exotic foods—calls his favorite fruit. By the middle of the eighteenth century Green Gage was celebrated in the New World as much as in its French homeland, and George Washington and Thomas Jefferson grew it on their plantations. What more can anyone ask?

By now it's January 2010, peak season for the mail-order nursery trade, and my newfound enthusiasm for fruit trees raises some difficult questions. The window for ordering plants through the mail, typically the only way to purchase interesting fruit varieties, comes around only once a year. In a month or so many of the most desirable plants will sell out, and these will need to ship before they break dormancy in the spring. Although it isn't clear where I can plant trees—the only space available is my third-of-an-acre garden plot, which is already maxed out with vegetable plantings—holding off another year to get started is a discouraging thought.

Waiting would be prudent, as would signing a lease on some land, writing a business plan, and developing a carefully selected list of fruits tailored to the market. But then again the best-laid plans often go awry in this line of work. Life is short, fruit trees take many years to mature, and flying by the seat of my pants may not be such a bad alternative. In the end the decision effectively makes itself. I throw caution aside, finalize varietal lists, settle on nurseries with good reputations, place my orders, and leave just one thing to chance: where to grow and what to do with the approximately 250 fruit trees and 750 berry plants that will arrive on our doorstep in the early spring. Not having a clear plan is a little disturbing, but, worst-case scenario, the plants can remain in pots for a season or two.

In the midst of this activity the Maine Farmland Trust sends an updated FarmLink list of properties for sale or lease. This includes

descriptions of 167 farms scattered throughout Maine's sixteen counties, ranging from a ninety-five-acre Christmas tree operation and
hunting lodge in far northern Aroostook County to a saltwater farm
with deepwater ocean frontage on Beals Island near Jonesport, close
to the Canadian border. These properties run the gamut of Maine
food production: potato fields, orchards, greenhouses, cornfields,
woodlots, dairy and cattle operations, vegetable and berry fields.
Some are for sale, but most offer long-term leases and a variety
of creative partnerships and living arrangements. Descriptions
range from low-key to boisterous. "This gorgeous saltwater farm is
ready to be brought back into action!" reads one. "Owner is VERY
enthusiastic about getting someone on the land and seeing it remain
active. Call today!" Prospective farmers can move into "wonderfully
livable" farmhouses, cabins, yurts, and trailers, or build something
on their own. One of my favorites is a homesteader searching for
others "who want to develop a viable peasant lifestyle for our area."

While scrolling through listings for Portland's Cumberland
County, one of the descriptions immediately catches my eye: "2
tillable acres in Cape Elizabeth, looking for a manager or business partner. Continue current cut flowers and expand vegetables
inventory. Not opposed to a greenhouse. Property is less than 15
minutes to Portland. New drilled well, with 12-15 gal/min. Might
be suitable for field trials or permaculture." Farm ID: 888.

I know Cape Elizabeth land well, and can't imagine this could
be anything but Rodney Voisine's property. Have Mary Ellen and
Austin Chadd moved on? If the listing is correct and his land is
available, it could work out perfectly. Rodney's field is about a
quarter mile from my existing garden, nearly connected by an
old logging road through the woods. It would be easy to borrow
equipment at my current site and drive to Rodney's for occasional
tilling and tractor work. The listing seems too good to be true, but
an e-mail from MFT confirms it. They forward Rodney's address
and phone number.

"I'm not actually looking for someone this season," Rodney
tells me when I reach him on the phone the next day. He didn't
realize the post was still up on FarmLink. It was more than a year
old and predated the Chadds' arrival. He confirms that Mary Ellen

and Austin have moved on, however. They've found a larger piece of land for themselves where they can expand their vegetable operation. "I've been planning to let the field go back to meadow," Rodney tells me, "but I'm happy you called." He's willing to sit down to talk over ideas, and maybe we can work something out. "Are you available next week?" he asks.

It feels a little strange to enter the stone gates at the entrance to Rodney's property and make my way up the winding driveway to his imposing house in search of farmland. Nevertheless I park beside the large barn and knock on the door to meet with him. Inside the kitchen three Portuguese terriers swarm around me in greeting, wagging their tails and competing for attention. Rodney offers me coffee and we sit at a nearby table looking out over the snow-covered gardens and fields. His demeanor is at once warm and business-like, no-nonsense but flexible and open to ideas—a winning combination. His energy is infectious. He talks rapidly and seems tireless; it's impossible to guess from his appearance that he's just returned from a twenty-four-hour shift at the hospital. A full night's sleep behind me, I try to be lucid and pretend to keep up.

It takes less than half an hour for us to come to an agreement. "We'll want to keep the edges of the field mowed off, to control the bittersweet vines," Rodney tells me. In return for loaning his van, letting me cut and sell flowers from his extensive perennial beds, covering the insurance, sharing space in the barn, helping to buy vegetable seedlings, lending me tools, and leasing over an acre of land, he's asking $500 in rent. One invaluable bonus is access to the Portland Farmers' Market through his long-standing flower business. It's nearly impossible to acquire a permit at this crowded market. He'll let me plant fruit trees and berries, and we agree to discuss some kind of buyback plan by which he'd reimburse me for tree-planting costs in the event of my departure. He also offers to front money for a seasonal loan, and harvest fruit from his 4,000-square-foot planting of saskatoon berries, otherwise known as serviceberries or shadbush. From Rodney's perspective, I'll promote his Old Ocean House Farms brand, keep the fields tended and weeded, and preserve his spot at the farmers' market. All of this seems more than fair, a good exchange.

Over the course of the next month we finalize details and make plans for the year ahead. In March I'll pot up as many trees and berries as can fit inside my greenhouse, getting a jump on the season and prepping them for nursery sales. By late May they'll be large enough to transplant, and they can go to market on a utility trailer behind Rodney's van. Nursery plants will fill our stand at the farmers' market through the end of June, until vegetable and cut flower sales kick into high gear. I may hire occasional day labor, or work with someone Rodney suggests who's helped at the farm before, but largely I'll manage alone until I gain a better understanding of the cash flow. There's a sense of inevitability to all this, an easy decision. In one stroke the outlines of a season that seemed such a gamble, so full of uncertainties, are laid out before me like a road map. It feels right.

Nine

DIVERSE FOODS IN THE MARKET

*A*s snow begins to retreat off my garden beds in late March, revealing the remains of last fall's weeds, mulch, and plant debris pressed flat to the ground like a layer of parchment, everything seems deceptively straightforward. The fields look blank and clean, plant lists and stored racks of seeds promise a kind of order for the season ahead, and four restful months have dimmed my memories of last summer's hard work.

This year will be something altogether new and different. Already by early spring I'm scrambling to organize plantings, arrange permits and licenses, design and build a market display, and track down materials of all kinds, from ingredients for organic soil mixes to stakes for securing young trees. My time divides between the computer—searching online for planting pots, for example (which turn up cheaply through Craigslist at two recently closed nurseries)—and hands-on work like sorting and organizing planting materials in my nursery space.

I need mulch hay for berry plantings, but it's in short supply due to last summer's cold, wet season. Southern Maine farmers either couldn't mow in the rainy weather, or lost cuttings when hay began to mold and rot in the field. Living in rural Washington State back in the 1990s spoiled me, because land and hay fields are plentiful there and water-damaged bales are generally free for the taking. The same would be true farther from Portland here in Maine, but most of what's available in this area is clean hay or straw trucked from northern Aroostook County. It's hard to pay market price for feed hay stored several months in a dry barn, and it feels wasteful to use it as mulch. Nevertheless I track down someone selling bales, hook a trailer to my station wagon, and drive out to his small farm.

It takes a couple of minutes to turn the car and trailer around in his driveway, avoiding a tractor parked on one side and deep mud ruts on the other. Horse paddocks and a couple of acres of pasture fan out around his two barns. The first houses the horses, while the second is filled with hay. I leave my car at the hay barn and walk over to the house, where the farmer greets me brusquely at his kitchen door, breathing heavily from an oxygen tank. "If you want less than a hundred bales they'll cost $5 each," he tells me straight off, a dollar higher than he'd quoted over the phone. Factor in the cost of shipping and storage, he's barely breaking even, so I smile and nod agreement. He looks disappointed.

I drop the gate on the trailer and start hauling bales out of the barn, threading my way between puddles and the driveway's slick mud. A few minutes later the farmer watches from his kitchen window and, apparently, comes up with new reasons to be disagreeable. Whether it's my Subaru station wagon or something about my appearance, he's pegged me for an organic grower—in his eyes an innocent with a rosy view of the world's possibilities, full of half-baked ideas. Someone he needs to set straight. He stumbles out his door, hops on an ATV, and drives across the yard to look for an argument.

"You know, chemicals are safe, I've been spraying all my life and it hasn't done me any harm," he tells me as a conversation starter. Fine, I think, this isn't an argument that appeals to me. "You can't grow blueberries around here without chemical herbicides and pesticides, and you can't feed the world with organic agriculture," he says. In other words, we'd all starve if things were left to people like me. I want to ask him why, exactly, he'd want me to spray chemicals when there hasn't been any particular need to do so in my fields. Should I douse my raspberries and strawberries in captan to prevent fungal growth, even though good sanitation and crop rotations have kept the fruit clean year after year? I can't speak for problems encountered by larger growers, but my gardens get by just fine.

I avoid taking the bait, finish loading my trailer, write a check, and stick around for a few minutes to ask questions and see if we can find any common ground. Maybe I can learn something from him. In the end somehow we strike a positive note, even have a productive exchange. We talk about how to build a hotbed, an actively fermenting compost pile that supplies heat to a small greenhouse or glass-covered frame. At one time he'd built hotbeds using a mix of chicken manure and wood shavings. The compost has to be assembled with materials that jump-start biological activity in the early-spring cold, and the timing has to be right so it can generate heat for young seedlings. He explains his technique, stops looking for a fight, and shares what he knows.

My trailer is filled to the top with thirty hay bales. I pull slowly onto the road and drive carefully back to my gardens a few miles away. Parking close to the field, I stack hay along one edge and dig snow and ice away from the greenhouse door. Inside it's a different world, an emerging garden filled with hardy greens like kale, sage, lettuce, and chard, all of which survived the winter without supplemental heat. The sun is shining and it's topping seventy degrees in here under the single layer of plastic, though hovering in the low forties outside. Already some of the kales are sending out new leaves and starting to bud, their tips tender and sweet, as good as newly emerged asparagus shoots in May. Everything is returning to life quickly in the warmth and light of early spring.

I bought this seventy-five-foot-long, fourteen-foot-wide hoophouse—a simple, lightweight structure made from bent steel poles covered in plastic—two years ago from a ramshackle farm in Massachusetts. An AmeriCorps volunteer helped knock hornet nests off its frame, pull chest-high weeds away from its doors, hack away rusted bolts to free the posts, and break it down into pieces that fit easily in the back of a U-Haul truck. After several hours of demolition we carted everything back to Maine and reconstructed the frame in a sunny corner of my borrowed field. At first the structure looked very ragged, covered loosely in salvaged plastic tacked in place with scrap wood, but a new plastic sheet and doors for the end walls improved its appearance.

Thanks to the generosity of owner Peter Eastman and his son John, my gardens and greenhouse have found a semipermanent home on this small farm a few doors down from Rodney Voisine's property. In exchange for being here on this one-third-acre corner of the field, I've helped out with various projects—rebuilding rotting sills on the barn's doorsteps, fixing broken windows, tending flower gardens, and caring for the dozen or so apple trees Peter's father planted in the 1920s. This is my fifth year growing on this site, a continuity that's surprising in light of how much my other gardens have moved around.

As fog begins to roll in and wind whips the treetops, I pull on extra layers and head outside to finish inspecting the gardens. In a corner of the field near the woods one of my young Montmorency cherry trees has been ripped to shreds—the work of a raccoon or skunk looking for insects, or hungry enough to feed on the bark? Nearby rows of parsnips show emergent green leaves even as snow retreats off the beds. I dig a few out and my fingers numb instantly in the half-frozen mud. It's well worth the trouble for these flavorful vegetables, their sweetness intensified by the winter cold, which raises their sugar levels. I walk over to the farmhouse, brush snow off the cellar entrance, and duck inside. "Can you check on my leeks?" the Eastmans' tenant Meghan calls out as she hears me descending the stairs toward our shared root cellar. These are her favorite vegetables. "I'll bring some up to the kitchen," I tell her.

Down in the cellar turnips have sprouted small, blanched leaves, potatoes look clean and firm in their paper bags, and Meghan's leeks, stored with their roots in damp sand, have lost their vivid green hues but nevertheless survived the winter intact. If we hadn't already eaten our way through beets and carrots they'd also be in fine shape. These will keep well into June in a good cellar. In comparison heavily mulched beets in the field are past saving, hollowed out and rotting, their remaining flesh nibbled down to nothing. Mice discovered this insulated cache and made nests among the frost-sweetened roots. I give up trying to salvage any of the beets outdoors, push their protective mulch back into place, and leave what remains of the feast to the mice.

What will it be like to dig root crops to sell and worry as much about the way they look as how they taste? Will this work remain gratifying and enjoyable when growing for market? My only previous experience selling at a farmers' market was in Washington State, when a girlfriend persuaded me to set a table among regular vendors one Saturday and pile it high with nothing but surplus collard greens from our garden. We stood around talking with friends most of the morning, and in the end sold just one bunch. "Ewww, collard greens," is the only comment I remember. This is going to be a steep learning curve.

After closing up the cellar I stop to pick some kale from the greenhouse, throwing it in my bucket next to the parsnips and potatoes and wiping my hands on the front of my pants. Nothing wrong with a little dirt on the leaves and on my clothing; it feels good to connect with the earth after a long winter indoors. I toss the vegetables in the car and wash everything later in our large kitchen sink, collecting mud from root crops in the bottom of the bucket. By now the sun is setting, so I open the side window in the kitchen, the one that looks out into a neighbor's untended backyard, and dump the muck and muddy water into the urban jungle.

Even now, at the end of March, the tail end of a long Maine winter, last year's season lingers in our kitchen, the dining room, and throughout the house. Harvests are months away, but canned fruits and vegetables, and storage crops like onions, garlic, and squash, are piled everywhere. A Boston Marrow squash, close relative of Hubbards brought to New England from Argentina in the 1780s, lived on the chest in our entrance hall until we gave it away. A forty-five-pound orange giant nearly three feet across, it was an awkward beauty that dwarfed the oven. Other squashes line the sideboard, and the last of the fall pumpkins hang on in a spare room. What's left is either art or clutter; depends on your point of view.

A week later Karla helps me set up a temporary growing station in our front bedroom to start heat-loving vegetables like tomatoes, peppers, and eggplants. The greenhouse won't be ready for seedlings until later in April, because until then nights will be too cold for tender new plants inside an unheated hoophouse. It's expensive to heat a greenhouse in early spring, and for my purposes unnecessary. Seedlings germinate well in small trays in a warm room at home, and can stay there for two weeks. When they outgrow this limited space, they can go into cold frames inside the hoophouse. These cold frames are essentially four-foot-tall, eight-by-twelve-foot mini-greenhouses constructed from rough-sawn lumber and polycarbonate plastic panels. They create a warm and protected environment that can be supplemented at night if necessary with a temperature-regulated electric space heater. In recent years I've raised thousands of seed-lings this way with minimal energy input and very little cost, using the heater only a handful of times during cold snaps.

Karla watches patiently as I pull back the edge of the rug in our bedroom and lay down a sheet of plastic to protect the floor. Together we lift the heavy bed frame, roll the rug to the side of the room, and set a piece of concrete fiberboard on two sawhorses to hold the seed flats. Karla picks up a spray bottle and fills it with water from the bathtub tap while I start sowing seeds into trays filled with potting soil. Soon our cheerful little bedroom is trans-formed into a horticultural production line, complete with buzzing fluorescent lights slung low over the containers farthest from the window. "Can we keep the door shut so the thermostat controls the room's temperature?" I ask hesitantly. The room will need to stay above seventy degrees for good germination. Patient and agree-able, somehow Karla takes all this in with a smile.

Karla pitches in wherever she can, wishing she could take a more active role in the gardens. She has wonderful memories of her great-grandfather's dairy farm and orchard, and childhood expe-riences of the countryside in central Maine. Secretly I'm relieved there's only one fruit and vegetable collector in the house, however. Her broader interests—from environmental science and computer programming to sea kayaking—are a healthy balance to my slightly obsessive tendencies, and her willingness to help with projects like this reinforces the strong bond between us. Keeping the pressures of our professional lives separate ensures that, when we do work together, it will be fun and pleasurable. It also doesn't hurt that she's an outstanding, creative cook. I'm not bad in the kitchen, but my place is at the sink washing dishes when Karla is around. She brings out the best in foods fresh from the garden.

My hoophouse won't be ready for heat-loving plants like peppers and tomatoes until the weather warms, but already by early April the soil within it registers nearly twenty degrees higher than the ground outside, more than warm enough for cool-weather crops. On a clear day I return to plant under one of the cold frames. I ditch my coat to bask in the warm sunshine and take time to savor the work, slowly loosening the soil with a pitchfork and feeling neglected muscles come back to life. The ground is baked dry, and it raises dust with every turn. Watering in newly planted beds of arugula, Italian flat-leaved parsley, celery, spinach, mustard, and lettuce seems to take forever. After several passes with a garden hose the soil finally reaches its saturation point. The earth feels dark and rich, warm to the touch. Seedlings will sprout quickly in this protected space.

Owning a greenhouse means no more begging for space at local farms in early spring, or sharing a corner of a tired old hoophouse at a local garden center, surrounded by piles of flea-market junk. Last year I used this greenhouse to start seedlings, grow early-season vegetables, ripen heat-loving plants like tomatoes over the summer (despite the outbreak of late blight), and extend the growing season with hardy greens. This spring I'm adding another use, and every square foot of available space not devoted to vegetables is now filled with fruit trees and berry bushes. In the middle of March I potted roughly half of my 250 apple, peach, pear, cherry, plum, and apricot trees, as well as hundreds of berries, to sell at the farmers' market. The rest are stored in the root cellar until they can go directly into Rodney's field alongside flowers and vegetables. The trees have leafed out quickly in the greenhouse warmth and by early April have already started putting on new growth.

With new beds in the greenhouse planted and watered, I head over to the root cellar to collect apple rootstocks and begin grafting. The remainder of my mail-order nursery trees and berries are crowded into a corner of the cellar, their roots buried in damp compost. They need to remain dormant in cool, dark conditions until the ground warms up enough to plant in another couple of weeks.

The apple rootstocks I've purchased through the mail are easy to distinguish from the rest—they're tied into bundles of what look like half-inch-diameter sticks, clipped neatly at a height of about twenty inches, with spindly roots trailing from their bases. I carry them outside and close the cellar to keep it cool.

Spring grafting of dormant fruit tree cuttings (scions), attaching them to newly propagated rootstocks, is called bench-grafting. This is a common way to acquire new varieties, because scions—cuttings taken off tree branches in March from the previous season's growth—are easy to store and ship, and can keep up to two months if they remain moist and cool in a cellar or the back of a refrigerator (they need to remain away from fruits and vegetables like tomatoes, which release ethylene gas that can cause scions to break dormancy). The scion determines the variety of fruit, while the rootstock it's grafted to governs its mature height and other growth habits. Though some fruits like plums and peaches can share rootstocks because they're in the same genus, apples must be grafted to apple rootstocks, and pears to pears. A scion from an antique apple like Fall Wine, for example, could be grafted to a modern dwarfing rootstock like Geneva 16 to produce a tree roughly eight feet tall. The same scion attached to a standard-sized rootstock will produce identical apples on a much larger tree.

Grafting trees is often the only way to acquire obscure varieties, and it immediately opens up a world of collecting possibilities. Having learned to graft over the past few years, this season I've acquired all sorts of unusual fruits from other growers to expand my trials, and scoured the Seed Savers Exchange *Fruit, Berry and Nut Inventory* for varieties that remain commercially available. Although this SSE publication lists thousands of fruits, many of these are available only as scions or for custom grafting, because market niches are too small to sustain nursery production. The fruits listed here are a true cornucopia, but their future is precarious because large numbers are available from only one or two sources. Retiring hobbyists and shifts in the nursery business can lead to losses for all kinds of rare fruits.

One small nursery in Yoncalla, Oregon, crops up repeatedly in my search. The Spearheart Farm and Orchard, Nick Botner's one-man operation, offers thousands of apples, pears, cherries, plums, quince, and grapes, thirty-three hundred varieties in all. His is the largest private collection of fruit in the country. Send him an envelope and $5, and in exchange he forwards his "catalog"— fifteen pages of varietal names, single-spaced in a small font, five columns, no descriptions. If you don't know exactly what you're looking for, information may be available somewhere else. Or it may not; much of what he sells is very obscure. Spearheart sells only scions, no grafted nursery trees, and the cost is $5 apiece. If you want any of these rare fruits, you need to buy rootstocks through another nursery and graft them yourself.

Now in his mid-eighties, Botner has been collecting trees for thirty years, ever since moving to his seven acres of land in Oregon from a homestead in Alaska. He plants as closely as three feet apart on dwarf rootstocks to maximize diversity on his limited land. Many of his trees are available nowhere else: Sweet McIntosh apples, whose balanced flavor and crispness captured my imagination at the Geneva plant station; Duchess D'Angouleme dessert pears, a variety historically grown in New England; and cider pears like Winnals Longdon and Taynton Squash. I order these and thirty other varieties, recognizing them only through written descriptions published elsewhere, if that. Some I know nothing about; their names captivate me and I take a chance. (Note: In the following year, 2011, Nick Botner retired and closed the nursery. An organization called the Home Orchard Society is now working to preserve his collection.)

As I head outside from the cellar with rootstocks in hand, I stop by the barn to grab my tools and two packages of scions, which are wrapped in damp paper towels and plastic bags. After setting up a grafting station in the sunshine, I heel the rootstocks into damp mulch in a wheelbarrow to keep them from drying out, arrange Nick Botner's scions on the bench, and organize a variety of supplies: grafting tape and wax, a Swiss grafting knife, masking tape and markers for temporary labels, and a bleach solution to keep the tools sterile.

One by one I select a scion whose diameter matches a section of rootstock, cut each on the diagonal, align the two pieces so they fit together precisely, wrap the joint with grafting tape to secure it, and cover the union with grafting wax for good measure. I label each new tree and place its roots back in the mulch. At the end of the day the wheelbarrow fills with what look like rows of bandaged sticks, and they're nearly as vulnerable as they appear. Grafting demands care and craftsmanship. Doing it well, seeing buds break open successfully and new branches emerge over the course of several weeks, is one of the most gratifying of all experiences in the garden. Aligning grafts poorly, or planting too early before hard frosts have passed, limits the percentage of grafts that will "take" and grow. When all the grafts are finished I return the trees to the cellar for safekeeping until it's time to set them in the garden toward the end of the month.

My pace accelerates as the weeks go by and the weather warms. Toward the latter part of April I move young seedlings into the greenhouse, transplant newly grafted fruit trees, and start planting rows of greens and peas directly in the garden. None of this can wait, and neither can business planning and paperwork. Vegetables and flowers will sell at the market under Rodney's Old Ocean House Farms label, but I've set up my own business for the nursery, giving it the name Origins Fruit. This required registration as a limited liability company, licensing for nursery production, and filing for state sales tax payments. My new website, www.originsfruit.com, advertises nursery plants. It lists pears, peaches, cherries, apricots, plums, and small fruits like strawberries and highbush blueberries—every fruit tree and berry that I'll sell this year, from old-time cooking apples like Rhode Island Greening to more recently developed dessert varieties like Keepsake. It's hard to guess which fruits will sell or in what volume, but no one else at Portland's busy farmers' market is carrying any of these plants, and local nurseries stock a limited range. It's worth a shot.

On a warm sunny day later in April, the twenty-year-old son of a friend of mine parks in the driveway by Rodney's barn and walks over to say hello. A sometime horticulture student, he's helping me plant trees for the day and begin prepping ground at my new site. He stands a bit hunched in the cold with his hands buried deep in the pockets of his hoodie, and we talk about orchards and fruit trees, which seem to interest him. This is something different from the landscaping jobs he usually picks up. He's had a rough night, though, and needs to make a few phone calls before starting work, something about a break-in at his apartment.

While he sorts things out I start digging planting holes and setting posts. Time is short for getting the remaining half of my tree order into the ground before the season becomes any busier. The farmers' market starts in two weeks, and meanwhile there are 125 trees to plant and secure to permanent stakes, hundreds of berry bushes to pot up or plant, cool-weather vegetables to transplant and direct-seed, ground to prepare, and a market display to construct. I feel reasonably confident about staying on top of everything, but a little help isn't such a bad idea from time to time.

Each of my newly purchased two-year-old apple trees on dwarfing rootstocks needs support, because their roots won't be deep enough to stand up against heavy wind. There are many ways for growers to do this, and after much research I've come up with an approach that seems reasonably affordable and effective. Planting holes will be spaced closely, varying somewhat with the four different rootstocks I'm using, but averaging seven feet between trees in a row. A fourteen-foot distance separating rows should suffice to allow a tractor and tiller to pass once the trees grow in. This will also leave enough room to grow vegetables, at least in the first few years. Roughly a third of the gardens will eventually switch over entirely to fruit as trees gradually shade the ground. Most apple trees will grow using the "central spindle" method, in which the main trunk winds around a post, with the leading branch (called the central leader) tied off at roughly a sixty-degree angle. Tipping the leader slows the tree's growth, further dwarfing it, and sends a hormonal signal to the tree to produce more fruit.

Commercial growers often use preservative-soaked, pressure-treated posts as tree supports. These are relatively cheap and can last many years in the ground. In recent years chemical treatments have become less toxic, but nevertheless using pressure-treated wood voids organic certification, and I wouldn't want to introduce these chemicals to my garden. Instead I'm substituting two-foot sections of plastic pipe buried vertically, with the ends protruding slightly above ground level. Once my trees outgrow shorter stakes I'll drop eight-foot-tall, untreated hemlock posts into the buried pipes. Eliminating ground contact helps posts last longer, and they can slide out for replacement without disturbing the soil or tree roots.

Finished at last with his other business, my helper comes over to dig postholes and plant apple trees with me. One by one we dig two feet down, tamp a pipe into place with a heavy bar, slide in a stake, and plant a tree beside it. It's hard work for little-used muscles, like waking up one day to drive spikes for the railroad. We make good progress, however, planting a dozen trees in the first three hours, tying them off to their stakes with one-foot sections of bicycle inner tubes, and bending the central leader to its desired angle. At one time I used to secure trees to stakes with lightweight garden twine, but this doesn't work very well. When the twine isn't rotting and falling off, leaving trees at the mercy of the next strong wind, it tends to bury itself deeply in the bark, requiring surgery with a grafting knife. Two abandoned inner tubes tossed in a neighbor's trash bin suggested this better solution, and the owner of a local bike shop is more than happy to provide a steady supply of punctured tubes. He disappears into the basement when he sees me coming and returns with an armload slung over his shoulder.

It's impossible to know exactly what the coming season has in store. Drought or heavy rain, a cold summer or intense heat—each season is variable and unpredictable. I face the next few months with a cabinet of heirloom seeds, a greenhouse filled with plants, an assortment of newly purchased or borrowed tools and equipment, the approximation of a business plan in my head, and the goodwill of generous property owners. Will my nursery plants find a receptive audience at the market stand, and will there be enough products to stock it fully week after week? Covering the season opening in two weeks will be easy enough, thanks to squashes and root crops left over from last season, plus berry plants and early-season greens. But will my supply last until the next round of early-summer harvests? And how many customers will buy vegetables from me at Portland's very competitive market?

A couple of months later the sound of a marimba wakes me out of a deep sleep. Our bedroom is pitch black as I fumble for my phone and turn off the alarm, then roll out of bed and pull on my work clothes. It's four forty-five Saturday morning, about four hours before I'd like to get up. Time is short, however. The earliest farmers will have already arrived to set up their stands in Portland's Deering Oaks park. My travel time is less than anyone else's, about five minutes, but competition for space can be intense in this busy market. I hurry downstairs, grab something out of the fridge to eat later on, carry my cash box to the loaded van, and drive through the city's deserted streets to reach the market by five fifteen.

As usual I'm one of the last to arrive. Space at my end of the market has gotten tighter each week as surrounding displays have expanded with the season. I jockey for position along the park access road that serves as Portland's Saturday market, angle in as close as possible to a neighboring farmer's truck, and start unloading my utility trailer. A few of the farmers banter back and forth, while others are lost in their own worlds, arranging tables, sorting produce, chalking up signs. Most enjoy the chance to interact with the public, though some shy away from intense social immersion and look forward to returning to the solitude of their fields. On the whole they look pretty tired, and with good reason—in many cases they've been awake since 2 AM loading trucks and traveling up to three hours from distant farms in central Maine.

One of the farmers stops by with a clipboard in hand. "I'm taking orders for breakfast sandwiches," she tells me. This is something new, an experiment. She's placing a group order with a local cooperative restaurant. "Can't say no to that. How soon will they be ready?" I ask. "About two hours," she tells me, factoring in the time involved in collecting orders, waiting for the food to cook, and driving up the hill to retrieve it. A little deflated, I tell her that's okay. Delayed gratification will only improve my appetite. "Do you want bacon with your eggs?" she asks. Um, yes. It's local, sourced by people I trust, too hard to resist even though I'm placing my order with a vegan Rastafarian. She smiles warmly and promises to come back as soon as she can.

After setting up my market display I take a few minutes to walk the length of the market, see what's available at other stands, check on prices, and say hello to friends. The breadth and quality of produce on display here is humbling—particularly the outstanding selection of early-season vegetables offered by farmers like Chris Cavendish and Daniel Price. Daniel, dressed as always in Carhartt work pants and a T-shirt, a baseball cap pulled low over his eyes and his hair pulled back in a ponytail, is carrying a handful of hybrid Japanese turnips. "Take the Hakurei challenge," he says with a smile, urging me to try one of these perfectly round, smooth white roots for breakfast. The texture is excellent, crisp and not at all fibrous, but to my taste it could have a little more bite, even at six thirty in the morning. I'll hold out for the deep flavor of rutabagas sweetened by cool fall nights.

Having never imagined that retail would suit me, my pleasure in the past few weeks selling Rodney's cut flowers and my now certified organic vegetables, as well as nursery crops, has come as a surprise. To be honest this work isn't exactly representative of most direct sales, though—the Portland farmers' market is as much a weekly street festival as shopping venue. Nothing in this scene would be familiar to the guy behind the counter at the auto parts store down the road: the energetic buzz, musicians stopping by to play everything from banjos to double bass, cheerful customers trying to pay more than the asking price. What feels like half the town parades in front of my stand each week, friends come over to say hello, and people reach out from all directions to hand me cash. That it's mostly ones and fives doesn't seem to matter; it still feels like Christmas.

Nursery plants have sold well. I bring a few fruit trees to market each week and hand out lists printed from my website to describe the rest of the inventory. Customers arrange times to meet later at the garden to select their trees. My market display also includes as many berry bushes as can fit on the trailer, and these sell quickly. Prices are typically lower than local nurseries, and the fruit selection emphasizes flavor. Upon tallying the cost of blueberry bushes, grapevines, or raspberry canes, many customers ask "That's it?" Maybe my margins could increase a little.

Every week through midsummer I answer the same frequently asked questions about nursery plants, and yet everyone's enthusiasm generally keeps them from becoming tiresome. How much sun do strawberry plants require? How much sun do apple trees need?

And how about raspberries, do they need a lot of sun? Can you grow blueberries in pots? How do you prune blackberries? Other conversations provide unexpected leads, like information about a pear tree growing in someone's yard, an unknown variety, a tree roughly sixty feet tall that produces bumper crops of good fruit. A Russian woman stops by to ask about sour cherries. When she inquires about black currants I tell her I'm sorry, I can't sell them legally in southern Maine (because currants can be host plants for white pine blister rust). "Then sell them to me illegally," she says quietly, leaning in close with a knowing smile.

In my mind every peach tree, grapevine, or strawberry plant sold this year has become part of a network, a link that extends my own trials and experimentation. Customers stop by frequently over the summer to tell me how their plants are faring. One tiny elderly woman in oversized dark glasses peppers me with questions and struggles to select exactly the right strawberry plant from a flat of virtually identical clones in early June. She provides updates about its good health every time she sees me. "My plant looks good," she tells me. One day in August, however, she pulls me aside to say, "I think my plant is dead." The leaves have disappeared, and she has no idea what happened. "Does it look like something ate it?" I ask her. No. "Did you give it plenty of water?" Yes, it was in a small pot that dried out quickly on the deck, so she was very careful. Except, oh, yes, she did recently leave town for two weeks to visit her daughter. On her return she noticed the plant had died. I tell her if it doesn't bounce back to let me know and I'll replace it (which I do two weeks later). "You're honest," she tells me, "I'm going to buy something else." For a brief moment she eyes my stand, scanning the remaining nursery plants and a variety of peak summer vegetables like tomatoes, peppers, and summer squash. "But there's nothing else I want," she says with a grimace, and walks away.

A large part of my goal in starting this nursery has been to harness the power of the market to help spread biodiversity and bring it back into the community. While selling trees and berry plants I've started a database of people interested in growing fruit and preserving historic varieties. As much as this is a commercial enterprise, and my goal is to make money doing it, it's also a stab at collaboration—helping customers plant, prune, and maintain trees teaches me about their idiosyncrasies (the plants, not the customers, although I see and learn from both). My customers gain access to interesting foods; I gain sales and information.

Last winter I could have started a nonprofit, formed a board, written a few grants, given heirloom trees away, and taught people how to maintain them. This might have met with some success, but is there really any better way to find motivated growers than by asking them to pay for the privilege of participating? It keeps everyone honest and gives others a stake in the plants' survival. A farm stand feels like the purest form of market capitalism, the win–win of mutually beneficial trade. Most customers have no idea they're supporting a project trying to preserve agricultural diversity. They're simply buying desirable trees and berries.

By late summer it's clear Maine farmers are having one of their best years in recent memory. The season has been warm, the rainfall adequate, and pests and diseases have stayed in check. My sales of vegetables have been weaker than expected, mostly due to stiff competition, but nursery sales are in line with my supply. Rodney has been unfailingly helpful and supportive. His flowers have added immeasurably to the market display, while chefs have loved his saskatoon berries, known for their sweet, nutty flavor and high antioxidant values. In September customers can't get enough cider from my new press, and honey from Karla's two hives. Her bees forage mostly from Japanese knotweed, an invasive plant related to buckwheat, and produce from its flowers some of the best honey we've ever tasted.

"Can you explain what you're doing these days?" a friend asks as we linger in an old Grange hall near Portland following a local foods event, a week after the end of my first season. Another stops simultaneously to ask whether I've recovered. "What do you mean; recovered from what?" I ask him. "The growing season," he tells me. Of course, as though gardening is an affliction. The three of us laugh, even though he meant this as a serious question. "It's too soon to tell," I say. And my reply to the first question, what are my plans? I go through the litany and follow up with "in other words, I'm not exactly sure yet."

This first foray into the market worked out very well, in my opinion. Physically I held up fine, and somehow never felt rushed or overly stressed because the gardens were sized about right. They covered only about three-quarters of an acre, with the remainder of my leased space pulled out of production, cover-cropped and tilled to suppress weed growth. This much land produced more than enough seasonal vegetables and herbs to fill my busy stand and sell to a few small restaurant accounts. Springtime nursery production flowed smoothly into summer vegetables and cut flowers, and as these tapered off in the fall cider and honey picked up the slack. Everything played out as I'd imagined. The work felt manageable and on many levels satisfying. Setting plans in motion and turning ideas into tangible results has been very pleasurable and rewarding.

And yet many hours spent alone weeding a market garden provide something more than an opportunity for reflection. Two things have become abundantly clear from this year's experience: (a) For me the isolation is unsustainable; and (b) pressure to produce marketable products works against my collecting interests. Although my gardens nearly tripled in size this year, their diversity dropped roughly by half, at least among vegetables, as I focused on those with the highest yields and best sales potential. It was a worthwhile sacrifice for the market experience and the opportunity to maintain an active stand, for one season. Next year I'll want to stay true to my conservation goals while finding ways to make the work more sociable and enjoyable. What will this look like?

A persistent question that nagged me throughout the season, and haunts me still, is how efficiently backyard gardening can scale up. Financial questions are part of the calculation, because small-scale farming is a tough way to earn money. This season's work returned a modest wage that beat breaking even or losing money in the best small-farm tradition, but I wasn't exactly wearing a path to the bank. What's unfortunate is that, looking ahead, it's not clear how to increase margins for vegetable production without greatly expanding the work. Triple your workload to earn a living wage isn't much of a rallying cry, but it's the farmer way. Already I'm borrowing equipment, swapping for land, and using someone else's van to get to market, so there's not a lot of low-hanging fruit on the cost-saving side either.

Another concern is that the Portland area is becoming saturated with seasonal vegetables. Plenty of very talented and hardworking growers live within driving range of the city. They've spent years developing their businesses. Bringing tomatoes to the farmers' market in August, or carrots in October, or lettuce anytime other than early spring and late fall, and lining these up alongside the wealth of produce grown by other farmers feels like an exercise in futility. It can be a little heartbreaking to pack up unblemished, flavorful produce at the end of the market and haul it around to local restaurants, only to find that chefs have purchased all they need from other growers. In the end Karla and I sold or ate just about everything my gardens produced this season, and customers were on the whole very receptive and enthusiastic. But it seems a little ridiculous to continue to hawk many of the same products others grow in abundance.

Nevertheless, some viable alternatives are starting to come into focus. No other market vendors sold raw cider, fruit trees, or berry bushes this season, for example, and few carry honey. The move into fruit seems particularly promising. I'm finding that I enjoy the rhythms of tree planting and care, and its workload spreads more evenly throughout the year than vegetable production. Orchard work seems like something I could continue into old age, emulating nurseryman Nick Botner, if fortune is on my side. Next year will be different, and every year after that, as trees mature and come into their own.

The seeds of something new are here. Ten years from now I don't want to find myself alone in the field, breaking my back over rows of vegetables. The way forward seems to lie in specialty products and niche markets, in developing a distinct identity around rare food conservation that can set me apart in a maturing business. Looking ahead, I'd like to explore products like aged cider vinegar or chutneys, foods that customers will be excited to buy and that can't be found elsewhere. I'm beginning to understand where all of this is heading.

THE MEANING OF LOCAL FOOD

*I*n the middle of August 2010, on a hot summer afternoon, I
pull up to the curb in the Deering neighborhood on Portland's
western outskirts and jump out to check on my trailer. It's empty
except for two apple-picking ladders tied to the wooden framework
and angled precariously over the back of my car. I lift the longer
of the two over the side, prop it against a nearby tree, and return
to the car to fetch picking bags and buckets. Meanwhile my friend
Eli Cayer walks quickly over to the nearest house and rings the
doorbell. He disappears inside.

After a few minutes, someone reclining on a garden lounge
behind the house points me toward the kitchen door. Inside Eli is
laughing and talking with the owner, a fortyish woman named
Beth. She pours something from an unmarked bottle and hands me
the glass. "It's vodka," she tells me, "infused with honey and juni-
per berries." Which sounds like something closer in spirit to gin,
but whatever it is we knock it back and smile. The recipe came from
a Polish friend of hers, and it's delicious. Evidence that Beth's of a
like mind, another foodie, and that we've come to the right place.

Eli walks out front to the edge of her yard, where a solitary
crab apple tree juts over the sidewalk on a busy road near the high

school. He spotted it a few days ago and stopped by to knock on the door. Ordinarily Beth makes a "musky" apple jelly from the fruit, but she's too busy this year and won't get around to it, so we're free to pick all we want. The tree is large, about twenty feet tall, with abundant small red fruits that look for all the world like sweet cherries. Already by late summer dozens of apples have dropped to the sidewalk and the pavement is splattered with crushed fruit. Those remaining on the tree are at their peak of ripeness and flavor, a little too tangy and acidic to eat without puckering my mouth, but also tasting of sugar: sweet and sour.

We raise the ladder, angle it against the crook of one of the branches, and I climb up with my picking bag slung around my neck. It feels strange to do this in such a dense residential area. "Any idea how close we can get to the electric line?" I ask while eyeing the wires running through the foliage a few feet above me. Eli shakes his head and I move carefully, keeping what seems like a good precautionary distance. Enough anyway so we could reasonably tell Karla we'd been prudent if an accident lands me in the ER.

A young couple with a baby stroller walks quickly past us, avoiding my gaze. Eli hands me a pair of scissors, and we start neatly snipping off fruit. Ordinarily I'd grab whatever is within reach and toss the apples by the handful into the bag, but this extra care feels right, ceremonial. It's our first street tree harvest and the inauguration of Eli's hard cider winery. Good cider requires a balance of flavors, with acids and tannins as well as sugar, so we're going to press these crab apples out of curiosity to see what kind of juice they'll produce for blending. It takes about twenty minutes to pick all the fruit within reach of the ladder. I climb down and empty my bag into the five-gallon bucket Eli has been filling. One bucket of fruit, that's all we're going to get. Just enough for a trial run of my new press, and a bit of experimentation with some unusual fruit.

"Let's set the press right here, on the edge of the dock," Eli tells me half an hour later. We've driven back through town to his newly rented warehouse space. It's located in Portland's Bayside neighborhood in a low-slung building with several bays fronted by a covered loading dock. Above us birds roost on steel girders under the eaves, leaving feathers and droppings scattered across the concrete, and below us debris from the parking lot collects against the wall—piles of cigarette butts, waste plastic cups, and scrap paper. At least we'll be pressing under blue skies in the fresh air—when the wind is blowing from the right direction, that is, away from the wastewater treatment plant over the hill.

Eli connects a hose to the sink, opens the bay door, and starts washing down the pressing area. We're producing cider only for our own use today, and it won't touch anything that hasn't been cleaned and sterilized, but I dislike handling food in a place like this. We wash everything as well as possible, running hot soapy water over the concrete and scrubbing it with a stiff broom. After a few minutes everything seems pretty clean, and certainly more hygienic than cider production of generations past, dependent as it was on horse-driven equipment and wooden presses rigged up inside old barns, or set up directly in the orchard.

We wheel my new equipment to the edge of the dock and set up the grinder beside the bay door. Already I'm in love with this elegant press, a stainless-steel beauty purchased slightly used from Orchard Equipment Supply Company (OESCO) in western Massachusetts. It's designed for crushing grapes in small-scale wineries, and it operates by water pressure. Connect the internal rubber bladder by garden hose to any ordinary household faucet, crack the valve, and gradually the fruit squeezes against an upright stainless-steel cylinder, running juice through narrow openings in the drum into a collecting tray.

Small enough to fit in the back of a car, this Lancman press is nevertheless large enough to hold four bushels of apples, or roughly the capacity of a large washing machine. It's far cheaper than most alternatives, can be operated by one person, and it produces about ten gallons of juice per hour. OESCO started importing this equipment from Slovenia a few years ago and experimenting with apples. Whole fruit runs first through a grinder driven by a small electric motor, which breaks it down, and after this the crushed mash goes into the press. Squeezing the juice takes about twenty minutes. The size, price, and portability of this press are perfect for our experiments and limited production for my market stand.

Our first run of apples will be quick, because this five-gallon bucket of street tree crab apples will fill only about a quarter of the drum, yielding less than two gallons of cider. It's almost not worth the trouble, but we're anxious to sample the juice and test the equipment. So we fire up the grinder and run the apples into a clean bucket. The stream of finely chopped fruit that comes out is surprisingly dry. It's hard to imagine these little crab apples releasing much juice, but over the course of the season I'll come to discover that the appearance of newly crushed fruit can be deceptive. This seemingly dry fruit is in marked contrast with late-fall dessert apples, which often dissolve into a thick slurry and start running juice as soon as they're loaded into the press. Late-season apples don't necessarily produce more, however, because the wetter mash is due primarily to the partial breakdown of cell walls. In fact it's often more difficult to extract juice from softer fruits. By the end of October little pulp bombs sometimes explode without warning from the top of my press as its vents become clogged with macerated fruit. Pressure builds as the juice can't escape. The timing of this is unpredictable, the dominion of the cider gods. (Two months later a wad of wet mash explodes during a festival at a local pub as I demonstrate my press to the owner, splattering against the back of his friend's head twenty feet away. Luckily both of them find it funny.) Commercial producers often add rice hulls to a challenging late-season apple mash to improve its texture and pressability.

"Come taste this stuff!" I cry out to Eli. He grabs a glass and fills it from the stream that runs into a gallon-sized bottle, capturing the rose-colored juice and holding it up to the light. (In most of the world, cider refers only to the fermented product; newly pressed juice is just that, juice.) I'm struck by its beautiful color and absolute clarity, and take small sips to evaluate the flavor. This is nothing like the pasteurized product that passes for cider at the supermarket. It's much lighter and more delicate, at once mildly acidic and sweet, with a pleasing aroma. Eli grabs a refractometer and checks the Brix reading (a measure of its sugar content): fifteen degrees Brix, sweeter than any other apples we'll test through the rest of the season. These are supposed to be sour crab apples? The juice compares to a naturally sweet cranberry, translucent and clear, refreshing like a light sparkling wine.

That any cider could have such unusual flavor and character surprises me. Having lived most of my life in New England, I should know the nuances of this drink. I've tasted fresh juice many times over the years, and while the difference between fresh-pressed and store-bought, heat-pasteurized cider is obvious, much of what we drink comes from a relatively narrow selection of commercial apples. This fresh-pressed juice from a largely neglected Portland street tree is something entirely different. "We need to get out and find more apples," Eli tells me. Our first experiment suggests a world of possibilities, a range of previously unimagined flavors to explore.

Though this crabapple tastes great right out of the press, our primary interest is to see what will happen once the sugars in the juice ferment to alcohol. Eli fills two bottles, caps them with air locks, and puts them aside in a cool room. He adds nothing at all, no sulfites or yeast, because our goal is to learn as much about this particular fruit as possible, leaving fermentation to its own devices. The simplest hard cider production involves nothing more than pressing high-quality juice and preventing contact with oxygen during fermentation (exposure to air will ultimately produce apple vinegar). Natural yeasts in the air around us can do all the work. Because this is about as far away from commercial production as you can get (typically juice is sterilized with sulfites and fermented with cultured yeasts), the outcome will be somewhat unpredictable.

Eli's new business is called the Urban Farm Fermentory. His business plan calls for using every inch of available space in his rented three-thousand-square-foot warehouse and its small backyard to produce food. Fish tanks in the entrance will raise tilapia, a side room will grow culinary mushrooms, and the newly constructed hoophouse out back will grow herbs and vegetables. Thus the "urban farm," and he explains the rest by saying, "We're going to ferment everything." He'll experiment with sauerkraut, hard cider, honey mead, vinegars, and a fermented health tonic called kombucha. Throw everything at the wall and see what sticks. Eli's friends collaborate on the project, like designer and gardener Dave Homa, who maintains the greenhouse and pitches in to help with just about everything else. Karla is keeping her two beehives out back. The UFF is a busy place; at any given time it's impossible to guess what experiments might be happening inside.

Eli's a born entrepreneur, the kind of guy who knows everyone and starts one venture after another. Just a few months into this new business and not yet selling any products, he's generated a business following of several hundred Facebook friends and gotten some great press, even a short write-up in *The New York Times*. A steady stream of curious visitors stops by to visit the gardens and admire the space, which his friends have decorated on every available surface with graffiti art. Eli is always in a hurry, trying to do too much in a short time. To compound this, last week he and his girlfriend Anna had their first baby, Arlo, and the surf has been up. His wetsuit hangs on a railing out back with a puddle of Casco Bay seawater collecting beneath it.

"Strong like moose," Dave Homa says in a mock Eastern European accent, smiling as he rolls an oak barrel into place. A month has passed since our street tree harvest, and the cider season is in full swing. Dave and Eli are putting the finishing touches on a three-tiered welded steel rack in the cider house (technically licensed as a winery), which will hold two dozen fifty-gallon stainless drums and several used wooden bourbon barrels. In the adjacent testing room ciders of varying hues fill carboys and salvaged one-gallon wine bottles, each topped with a fermentation lock to keep out oxygen and contaminants while allowing carbon dioxide to escape. Some of these juices we've pressed from individual trees around town, while others are samples from commercial sources.

Eli and I close up the sliding door on the dock and jump into my car. We've loaded it once again for picking, the trailer filled with ladders, buckets, and heavy-duty kraft paper bags. Today we're headed out of Portland to an orchard located thirty minutes away, near the south end of Sebago Lake. It's nearly ninety degrees, a late morning in mid-September, and Eli has brought along nothing but an empty coffee cup. "Don't you need something to eat, or at least a bottle of water?" I ask halfway into our drive, and he says, "Oh yeah," good idea. I park curbside at a supermarket, engine idling, while he runs in to grab an energy drink and some snacks.

We pull up to a gate marked by an ORCHARD sign and drive through to the barn. Weeds choke the entrance road, the market stand is locked up, tent caterpillars have colonized some of the trees, and the grass has grown knee-high between tree rows. The barn, covered in tar paper, looks derelict, but on closer inspection turns out to be cosmetically challenged but otherwise sound. It looks like no one has been here for months, and a large sign at the entrance confirms that the orchard and its pick-your-own operation is closed. The owner has agreed to let me salvage available fruit, on the condition that I keep things quiet to prevent the rest of the world from showing up in search of free apples. We back around to the first row of trees and start unloading equipment.

Dave Homa rolls in behind us with another friend, a freelance photographer for *The New York Times* and an enthusiastic home brewer. It's hot, much too hot. Dave's used to this; he runs a gardening business and designs permaculture plantings (permaculture being a system of ecological design, focused especially on perennial food plants). Heaving picking bags around under a midday sun is maybe a little new to the others, though. I work in my usual weather-oblivious uniform of Carhartt pants, long-sleeved work shirt, heavy work boots, and a broad-brimmed hat. My philosophy: Keep direct sun off my skin; better to bake than broil.

A member of the family that owns this orchard works for the Department of Environmental Protection with Karla. Until last year one of the largest orchards in the state leased and managed the site and brought equipment down as needed from their base half an hour away. They pulled out, however, unable to make a profit off these apples, which lean heavily toward Macs and Cortlands. The trees are reminiscent of the dated plantings I found in our property search— standard commercial varieties on large rootstocks, hard to prune, spray, and pick. This season the owner hired someone to prune trees on roughly a third of these twenty acres, but otherwise no work has been done. He's generously letting me salvage apples until he finds someone willing to take over the lease and run the business.

Many orchards here in central Maine lost all their fruit in this 2010 year, including a comparatively large operation located just a couple of miles down the road. A heavy May frost hit at the wrong time and devastated newly emerging apples. Here the Macs have almost no fruit, but somehow every other variety is loaded, thanks to a warm microclimate and a favorable hillside location, which drains away pockets of cold air. Most of the apples are surprisingly free of insect and disease damage despite the trees' lack of maintenance and the complete absence of insecticides. Pests like codling moths haven't yet caught on to their good fortune and built up their populations enough to cause visible problems.

Dave and I walk down the hill to the earliest-bearing block. A couple of rows of an apple called Paula Red are ready to pick, running a week or two ahead of nearby Golden Delicious and Empires. It's too steep to drive my car down the hill, so we're stuck hauling apples up to the trailer by hand. Eli hoists a bushel onto his shoulder, looking like a tattooed peasant farmer, while Dave talks about the Jamaican guys who work the orchards he used to prune. We work for a couple of hours, after which the others have something urgent going on and need to head out. I stick around awhile longer to finish picking and packing the trailer, then drive back to meet them at the Fermentory, somehow arriving before they do. "We found this sweet little swimming hole on the river," they explain later.

We'll press the apples Eli and the others have picked and use their juice as part of a blend for hard cider. For my purposes, however, juice will be bottled for fresh consumption. This year no other vendors are selling their own cider at the Portland Farmers' Market, largely because of regulatory complications, so it's been a very popular product. "It tastes like eating an apple!" customers tell me as they throng my stand, as though this is a revelation. Other farmers buy it by the half gallon and drink it on the spot, and mothers offer pint-sized servings to their appreciative children. Customers return each week for more and tell me they've never tasted juice this good.

My cider is light and sweet, nearly translucent. In comparison the pasteurized product other vendors buy wholesale from a handful of large operations, including the orchard that once leased the land from which we're picking, is typically cloudy and dark, kind of a grayish brown. Whether such low quality in the mass-produced drink is due to heat pasteurization (substituting ultraviolet treatment is markedly better), poor fruit selection, or something else about its pressing and handling, customers clearly recognize the difference. After tasting something really good it's hard to go back.

Even growers at the market who produce their own apples buy wholesale cider to stock their stands, because regulations have effectively shut down small operations. Back in the 1990s a sixteen-month-old girl died from drinking a smoothie containing unpasteurized apple juice produced by Odwalla, and numerous others were sickened by the *E. coli* strain that infected it. The result was a wave of reformist national regulations that all but destroyed the raw juice industry, forcing producers to purchase expensive pasteurization equipment or stop production. This is pretty disturbing, in my opinion. While it's true that scary, rapidly evolving bacterial strains have infiltrated our food supply, and ensuring safety is critical, pasteurization doesn't get at the root of the problem. The real culprits behind unsafe cider are poor worker hygiene, use of rotting fruit, and fecal contamination from dropped apples in orchards grazed by domestic animals. If you start with bad fruit and unclean processing, it's hard to understand how heat-treating the juice is supposed to make it any more drinkable.

I keep my food safe by using apples picked fresh from the tree, discarding any that are split or damaged, washing them in a three-bay sink in Eli's commercial kitchen, and pressing them immediately after grinding. Juice collects in a food-grade brewer's bucket where solids settle out briefly before bottling. From there it goes into a chest freezer running nearby in our market van, where it cools overnight to a temperature in the upper thirties. Anything that doesn't sell within twenty-four hours finds its way to our basement, where it bubbles away intoxicatingly for months. I know this food, know where it's been and how it's been handled, and can speak for its quality and safety.

My cider sells legally at the market due to a regulatory exemption that few other growers can use. A loophole enables those who produce their own raw cider to sell it directly to retail customers. For most growers the resulting sales can't generate enough volume to support a licensed commercial kitchen and equipment. Thanks to my borrowed space in Eli's facility, low-cost press, and salvaged apples, however, I'm able to make good use of this exemption. Six days of sales at the market in the fall of 2010 pay off all my expenses and investment in pressing equipment.

This is clearly a promising new direction. As I look back over my first season at the market, sales of distinctly regional products like cider, honey, and nursery plants feel most gratifying. Finding products that expand the market range and fill an as yet unmet (or unrecognized) need is much more satisfying than trying to one-up the competition. Improvements to my display and other marketing tricks can help me compete against other growers, but when customers want something different like raw cider, they seek it out. This is one of the beauties of the market—instant feedback about what's needed, what works, and what the public desires.

Are there other value-added products based on rare and unusual foods that could find a receptive audience at my stand? Until a few years ago restrictions on sales at the Portland Farmers' Market imposed by the city prevented most vendors from venturing much beyond vegetables, cut flowers, and spring seedlings for home gardens. (Over the past few seasons Portland has eased restrictions and opened the door to foods like milk, cheese, and meat.) Because of this history the market still leans heavily toward vegetables. It should come as no surprise that it's difficult for me to sell beets, carrots, or even high-value crops like tomatoes. After a few Saturdays watching produce languish in its display, like beautiful peppers in a rainbow of colors, I come to accept that either someone else is filling that niche, or the demand just isn't there.

Despite the strength of the competition in this market, gaps remain—there's very little fruit beyond strawberries, blueberries, and apples, for example, and little or no prepared food, jams and jellies, baked goods, or wine. There are serious challenges involved with any of these products, however. Value-added foods often represent a lot of work with narrow margins (as anyone making home preserves can attest), and they require permitting and licensing. Fresh fruit tends to have low returns and it can be very hard to transport. Even with careful handling, the few pints of raspberries I carried to market as an experiment softened and started running juice all over the coolers after a few hours. After so much work, they sold poorly. Another lesson learned.

And yet some interesting fruits deserve attention. One of the rarest in my collection is a strawberry called Marshall, described by Gary Nabhan in a 2004 publication of the Renewing America's Food Traditions coalition as one of America's "top ten endangered foods." It was also once known as "the finest eating strawberry in America ... exceedingly handsome, splendidly flavored, pleasantly sprightly, aromatic and juicy." The Marshall dates back to 1890 in Marshfield, Massachusetts, where it was a chance seedling found in the fields of farmer Marshall Ewell. According to an excerpt from a 1924 meeting of the Marshfield Historical Society, a workman discovered the original Marshall strawberry plant while digging in a field, and later discarded it in a ditch, where Marshall Ewell's wife rescued it. From there it went on to win prizes at the Massachusetts Horticultural Society. It entered the commercial trade and became a major production fruit for half a century, particularly in the Pacific Northwest.

Today the Marshall is nearly extinct, and the identity of remaining plants is in dispute. The USDA's germplasm repository in Corvallis, Oregon, maintains one line (the source of my plants), while its counterparts in Beltsville, Maryland, and Bainbridge, Georgia, have others that don't match up genetically. The only other known potential source as of this writing is the Bainbridge Island Historical Society in Washington State, which maintains a small plot of berries presumed to be Marshalls, acquired from a Japanese farmer who relocated to eastern Washington during the Second World War to avoid internment in West Coast prison camps. No commercial sources or growers remain today for this berry.

It took less than the span of a generation to bring the Marshall from prominence to near extinction. Why would such a widely celebrated, flavorful strawberry with a rich history completely disappear from small gardens as well as commercial farms? Doesn't everyone dream of the perfect strawberry? Part of the answer lies in the very qualities that make great fruit. Marshalls are juicy and less firm than modern strains, not well adapted for storage and long-haul shipping. *The Small Fruits of New York,* published in 1925, says they require heavy, rich soil, and don't perform as well in unfavorable conditions. They're also susceptible to viruses introduced to the United States in the wake of the Second World War.

In my gardens Marshalls have yet to show disease problems, and they live up to their culinary promise. Whether or not these plants descend directly from their nineteenth-century namesake, they're quite sweet, but not to the point of overpowering their tangy, rich flavor. This variety wins blind taste tests among strawberries in my fields, although others include several known for their high quality, like Sparkle and Earliglow. To date the Marshall strawberries have been prolific and healthy, and they produce well, if not as abundantly as newer cultivars. Arguably their greatest strength is also their downfall—these berries are soft and juicy, very flavorful but delicate. It's difficult to bring them to market even for same-day direct sales, because with so much juice they start to break down as soon as they leave the field.

This shortcoming suggests another approach: freezing. The Marshall strawberry holds its flavor and color after processing, so historically it was a mainstay that helped establish the frozen food industry in the Pacific Northwest. Could there be a useful lesson in this history? Freezing could be the answer to my ongoing dilemma about what to do with so many finicky and diverse fruits in my fields. Instead of struggling to develop markets for older varieties that don't look as pretty as modern strains, and don't hold up well in handling, but have exceptional flavor, in processing I might develop value-added products. Throw frozen Marshall strawberries in a blender to make fruit smoothies, for example, and it would not only be a winner at the market but also support rare fruit conservation. Perfect, problem solved. No one else sells prepared foods like this at the Portland Farmers' Market, and on a hot summer day smoothies would fly from the stand.

In January 2011 a friend interested in helping my project suggests making smoothies with a blender rigged up to a stationary bike. This is a fun idea, and it offers a quick and simple setup for the market. In addition to the bike and blender attachment, we might get by with nothing but a cooler and some sort of simple washing station. Someone did this, albeit illegally, for a season or two at another market nearby. Sounds good, but a few phone calls kill the idea. To stay within the law I'll need a permit from the Department of Agriculture to process fruit, as well as access to a commercial kitchen.

The Department of Health licenses vendor sales at the state level, and Portland's City Clerk and Code Enforcement offices handle local regulatory compliance. Smoothie sales will require a city vendor license and a food cart that meets strict codes. I'll also have to take a class to become a certified food protection manager. My cart will need running hot water on demand, a three-bay sink for sterilizing equipment, a separate hand-washing sink, and two 20-gallon tanks for potable water and waste. Its surface will have to be steel—no wood—with smooth, easy-to-clean sides without exposed screws or hardware. Sounds like a regulatory nightmare with no end.

Luckily I enjoy this kind of puzzle. I get started right away, knowing that completing the permitting and building my cart could take several months. My plan breaks some new ground, and from the start it's clear no one at the state or local levels knows exactly how to process my applications. They're as helpful as they can be, but at least twice over the next three months they tell me a cart at the market definitely won't be permitted. With my state mobile vendor license in hand, I bounce around from office to office at the city level, searching for approval. The City Clerk's office tells me it's fine to sell fruit smoothies with a vendor permit, and that no restriction prevents farmers from doing the same with their own fruits, but it's impossible to be a farmer and vendor simultaneously because regulations state that pushcarts have to remain at least sixty-five feet away from other food purveyors, including stands at the farmers' market. "In other words, I have to stay sixty-five feet away from myself," I say. Essentially, yes, comes the reply. "And what's the appeal process? Do I need approval from the city council for a variance?" No, they say, start with the city attorney.

This runaround doesn't bother me, because regulations on the whole make good sense. Everyone is just trying to do their job. That, and the devil in me is more than a little gleeful that these restrictions mean I'll enjoy a smoothie monopoly for at least the coming year. In the end answers come quickly and easily when I reach the right person on the phone. After getting past the front of the office at last to speak with the city attorney, she tells me, "I don't see any problem with what you want to do," and says she'll stand behind me if further problems arise at the city level. She has the power and authority to push this through, and when it comes time to inspect my cart and commercial kitchen base station (at Eli's cider house), she'll vouch for me with code enforcement. "If you run into any more trouble, just give me a call," she tells me.

As soon as the city gives me the green light in early April, I start building a cart. No prefabricated vendor setup fits my needs—most are designed for hot dogs or tacos, and have to be towed with a hitch. It would be much more desirable to build something small and light enough to wheel through doors for indoor storage, and roll onto my trailer for easy transport. The bike blender idea has gone out the window, too, because commercial models are slow and awkward. Instead my plan is to use handheld Cuisinart immersion blenders, which draw minimal power, only two hundred watts, and work quickly and efficiently. The cart will need a power source anyway to run a water pump from portable storage tanks. There's no power or water available at the market site in Deering Oaks park, so my cart has to be entirely self-contained.

State codes for vendor carts include minimum and maximum size requirements for all dimensions, including height. For some reason no one can explain to me, regulations require that carts must be at least thirty-two inches wide. Since the door to our basement workshop is thirty-three inches edge-to-edge, the design of my cart can be any width—as long as it falls between thirty-two and thirty-three inches. Height and length restrictions are a little more flexible, but the counter can't be too tall, and a very long cart would be unwieldy. Over the next two weeks I collect the necessary plumbing and electrical parts by mail and at the local hardware store and marine center—two 20-gallon water tanks, four sinks, two faucets, a twelve-volt pump, an on-demand water heater and vents, a propane tank, water lines and drains, two heavy, deep-cycle marine batteries, a charge controller, and an inverter (to convert power from the batteries' direct current to 110-volt alternating current). It's hard to see how everything can possibly fit into the limited space of a hand-wheeled cart.

In the end, somehow, everything works. By the time my strawberries are ready for harvest in late June, the city's code enforcement officer has inspected and approved my cart. It has a wooden frame with steel sides and a slate-gray countertop made from an environ-mentally friendly, food-grade composite called PaperStone. I've cut the steel with shears, secured the edges with countersunk screws, and covered the seams and screws with aluminum trim. Handles at one end of the cart and two heavy-duty tires set below the frame allow it to roll around, even with a full tank of water, which brings its weight to several hundred pounds. A row of sinks set a few inches below the counter offers good working space. Clean, food-grade surfaces, running hot water on demand, and power to operate small blenders are worth all the trouble. The truth is, this cart is much better than anything I would have dreamed up in the absence of regulations.

We roll the cart out for its test run at the market a few days later, on the Fourth of July holiday weekend. It's hot, and a line forms quickly. High demand keeps me and three friends working as quickly as we can: one to pull frozen fruit from the coolers and combine it with a light syrup, two to work the hand blenders, and one to handle cash and deal with customers. We advertise only one option, a blend that includes my peaches from last season, heirloom Marshall strawberries, four kinds of mint, maple syrup, and raw sugar. Everything is organic, there's no dairy, and fruit supplies most of the sweetness. The smoothies taste really good, like sorbet, and at the peak of the market we average three sales per minute, grossing nearly $1,200 in our first four hours. "Why hasn't anyone tried this before?" comes the refrain from customers. They have no idea. I don't even try to explain.

Raw cider. Smoothies. This becomes my new direction: collect-ing rare foods and creating value-added products that depend on their best characteristics and exceptional flavor. Giving new life to plants like the Marshall strawberry, using its natural sweetness to enhance a summertime drink, and thus justifying the time and expense of growing it. When I occasionally have to substitute other commercially purchased frozen strawberries, it's striking how flavorless they seem in comparison.

So what's next? For this I turn again to Eli Cayer. The more we press and ferment cider, the more fascinating its variations become. Through the season blends change, flavors evolve, and we learn the personalities of apple varietals. Jonagold produces a sweet, clear juice. Cortland lightens the mix, while astringent fruit from crab apples and a friend's wild tree creates complexity. Even Red Delicious contributes something of value, because its cider has a nice bouquet. The differences among these foods, sometimes subtle, sometimes dramatic, add immeasurable richness to our table. The deeper I go, the clearer becomes the French concept of *terroir,* the idea that a place can impart a particular taste, informed by the realities of ecology and climate as well as culture and tradition. Local food at its best is different from products shipped halfway around the world, not just in quality but also in kind.

In the summer of 2011 my experiences licensing raw cider and fruit smoothies at the farmers' market embolden me to expand further and bring fermented cider to my farm stand. Cider is true New England *terroir,* as much a reflection of the taste of this particular place as French Champagne or English Stilton cheese. Growing apples and fermenting their juice is a long-standing tradition here that dates back to earliest colonial days—a rich history that's all but disappeared. It's also a fascinating horticultural puzzle, because the taste of fruit varies from place to place and among varieties. To say that we know hard cider after drinking one of the insipidly sweet mass-market brands available today is like equating all wine with Manischewitz. The possibilities for blending hard cider are as myriad as wine.

My trees have yet to begin bearing, and many of the finest cider fruits in my collection are newly grafted, at least five years away from serious production. Most of my fifty Harrison apple trees, for example, the variety I'd first encountered at Ben Watson's Ark of Taste committee meeting, are no more than two feet tall. Yet it's never too soon to start clearing regulatory obstacles. Bureaucratic change can at times seem slower than watching trees grow. So one day in early July 2011, I stop one of our Portland neighbors who serves on the city council and ask what it would take for the city to grant me a variance to sell alcohol at the farmers' market. Would he support me? "Yeah, I'll bring this up with our Health and Recreation Committee," he says. He's one of its three members, and, for reasons that are hard to understand, this is the right place to start. Does alcohol fall under health or recreation? Apparently both, particularly when we're talking about sales at a farmers' market in a public park.

Eli gets behind the idea, and within four months we have our hearing. I tell the committee and a handful of local reporters that hard cider is a traditional drink, relatively healthful, with low alcohol, and that it pairs very well with food. Letting us sell at the market will support my efforts to collect and preserve rare trees. Recent regulation at the state level opened the door to wines at farmers' markets, and the only obstacle in Portland is a regulation prohibiting alcohol sales on city property. At the end of the hearing the three members of the committee unanimously grant their approval, legal counsel lends its support, and we're on to the full city council for their vote.

This is one of the main lessons I've learned over the past few years—don't wait, jump. Even though it's unclear when or whether we'll receive final approval to sell cider at the market, the harvest season is passing and time is short. Eli and I set for ourselves a goal of pressing and fermenting a hundred gallons to test the market, or about five hundred wine bottles. The challenge is to find the right fruit, because typical dessert apples like McIntosh and Cortland don't make very good cider. They're fine for fresh juice, but after fermenting not much taste and depth remain. We start scrounging around for more interesting trees and find a few bushels here, a few there, primarily older varieties from abandoned trees like Golden Bellflower and Northern Spy. Toward late fall I come across a windfall of about twenty bushels of Baldwins that puts us over the top, with a total of close to 120 gallons. With the help of friends we press the juice and Eli racks it into barrels, glass carboys, and gallon-sized bottles to ferment. Then in February 2012 the city council votes seven to two in favor of alcohol sales at the farmers' market. We're on.

"Do you have any gallon-sized Carlo Rossi bottles?" I call out to the Vietnamese guy working the counter at a local recycling redemption center. It's November 2011 and I've run out of containers to test small batches of fermenting cider at home. The place is noisy with clinking glass and a loader moving shrink-wrapped pallets. He pulls me off to the side in another windowless cinder-block room, and we find four sticky bottles. "How much?" I ask. He tells me they're mine for 60 cents. Each has the capacity of more than five ordinary wine bottles, which is hard to visualize until you transfer their contents. Carlo Rossi glass jugs are perfect for fermentation, sturdy and clear, with easily gripped handles. And sterilizing bottles from the redemption center is much preferable to drinking this wine myself.

After pressing, Eli adds commercial yeasts to the raw juice we've pressed and fits rubber stoppers and air locks to the barrels, bottles, and glass carboys. Within a couple of days the cider starts bubbling vigorously as the yeast goes to work converting sugars to alcohol, expanding into the two inches of headspace in each barrel and sometimes running up into the air locks. The yeast strains he's testing range from those typically used for English ciders to Trappist ale, wine, champagne, and even sake. Each imparts its own particular flavor to the finished product, a character that depends equally on the choice of apple varieties, temperature, and time. Row upon row of different blends fill Eli's warehouse, and as fermentation progresses he takes samples, tests for sugar levels and acidity, and records notes about color, clarity, taste, and aroma. Meanwhile in my own basement other experiments bubble away, and last year's bottles age in a dark corner.

It feels like we're being carried along by a growing tide. In 2012 as the new season begins my stand includes an ever-increasing range of distinct foods and nursery plants. Apple, peach, and pear trees I grafted two years ago from endangered varieties broaden the range of nursery stock. A freezer filled with fruits like strawberries, serviceberries, red and black raspberries, and peaches sits in the corner of our basement, ready for early-season smoothies. Karla bottles honey for market sales and gifts to friends. Again next fall we'll find neglected fruit trees to press raw juice. If Eli's newly fermented cider turns out well enough, it can go to market by midsummer. Other heirloom fruits and vegetables continue to round out my stand at the farmers' market. To me all of these products, which taste of this place and often trace their roots back to the hands of local people, redefine regional food. This isn't simply food from a nearby source—it is instead *of* this land, dependent on the community, and deeply tied to local history and culture. In this sense of place is the meaning of local food.

Eleven

THE CIDER TREE

"That's a Milden," John Bunker says as he bites into an apple in an abandoned orchard in Cape Elizabeth, Maine, in October 2011. He recognizes the variety from its pale yellow color splashed with red, its conical shape, and the flavor, color, and texture of its crisp, juicy flesh. Once relatively common in New England orchards, Milden has all but disappeared. West Coast plant collector and nurseryman Nick Botner sold scions of this variety until his retirement last year, but it's now commercially unavailable. Little information about it remains.

According to John the next tree is a Baldwin, as are most others in this abandoned orchard. Four of us trail behind him as he walks from tree to tree, tasting apples, examining characteristics of the fruit, unlocking their secrets. We walk carefully to avoid tripping over dense roots and stumps. Until recently this acre or so of land was heavily overgrown, its Mildens, Baldwins, and other as yet unidentified varieties forgotten in the woods. Over the past two years property manager John Greene and his crew have cleared the brush, revealing three dozen stately old trees loaded with surprisingly blemish-free fruit.

John Greene picks one of the Baldwins off a low-hanging branch, shines it on his shirt, and smiles broadly. He knows these trees are unlikely survivors. By John Bunker's estimate they date back over a hundred years, which means that in addition to escaping the past few decades of rampant development, they lived through the 1934 freeze that destroyed most Baldwins in Maine. Surrounding ocean currents moderate the winter climate here, and the family-run corporation that controls these two-thousand-plus acres has protected it from subdivision. John Greene supervises managed forest, open fields, farmland, and wildlife habitat, including areas designated for the protection of an endangered species in Maine, the New England cottontail rabbit. These Baldwins and Mildens produce fruit year after year that supports other wildlife, like wild turkeys and white-tailed deer. The ground under our feet is covered with apples in varying stages of decomposition, and dozens of bushels remain on the trees, weighing down branches up to twenty-five feet above our heads. Some of the larger trunks, a foot or more in diameter, have tipped over and rooted in place, sending new shoots skyward. Clearly no one has come into this orchard with a pruning saw for the better part of a generation.

John Greene pulls me aside as we finish in this area. "There's a much older apple tree in the woods near the water," he says. He describes it as a giant several feet in diameter, near the site of one of the oldest homesteads on this large property. "It's probably the oldest apple tree in Cape Elizabeth," he tells me. "Want to go take a look?" Of course I do. He's never seen any fruit on this ancient tree, so it isn't worth John Bunker's time, but maybe I can help figure out if it was ever grafted and pruned. We leave the rest of the group as they head to a younger orchard in a nearby field, hop into the cab of John's truck, and make our way through a maze of access roads winding through beautiful spruce and fir forest. The roads peter out as we approach a tidal river that links the ocean to nearby marshes. We park and jump out, eyeing the dense underbrush.

"The tree is somewhere over there," he says, pointing to a nearby clearing. Mindful of tick-borne Lyme disease, which is increasingly common in this area, I wander down the road searching for a break in the vegetation. Meanwhile John forces his way directly into the thickets, and a couple of minutes later shouts that he's found the tree. "There aren't any apples," he confirms, and not much else to see. "Don't bother trying to get in here," he shouts. "It's not worth the trouble." Soon he bursts out of the brush again, swiping at the front of his pants and clearing away by his estimate more than a dozen ticks.

"What would it take to rescue this tree?" he asks as we climb back into the truck. He wants to know if I'm willing to graft it.

"Easy," I tell him, "we'd come back in March and take cuttings from the new growth. I could graft scions to new rootstock for you next spring."

"Are you willing to do that?" he asks.

"Sure, love to," I say. A stately old apple tree, standing alone in the woods, full of untapped secrets: irresistible.

We know nothing about this tree. It might have been grafted and grown intentionally, or it may have sprouted wild from a seed dropped by a passing deer. But John is a professional forester, and if this apple tree is as old as he believes, it dates back to the days when most surrounding land was cleared for agriculture. Even if this is a wild seedling, there may have been good reason to spare it from the woodsman's axe. We could be looking at a favorite old dessert fruit, an apple settlers stored for winter eating. Or, more likely, fruit they pressed for cider and fermented into alcohol. Since this tree no longer bears, there's only one way to know. "I'll call you in March," I tell John. We'll collect scions, graft trees to new rootstock, and in three or four years, if all goes well, taste the fruit.

As I think about this ancient tree over the coming winter, it looms large in my imagination as a potent symbol of all that we've forgotten and neglected. To me it represents an enduring sense of place, a relationship to food very different from our own, and ways of living on the land that have all but disappeared. This tree symbolizes resilience, the ability to survive trends and cultural shifts to maintain something of lasting value. I start thinking of it as the cider tree. Cider, not only because most early orchards were planted from seed for this purpose, in a grand, unintentional breeding experiment, but because at one point or another most apple varieties found their way to the press. Cider is at once the humblest of uses for the apple, our most adaptable fruit, and its most forgiving.

Whether tannic little crab apples or fine dessert varieties, every fruit can add something of value to the whole in a cider blend.

The winter of 2011–12 is extraordinarily mild in Maine. By early March our limited snowpack is melting away, and spring is stirring in the air. Not a lot of time remains to collect dormant scions before sap starts running in the trees and buds begin to break into new leaves. My brother is in town, and we call John Greene and arrange a visit the following afternoon. We'll meet at his office, located in a barn at the end of a long private road.

The next day at the appointed time we pull into a muddy parking space and take a look around. John's office is in a breathtakingly beautiful location, two hundred feet from the shoreline, surrounded by open fields, with an unimpeded view of the ocean and nearby Richmond Island and Scarborough Beach. Today the sky is cloudless; bright sunshine reflects off the remaining snow. The temperature is rising well into the fifties, and the smell of the ocean fills the air. I head into the barn to find John as my brother talks with a friend who's come along for the visit, a recent transplant to Portland deeply interested in place-based foods and regional culinary traditions.

My friend jumps into the cab of John Greene's truck with his dog while my brother and I clamber onto the wooden flatbed. We hang on for the ride down an unplowed road as the truck cuts slowly through several inches of remaining snow. John parks at the edge of a field, and we grab our gear and head into the woods. I carry a saw and pruners but leave the aluminum extension ladder on the truck, hoping to avoid lugging it with me.

With the leaves off the trees and a blanket of snow holding down the undergrowth, the late-winter landscape looks very different from last fall. The tree is easily accessible in its small clearing, easy to spot from even a hundred yards away. This is a huge apple tree, standing over thirty feet tall with a trunk about seven feet in diameter. Curiously, we find two other, younger apple trees perfectly aligned in a straight row with their much older cousin. They look like wild seedlings, misshapen and unkempt, never pruned. Could they have sprouted from the stumps of older cultivated trees?

We decide to remove scions from each of these three trees, so one day we can compare the fruit. If any of the apples are identical, or nearly so, this would suggest they were planted intentionally. I squint into the bright sunlight at the base of one of the smaller trees, searching for new growth suitable for grafting. Success depends on finding healthy, year-old shoots at least three or four inches long. The first small tree has a bit of recent growth near its crown, atop a twisting, half-dead trunk. Despite knowing it would be easiest to reach it with the extension ladder, nevertheless I'm feeling either adventurous or too lazy to walk back to fetch it. So I clamber into the branches, lean out precariously to reach the topmost growth, and with a few saw cuts remove enough wood for several grafts.

The next tree is starting to rot, and there's only one branch worth taking. The trunk sways while I climb and make the cut, removing enough wood for two grafts and throwing it down to my brother. Before I reach the ground and head for the oldest tree, my cider tree, John Greene walks over to it, jumps up, grabs the lowest branch, and pulls himself up. Neither of us likes to stand by and watch; this is too much fun. John reaches for the saw, makes a couple of cuts, and drops enough wood to the ground to graft several new trees. Our work is done. I clip young shoots off the larger branches, add labels, wrap them in plastic bags, and later store them in our refrigerator to remain dormant for another month, until the weather warms and it's time to graft. If all goes well, in three to four years we'll return new trees to this site, and give this old variety a chance to persevere into the future.

Like the Endecott pear tree, which has survived every era of American history from the Pilgrims to the post-industrial twenty-first century, this tree has stood alone in the woods for generations as everything around it changed. How fortunate for us that it remains alive and healthy, that we have this opportunity to collect scions and taste the fruit. With luck this apple can escape the fate of so many other historic foods—seeds that died in a cupboard, trees cut down for firewood, animals bred out of existence. As heartening as this is, however, finding such a tree as yet uncollected also reminds me of all that's been lost. And not only of extinct plant varieties themselves, but our understanding of the place-based traditions that sustained them. While collecting these foods, it's important that we preserve a working knowledge of their stories, because we protect what we understand and value.

Twenty years ago, when I set out to build a plant collection and regain a sense of place through food, it didn't work. This was in part because central Washington State wasn't really my home, and I'd made no long-term commitment to remain there. Even after six years in that beautiful valley, an eternity for anyone under the age of thirty, when asked where I came from the answer was always "Boston." I understand New England, know that I belong here, and have always felt somewhat rootless when living anywhere else.

Today the only trace that remains of my gardens in Washington, and of the heirloom beans, grains, vegetables, berries, and fruit trees that grew there, is a muddy old planting journal that rests on our bookshelf. Its pages describe my first fledgling efforts to collect and grow rare foods, and they include crude maps listing trees and berries from eastern Washington's now defunct Bear Creek Nursery. I worked hard to keep those plants alive, watering faithfully by hand from the nearby irrigation ditch, but their continued survival depended on my care. After my departure the twenty or so fruit trees—varieties like Duchess of Oldenburg and Haralson apples, Flemish Beauty and Clapp's Favorite pears—withered and died. It was a good lesson about stewardship. I didn't really belong in that place, and didn't have within me the commitment needed to adapt to it.

What was missing? The answer seems to be partly about ecology and sense of place, partly a larger cultural connection to the community. Although some of the best friends I've ever had were in that Washington valley, something about the American West always felt alien to me. I was as displaced as the fruit trees in my gardens. No more a native than the varieties listed in my old journal—Duchess of Oldenburg apples, originally from Russia, imported to this country by the Massachusetts Horticultural Society in 1835 and widely grown in northern Maine; Haralson apples, developed in the early twentieth century at the University of Minnesota; Flemish Beauty pears, originally from Belgium; and Clapp's Favorite pears, bred in Massachusetts in the nineteenth century by Thaddeus Clapp from a Flemish Beauty tree. Eventually these trees could have adapted and thrived in their new home, but not without ongoing attention and care.

When I left behind my gardens in Washington, it seemed that time had passed by these heirloom foods, and they would never make their way back to most tables. But over the past decade so much has changed. My decision to return to this work several years ago was due in part to deep cultural shifts in our approach to food. These days old hippie co-ops have gone mainstream with chains like Whole Foods, cooking shows attract audiences from all walks of life, and even corporate campuses sprout vegetable gardens and orchards. Today most Americans are aware of what they eat in ways that would have been unthinkable just a few years ago. We look at agriculture, cooking, and land use with new eyes, and this has transformed everything for me. It's possible now to believe that, after I'm gone, others will plant and save seeds from my vegetable collection, care for my fruit trees, and appreciate the stories and rich history behind them. We're beginning to reclaim traditions that once seemed irretrievably lost. And when these stories have in fact disappeared, we're picking up the threads and beginning anew—taking scions from old apple trees, experimenting with heirloom seeds, and learning their secrets.

These cultural changes play out for Karla and me every day in the way we cook, eat, and think about our food. After collecting scions with John Greene, my brother and I return to the house and pull out a bottle of hard cider. He brought it with him to Maine from an orchard near his home in Maryland. Karla fills the oven with lamb from a friend's farm and roasting vegetables from my gardens, regional heirlooms like Canada Crookneck squash, Gilfeather rutabagas, and Early Blood beets. The smell of garlic fills the air. We taste the commercial cider side by side with bottles from our own basement, sampling from trees Eli Cayer and I picked together last fall, and pairing each with aged cheeses from small farms in Maine's midcoast region. Musty yet sweet, with alcohol levels hovering around 5 percent, the ciders go down easily. We pour glass after glass, comparing respective aromas and flavors, imagining what each apple contributed to the whole.

"Eat it to save it." This line from my irrepressible friend Poppy Tooker, a chef, preservationist, and food activist from New Orleans, immediately comes to mind as we enjoy the feast. Eat these delicious frost-sweetened beets and rutabagas, these rare squashes, so they can reclaim their place in our fields and on our tables. To this I might add another twist: "Share it to save it." If these plants remain only in private collections and fail to find their way into the world again through our gardens, farms, and markets, then their richness will be lost to us. Sharing them, connecting them to our everyday lives, is the key to their survival. It's what matters most. The purpose of these foods is to be eaten.

Toward the end of March 2012, the coming season begins to take shape. Crocuses are blooming, lilacs are starting to bud, and Karla's two beehives are frenzied with activity. Mustard, lettuce, and arugula sprout in my greenhouse, surrounded by nursery plants showing their first signs of new life. Dozens of fruit scions lie dormant at the back of our refrigerator. These include apples and pears I rescued last week by chance from seven trees in Massachusetts, which may be more than two hundred years old. Most were completely hollowed out and rotting, waiting for someone to come along and save them. Meanwhile many of the trees I planted two years ago are over eight feet tall. We may have our first taste of George IV peaches this summer, if their blossoms can escape late-spring frosts. All the pieces of this puzzle, my effort to create a "farm" to bring new life to rare foods, are starting to make sense. Seeds of an idea planted more than twenty years ago, on the far side of the continent, are bearing fruit.

This patchwork farm of mine isn't some re-created vision from the past, a romanticized pastoral life. It's based on the realities of this particular time and space, on collaboration and shared goals. As much as New England's lost farmsteads have important lessons to teach us, we no longer live in an agrarian world. But if we're going to reach some new, better place, build on our newfound appreciation for good food, then we need to find creative ways to weave the best of the past into our lives. This is what I believe, and what motivates me to continue my work: that even the smallest garden can express something nearly forgotten, become a pocket of diversity in a world that looks and tastes increasingly the same. It's up to each of us to decide what we'll leave to future generations. And the time to begin is now.

Acknowledgments

This book begins and ends in the garden. As an urban dweller with limited access to tools, equipment, and land, I'm very grateful to those who have opened their doors and shared valuable resources with me over the past five years. Without the generosity and good will of friends like Peter and John Eastman, Rodney Voisine, Frank Governali, Terry Ann Scriven, Eli Cayer, and Peter Moulton, the fruit trees, berries, and vegetables described on these pages would have remained nothing but names to me.

Ben Watson, Margo Baldwin, and the rest of the staff at Chelsea Green have been wonderful collaborators, believing in the mission of this book and working tirelessly to lend their voices to the cause of biodiversity and sustainable agriculture.

This narrative has unfolded simultaneously in the fields and on paper; I've lived it as I've written it. My deepest thanks go to those who appear on these pages, and to others who share the work. Friends from the Slow Food movement like Ben Watson, Gary Nabhan, Robin Schempp, Dominic Palumbo, Jeff Roberts, Jim Gerritsen, Jenny Trotter, and Cerise Mayo; members of the Ark of Taste Committee; farmers, local-food activists, and collectors like Tom Burford, John Bunker, Will Bonsall, Charles Boothby, Russell Libby, John Greene, Jeremy Oldfield, Mary Ellen Chadd, Austin Chadd, Roger Doiron, and Sonja Johanson; staff at the Maine Farmland Trust; researchers and plant breeders Michael Glos and Bill Garman; and gardening friends like the Sandoval family of Washington State and teachers at the La Providencia school in Garin, Argentina.

I'm indebted to Michael Sanders for his insightful editing of early drafts and for the extraordinary level of detail he brings to his work. He taught me how to find a voice and develop a narrative and translate my experiences to the written page. Michael's advice was immeasurably helpful to this first-time author. Many others have also contributed along the way, helping to steer the book through to completion: Russell French, Barbara Mahaney, David Mahaney, Terra Brockman, Roz Cummins, Don Lindgren, Samantha Lindgren, Rowan Jacobsen, Karl Schatz, Margaret Hathaway Schatz, Alex Novak, Ben Hewitt, and Dave Norman.

I'd also like to thank friends and family who read through early manuscripts and offered so much encouragement and support: Amanda Blaine, Tara Treichel, Marin Magat, Ian Houseal, David Levi, Liz Trice, Molly Smith, Joe Brunette, Emily Bernhard, Erica Corbett Klein, Christian Klein, John Buchanan, Kate Buchanan, Brendan O'Connell, and Emily Buchanan.

The past few years of gardening and writing would have been a lonely road without the love and constant support of Karla Hyde. May there be many more seasons filled with meals from the garden, drink from our vines and trees, and romps with our dog, Tica, through New England's fields and forests and along its sandy shores.

Finally, to my mother, Joan Buchanan, and in loving memory of my father, Eustace W. (Pete) Buchanan, I'd like to dedicate this book.

Index

"This logo identifies paper that meets the standards of the Forest Stewardship Council®. FSC® is widely regarded as the best practice in forest management, ensuring the highest protections for forests and indigenous peoples."

Chelsea Green Publishing is committed to preserving ancient forests and natural resources. We elected to print this title on 30-percent postconsumer recycled paper, processed chlorine-free. As a result, for this printing, we have saved:

10 Trees (40' tall and 6-8" diameter)
5 Million BTUs of Total Energy
906 Pounds of Greenhouse Gases
4,912 Gallons of Wastewater
329 Pounds of Solid Waste

Chelsea Green Publishing made this paper choice because we and our printer, Thomson-Shore, Inc., are members of the Green Press Initiative, a nonprofit program dedicated to supporting authors, publishers, and suppliers in their efforts to reduce their use of fiber obtained from endangered forests. For more information, visit: www.greenpressinitiative.org.

Environmental impact estimates were made using the Environmental Defense Paper Calculator.

For more information visit: www.papercalculator.org.